INTRODUCTION.

THE author happened, in the presence of a friend, to hint his intention of writing this life, when the latter instantly took the alarm, and exclaimed, " Why, you surely are not going to whitewash Judge Jeffreys ?" The author said, he certainly could not think of justifying that lawyer upon every occasion, whose character was, upon the whole, none of the best; but that he saw no reason why even such a man as Jeffreys might not have had some good qualities, as well as others.

Now, most will agree that this is a fair principle, not at all inapplicable to human nature; and, upon investigating the subject, some very redeeming traits soon showed themselves, brightening up with admirable lustre the conduct of a man who has been denounced by Protestant

writers, people of his own creed, as the most
wicked of mortals. Were all the histories un-
impeachable which profess to speak of him, and
the anathemas against him as prompt in their
fulfilment as in their descent from the pens of
ripe and ready writers, surely he might beg
from the Catholics a place in their purgatory,
and count it indeed a felicitous atonement for
his misdeeds.

But really it would be as absurd to predicate
of any person that he is entirely vicious, as that
we should desire to see Jeffreys at the head of
the King's Bench now, instead of the excellent
and patient judge who presides there. At the
same time, we are far from advising parents to
recommend the example of Sir George Jeffreys
to their children. Heaven grant that our country
may be for ever free from such tyranny as his;
and that whoever ventures to make him a pat-
tern may be impeached, and soon hanged, or
beheaded, as may suit! All we say is, that
whenever a cloud is spread over the political
horizon, some needy adventurer will appear,
ready to serve every turn; and that it is, nevertheless, the province of such as are pleased to
record his actions, to give him fair measure,
good as well as evil report. For were it otherwise, it need only be said of any one, as Bur-

net did of Jeffreys, that he is " scandalously
vicious;" and the terms monster, tyrant, ruffian,
a cohort of abuse, a condemnation full and
universal, would be poured forth against him,
without the scantiest endeavour to point out the
true sources of his errors; so that others would
never be the wiser, or better enabled to shun
them. If an inquiry be once set on foot, there
are kindly qualities even in the worst of men :
the depraved and degenerate (as some are
called) will often, in their mood, achieve generous and noble deeds which the excellent of the
earth have seldom contemplated, so sternly is
the Divine Image, all over beautiful and lovely,
stamped upon us. But, had the author even indulged in panegyric, the character of Jeffreys
would not have been the first, no, nor yet the
worst, which a solitary writer might have dared
to ennoble in the face of all others who have
agreed in an united theme of execration.

What said the philosopher Seneca of Claudius
Cæsar? Consoling Polybius, the emperor's
freedman, for the loss of a brother, he writes :—
" Since you are so anxious to banish all things
from your memory, think on Cæsar: see what
faithfulness, what diligence you owe him, for
his partiality. It is his watchfulness which
guards the dwellings of all; his labour the ease

of all, his industry the luxuries of all, his occu-
pation the repose of all. Add now, that as you
ever hold Cæsar to be more dear to you than
your own soul; it is not right, whilst Cæsar is
safe, to repine at fortune."[1]

This was the great philosopher who so far
scorned the world, as to declare, that there was
great pleasure in the very article of death; and
yet he wasted much such lavish praise upon a
drivelling idiot.

But not to harass the reader; does not our
own historian, George Buck, speak feelingly for
Crook-back'd Richard? " There is no story
that shows the planetary affections and malice
of the vulgar," says the panegyrist, " more
truly than King Richard's, and what a tickle
game kings have to play with them; though his
successor, Henry VII. played his providently
enough (with help of the standers-by); yet even
those times both groaned and complained, but
had not the sting and infection of King Richard's

---

[1] Cum voles omnium rerum oblivisci, cogita Cæsarem:
vide quantam hujus in te indulgentiæ fidem, quantam indus-
triam debeas. Omnium domos illius vigilia defendit, omnium otium illius labor, omnium delicias illius industria,
omnium vacationem illius occupatio.—Adjice nunc, quod
cum semper prædices cariorem tibi spiritu tuo Cæsarem esse,
fas tibi non est, salvo Cæsare, de fortunâ queri.

adversaries, who did not only contend with his immortal parts, but raked his dust, to find and aggravate exceptions in his grave."— "Julius Cæsar," continues he, "was, and ever will be, reputed a wise and a great captain, although his emulation cost an infinite quantity of human blood. He thought *crimen sacrum Ambitio.*"

> If right for ought may e'er be violate,
> It must be only for a sovereign state.

And again: "He wore the crown at Bosworth," says Polidore, "thinking that day should either be the last of his life, or the first of a better; but whatever was his mystery, it rendered him a confident and valiant master of his right."

Indeed, one might at this day be emboldened to ask—What had become of Richmond's memory, if he had fallen down slain in Bosworth-field, and, like Richard, had been

> Dragg'd by the hair to hostile swords a prey,
> And slain with barbarous wounds?

What had been told us of Augustus, if he had died less than Emperor of Rome? What of our Jeffreys, on the other hand, if the army at Salisbury had stood faithful to King James; or the Lord Dartmouth, blest with auspicious winds, had attacked the Dutch fleet, ere the Prince of Orange had landed at Torbay?

But it is for the public to judge: to their mercy we leave the great Chief Justice, and go on at once, lest some Christopher Sly should peep out, and say, " A good matter surely: come there any more of it? Would it were done!" When the answer must be, " My lord, 'tis but begun."

CONTENTS.

CHAP. I.

CHAP. II.

CHAP. V.

CHAP. VI.

CHAP. VII.

CHAP. VIII.

MEMOIRS

OF

JUDGE JEFFREYS.

CHAP. I.

Birth and parentage of Jeffreys—His love of splendour—Anecdote
—Goes to school at Shrewsbury, St. Paul's free-school, and to
Westminster—Recollection of Busby—Jeffreys a lawyer against
his father's consent—His remarkable dream—He is entered of
the Inner Temple—Sir Geoffry Palmer, attorney-general to
Charles II.—Studies of Jeffreys—His love of the bottle—He is
the zealous supporter of the democratic faction, who encourage
him and assist him with money.

GEORGE JEFFREYS was the sixth son of John
Jefferys, Esq. of Acton,[1] near Wrexham, in the

---

[1] Now the property of Sir Foster Cunliffe, Bart. Acton
had been for a long time in the family: and Pennant
is pleased to tell us of the obloquy which must have fallen on
the race of Jeffreys, by the production of the chancellor, after
it had so long run uncontaminated from an ancient stock.

A

county of Denbigh, by Margaret, daughter of
Sir Thomas Ireland,[1] Knight, of Bewsey, in the
County Palatine of Lancaster, and was born at
his father's house about the year 1648.

His paternal grandfather was a judge of North
Wales (though some call him a justice of peace
for that principality), and claimed on his father's
side a descent from Tudor Trevor, Earl of
Hereford.

John Jeffreys,[2] the father, was held to be a
gentleman in his neighbourhood; and although
his estate was not large, he lived contentedly
upon his fortune, improving it by industry and
frugality, till, having gained the good-will of his
acquaintance, he obtained so good a recommendation to his intended wife, through a person of
some interest who knew him, as to win her hand
very successfully. Whether, as some have said,
he indulged a niggardly and covetous disposition,
or was, according to others, prudent and economi-
cal (for men differ somewhat as to the bounds between thriftiness and parsimony), it is admitted
that he was a cautious and careful housekeeper,

[1] Probably of Gray's Inn, and the same who abridged
eleven books of Lord Coke's Reports, and the Reports of
Chief Justice Dyer.
[2] The original name of the family was Jefferys, although
the chancellor wrote his name Jeffreys.

that he prospered on the fruits of his exertions, and lived in peace and happiness with his partner at home. But he was decidedly a foe to extravagance; and we will here give an instance of the dislike which he bore to that fashionable vice. When his son George had supplanted that good old cavalier, Sir Job Charlton, in the chief-justiceship of Chester, he thought to dazzle his old companions and the unassuming natives of his birth-place with the splendour of his new state. Accordingly, he purposed a visit to his father, and went forth with a train so numerous, that the cider-barrels ran very fast, and the larder was in a state of perpetual exhaustion: on which the old gentleman put himself into such a fret, that he charged his son with a design to ruin him, by bringing a whole country at his heels, and bade him never attempt the like prodigality with hopes of success. The reverend old man lived to a very considerable age, having witnessed his son's eminence and downfall; but he ever withheld his sanction from those arbitrary measures which the chancellor pursued. Pennant saw a likeness of him at Acton House, taken in the year 1690, in the eighty-second year of his age.

George, who, were we writing romance, would be called the hero of these pages, showed very early that prompt address and activity which

were the causes of his rising: he was always
striving for the mastery over his young companions; and, although he inherited no ambition
from his parents, he was indebted to their diligence for the improvement of his enterprising
parts.

When yet very young, he was sent to the free-
school at Shrewsbury, where he remained some
time, we are told, not without credit; and on his
leaving that place, it appears to have been the
wish of his father that he should have settled to
some trade, for he had already evinced proofs
of a disposition far from tractable. This sober
career, however, would have been a sad check
to the untameable spirit of Jeffreys: no fatherly
admonitions would, probably, have hindered him
from becoming the idle apprentice; and he certainly possessed talents and propensities, which,
had he been kept in an inferior station, might
have procured him his quietus in those turbulent
times much sooner than the ambitious bearing
of his elevated fortunes. It seems as though
his mind was instinctively bent upon aggrandisement; and he was so fortunate as to discover,
youthful as he was, the importance of learning
and information: he is, therefore, described as
being addicted to study; so it was determined
to give him the benefit of a superior education
at St. Paul's free-school. Here he acquired a

fair proficiency in the learned languages;[1] and he imbibed also in this place that fondness for the profession of the law, which led him to fix on it as his future destiny. He afterwards went to Westminster school, then under the care of Dr. Busby, whose rod bears as high a character as his learning.[2] Of his improvement here we have no account; but many years afterwards he showed that he had not forgotten his old school-master, nor the knowledge of grammar he had acquired. On the trial of Rosewell, the dissenting minister, there was a little conversation about the relative and the antecedent on an objection taken to the indictment; and Jeffreys, the chief justice, referring to a treasonable sentence charged

[1] Not, as has been said, under the care of Dr. Gill. There were two Gills, father and son, successively masters of St. Paul's school; but the last was removed from his situation in 1635, and died in 1642, before the birth of Jeffreys. John Langley was the next, and he died much beloved by his scholars in 1657. He was succeeded by Samuel Cromleholme, or Crumlum, who, from his acquaintance with languages, obtained the name of πολυγλωττος,* and under him, young Jeffreys probably received his education. St. Paul's school was burnt in his time.

[2] There was another George Jeffreys, a lawyer, who was born at Weldon, in Northamptonshire, and who went to that school. He died in 1755, at the age of 77.

* Many-tongued.

to have been delivered by the prisoner from his
pulpit, said—" I think it must be taken to be an
entire speech, and you lay it in the indictment to
be so, and then the relative must go to the last
antecedent, or else Dr. Busby (that so long ruled
in Westminster school) taught me quite wrong;
and who had tried most of the grammars extant,
and used to lay down that as a positive rule, that
the relative must refer to the next antecedent."[1]

His desire for forensic debate was, however,
very far from being agreeable at home: often
and earnestly was he entreated by his father to
desist from a pursuit which savoured too much

---

[1] The words were—" We have had two wicked kings
together, who have permitted popery to enter in under their
noses, whom we can resemble to no other person than to the
most wicked Jeroboam ; and that if they would stand to their
principles, he did not fear but they would overcome their
enemies, as in former times, with rams' horns, broken platters,
and a stone in a sling."

And this is the observation of the lord chief justice :

" Suppose you were to speak it in English, Mr. Solicitor "
(indictments were then drawn in Latin)—" Now we have had
two wicked kings together, who have suffered popery to come
in under their noses (meaning the late king and this)—there
perhaps the inuendo is sensible, and no doubt of it ; then he
must mean *them :* but to say, If they will stand to their principles, they shall overcome their enemies ; pray to whom
does that ' *they*' relate ?"

of ambition to please a retired country gentleman; and when all dissuasions were found to be
unavailable, the signal of yielding to his wishes
was a gentle pat upon the back, accompanied by
these words: "Ah, George, George, I fear thou
wilt die with thy shoes and stockings on." Surely
the prophecy would have been accomplished,
but for the chancellor's sudden death in the
Tower. Some have said, that this legal impulse
arose from a dream which the ambitious boy
had whilst at this school. The substance of it
was, that "he should be the chief scholar there,
and should afterwards enrich himself by study
and industry, and that he should come to be
the second man in the kingdom; but in conclusion, should fall into great disgrace and misery."
This he told, when he came to the chancellorship: never imagining that the last part of it
could possibly befall him. But whatever might
have been his vapourings after his elevation, a
much more probable reason may be assigned
for his decision.

The profits of the law were greatly diminished
during the broils of the civil wars, and the
steady careful times of the Commonwealth; but
no sooner had the new system of things been
established, than the business of the counsellors
revived: they began to set up their equipages,

and to make a splendid show of the improved
fortune which had befallen them; and this,
doubtless, excited a youth who was never backward to discover the bright side of human life,
and who, being without an estate himself, was
thus stimulated by the hopes of acquiring one.

With all his constancy, Jeffreys needed one
essential towards the prosecution of that pursuit
which he had marked out for himself, and that
was the main-spring and engine of all human
action—money. His father, encumbered with
a large family, could scarcely have afforded assistance to his younger son, had he conformed
himself to the manners of his home; much less
would he create the means to promote an end so
hostile to his feelings. And, perhaps, it had
been happy for the state-prisoners of after-times,
if this aspiring youngster had been without
another relation :—but it happened, that he was
not only blessed with a fond grandmother, but
had either so far insinuated himself into her
good graces, or recommended himself to her
pride, that she came forward with an annuity of
forty pounds for him; and when his father found
this to be the case, he did not scruple ten
pounds a year more for decent clothing. Notwithstanding all these pushing efforts, he never
had the benefit of an University education.

He was entered of the Inner Temple, May 19, 1663; and, in an obscure apartment, commenced a study of the municipal law very diligently: while, at the same time, his pecuniary means were such, as to call upon his best wits for subsistence in a profession which bore a distinguished character for gentility. Templars of the present day can have a better idea of this dull lodging than of most ancient buildings; for, without the aid of Sir Walter's lively colouring, they can behold the very original of dulness in many corners of the learned spot which they people so thickly. Roger North, therefore, finds easy credit, when he applauds the good fortune of his relative[1] in coming into Sir Geoffry Palmer's[2] chambers, which were very commodious;

[1] The Lord Keeper.

[2] Geoffry Palmer was of Carlton in Northamptonshire. He was a very considerable lawyer, and the first attorney-general after the Restoration. He was employed against the unfortunate Earl of Strafford; and in November, 1642, was sent to the Tower for opposing " the Grand Remonstrance," after which he retired into Oxfordshire. In May, 1655, he was again imprisoned, on suspicion of being concerned in a plot against the Protector; and, we are told by a facetious writer, that he never could be persuaded to write Oliver any otherwise than with a little o. In 1660 he was knighted, made attorney to the King, and chief justice of Chester; and on the 7th of June, in the same year, a baronet. His wife was

having a gallery, and at the end a closet, with a
little garden. Here Sir Francis North could
turn about, and walk and talk with a friend: a
situation so eligible, that a few more such would
brighten up the countenance of many a recluse
of this day.

The saying of Juvenal—

> Magnis virtutibus obstat
> Res angusta domi —'

seems most applicable, where the sufferer is of
a modest and retiring habit ; but fails of its point,
when poverty drives forth the man of pleasantry
and humour to seek the pleasures of society,
and makes him acquire by his ingenuity an
access to those festivities he would vainly dream
of in his domestic solitude. Jeffreys was not
the man to sit silently in his chamber, either

Margaret, daughter of Sir Francis Moore, serjeant-at-law, of
Fawley, Berks, by whom he had four sons and two daughters.
He died, May 5, 1670, at Hampstead, aged 72, and was interred, having first lain in state in the Middle Temple Hall,
with great funeral honours. It was to a cultivated friendship
with Edward, the fourth son of Sir Geoffry, that the Lord
Keeper North owed an introduction to the family of that
great pleader, and much of his subsequent good fortune.

' " Slow rises worth, by poverty deprest."
JOHNSON.

mourning over the depths of the law, or indulging in that paradise of anticipation the advent of
clients: he was out and abroad in season and
out of season; grave with the grave, and cheerful
with the gay.

Most probably he was never a profound lawyer; and these holiday-makings were certainly
obstacles to the attainment of a difficult science.
But there were other reasons which diverted
him from a course of perpetual application—other
temptations which fell in with his ardent disposition, and easily seduced him from his abode of
silence.

The tide of conviviality had now strongly set
in: to refuse the social glass would have been to
court the martyrdom of Puritanism: every countenance was lighted up by the new-born hilari-
ties of the Restoration—every heart felt relieved
from the stern austerities of the republican tyrant; and this change agreed exactly with the
temper of our promising student. He was now
in a condition to consider every free dinner as a
boon of the first order, and was very willing in
return to enliven the entertainment with his
jests and sallies. Indeed, he was not the first
student who has readily deserted his apartment
to become an animated and welcome member of
the cheerful board; or who has forgotten to re-

turn thither when summoned to the drawing-
room, where his wit and address have made him
equally a favourite.

Yet these freedoms with Littleton and Coke,
truly hostile as they must be to the character of
a black-letter scholar, are calculated to give
the man who ventures on them an enlarged acquaintance with the world; and when a man
has determined to push his fortune unaided by
interest or influence, how much is done by ef-
frontery, and a certain easy indifference to the
rules by which others are governed, and abide!
These last qualities were eminently possessed
by Mr. Jeffreys; they accorded remarkably with
his versatile genius, which seldom failed to take
advantage of a beneficial change, or make any
sacrifice consistent with personal advancement.

The following whimsical lines are to be found
in an old poem, called "Jeffrey's Elegy."

> " I very well remember, on a night,
> 　Or rather on the peep of morning light,
> 　When sweet Aurora, with a smiling eye,
> 　Call'd up the birds to wonted melody,—
> 　Dull Morpheus with his weight upon me leant;
> 　Half-waking, and yet sleeping, thus I dreamt.
> 　Methought I saw a lawyer at his book,
> 　Studying Pecunia, but never Cooke;
> 　He scorned Littleton and Plowden too,
> 　With mouldy authors he'd have nought to do."

It might have been supposed, that as this lawyer was launched upon the world at the time when regal glories were revived, he would have lost no opportunity of proving himself a steady loyalist, and more especially as an indulgence in unrestrained pleasure was familiar with the career which he proposed for himself. But although the public voice was in favour of royalty, a host of discontented sufferers, angry republicans, and disaffected persons remained, to whom rest seemed a burthen, and tranquillity a crime. This is not the place for us to enter into the reasons of this disgust: it is sufficient to say that their labours were unceasing to procure converts to their cause; that their encouragement when they had found a partizan was no less abundant; and that, amongst the society which they had thus zealously drawn together, the needy and ambitious Jeffreys was numbered. He had now the means of turning his insinuating address to an excellent account; and he soon gained access to the chief of the party, with whom he so fully ingratiated himself, as to leave a conviction of his capacity and readiness to further their designs. Nor was he backward to perceive, that a great impression had been made by his blustering forwardness; and that their patronage would, at that moment, be of incal-

culable benefit to a beginner at the bar, to
whom the united efforts of a faction, however
obnoxious or inconsiderable, would be far pre-
ferable to the obscurity in which, unconnected
as he was, he might expect for some time to be
involved.

But this was not all: the difficulties of his
pecuniary means [1] were ever present with him;
and what scruples could be found sufficient to
deter a licentious adventurer from pursuing a
course likely to extricate him from the pressure
of want, and give free play to his luxuries?
Talents like his were not to be monopolized
without a speedy return for the services they
rendered; and thus he soon became a caressed
and cherished pensioner upon his new friends:
his allowance was no longer a source of apprehension: if he felt any anxiety, it was to display
all possible zeal and energy in the cause of those
who were so bountifully feeding him.

Thus, he would talk, write, or fight for them
if required; and it is further related of him, that,
in the hour of revelry, he would drink on his
knees the most approved toasts among the mal-

[1] His must have been at this time a perpetual "pecuniary
crisis." *

* The cant word during the great commercial panic of 1825 and 1826.

contents, which, as may be conjectured, were not a little treasonable: so that there quickly sprang from the rustic brood of a Welsh gentleman, a champion armed at all points for the destruction of kingly power.

CHAP. II.

Jeffreys pleads at Kingston at the age of eighteen, two years before
he is called to the bar—Paucity of lawyers—Boldness of his
carriage—His clear enunciation—Ingenious artifice to obtain
briefs — Cross-examining — Disinterested motive of Jeffreys'
marriage with the kinswoman of the heiress whom he first courted
—Amiable temper of his wife, Lady Sarah—He receives countenance from a namesake, Alderman Jeffreys—He is appointed
common-serjeant—His blustering in concealment of a bribe—
Jeffreys betrays the democrats, and accedes to the court party—
Friendship with Chiffinch, the King's page—Jeffreys, recorder
of London, owes his advancement to political tergiversation.

It has been asserted, that the young aspirant
was never called regularly to the bar; whilst,
according to others, he performed the exercises
allotted to students, and, having complied with
the customs of his Inn, was published in the
ordinary way, if we except his being promoted
over the heads of elder graduates through the
interest which he made with the benchers.
Perhaps this irregularity was alleged against
him in after-times, when every tale to his discredit met doubtless with a ready believer; but
the origin of the report may be traced beyond
question to his conduct at Kingston assizes,

during the plague. There, when the hearts of many, and amongst others those of the counsellors, were failing them, by reason of the neighbouring calamity, this youth, although but eighteen, put a gown upon his back and began to plead; and although he continued to act as an advocate continually from that time, it is certain that he was not called to the bar until two years afterwards; and he was probably admitted to speak upon that emergency, from the impracticability of inquiring into his qualification, which, on his own part, so far from denying, he most probably vehemently asserted. Indeed, the lawyers had been of late so much thinned by the calamities of civil war and pestilence, that the number of admittances at Gray's Inn had decreased from the usual quantity of one hundred and upwards, to a number nearly as low as fifty; on which account, a daring interloper might enter the field with a success to which in ordinary times he would have been utterly a stranger.

However gloomy the early days of Jeffreys's noviciate might have been, he could not be said to have embarked as an advocate without support; for he was backed in the first instance by the active confederacy, whose organ he had been. The party had been delighted with his zeal for

B

them, had foretold his future success, and applauded the choice of his profession; and they
now combined to give him their united confidence and interest.

It was at Guildhall, Hickes's Hall, and before
inferior courts, that he first essayed his powers;
and these he at first preferred to Westminster,
by reason of the frequency of their sittings, and
the comparative ease which attended the dis-
patch of business there; and there is good reason to believe that he went the home circuit.

He was of a bold aspect, and cared not for
the countenance of any man: his tongue was
voluble; his words audible, and clearly understood;[1] and he never spared any which were at
all likely to assist his client.[2] These advantages

---

[1] The following testimony to his loud voice took place at
the trial of Sir Patience Ward for perjury. It was necessary to call people as witnesses who had heard Sir Patience
give evidence at a former trial, and among these was Mr.
Northey.

Mr. Serjeant Jeffreys to Northey—" You heard my
question, when I said to him his invention was better than
his memory; upon your oath, upon what occasion was it?"

Mr. Northey—" I can't say, Sir George, what; but your
voice being much louder than other men's, I heard you
plainly."

[2] The description given of him by a poetaster of those
days has something in confirmation of this :—

soon forced him into notice: so that fees, the forerunners of legal preferment, soon crowded upon him; and we are even told, that persons would put a brief into his hand in the middle of a cause which they perceived likely to turn against them. He was not above adopting any artifice which might raise him in the estimation of those with whom he associated: so that, when he was sitting in a coffee-house, his servant would come to him under his previous direction, and say, that company attended him in his chamber, which was the signal for him to huff, and desire them to be told to stay a little, and that he would come presently. This ingenious trick helped forward his reputation for business; and it is not by any means an exaggeration to say, that he found himself in considerable practice sooner than almost any one of his contemporaries.

Nevertheless he sometimes received a check, in common with many others of his brethren, when they venture upon the occasional recreation of bantering witnesses, and in return meet

---

" But yet he's chiefly devil about the mouth."

And again:

" Oft with success this mighty blast did bawl,
Where loudest lungs and biggest words win all."

now and then with a smart stroke of humour, which coming from the intended butt of the auditory, seldom fails to disconcert the astonished assailant. A country-fellow was giving his evidence clad in a leather doublet,[1] and Mr. Jeffreys, who was counsel for the opposite party, found that his testimony was " pressing home." When he came to cross-examine, he bawled forth; " You fellow in the leather doublet, pray what have you for swearing ?" The man looked steadily at him, and, " Truly, sir," said he, " if you have no more for lying than I have for swearing, you might wear a leather doublet as well as I." Of course every body laughed, and the neighbourhood rang with the bluntness of the reply.

He had another rebuff when he was recorder. There was a wedding somewhere,—and those to whom it appertained to pay for the music at the nuptials refused the money, on which an action was brought; and as the " musitioners" were proving their case, the judge called out,—" You fiddler !" This made the witness wroth, and he appeared to be disgusted; but shortly afterwards he called himself a " mu-

[1] " His doublet was of sturdy buff,
    And tho' not sword, yet cudgel-proof."
                                    Hudibras.

sitioner," on which Jeffreys asked, what difference there was between a "; musitioner" and a
fiddler. "As much, sir," said the man of melody, "as there is between a pair of bagpipes
and a recorder."

One more story:—Some gentleman in the
course of his evidence was making use of the
law terms lessor and lessee, assignor and as-
signee; which might have escaped observation,
had not his testimony been directly against
Jeffreys's client: "You there, with your law
terms of your lessor and lessee, and of your as-
signee and your assignor, do you know what a
lessee or lessor is? I don't believe that you
know that, for all your formal evidence." "Yes,
Sir George," said the witness, in reply to this
gasconade, "but I do, and I'll give you this instance: if I nod to you, I am the nodder, and if
you nod to me, then I am the noddee."

A lucky advocate, such as we have just spoken
of, could scarcely hope for any better stroke of
fortune at this time than a successful marriage,
and he had been by no means unmindful of this
chance. He had acquired a very winning air
amongst the fairer sex, and was therefore the
more qualified to gain the hearts of women,
whose generosity will often pass by unheeded
the prejudices of birth and wealth, where they

meet with the plausible address of an affable and earnest suitor.

An opportunity was not long wanting; for Jeffreys thought the daughter of a merchant who had thirty thousand pounds, a prize far too valuable to be left unattempted. He accordingly prepared for the trial, and gained over a kinswoman and companion of the lady, through whom he silently addressed her. His cause was espoused so warmly by the disinterested relation whom we have mentioned, that it seems very likely that the heiress would have yielded to her friend's recommendation; but the suspicions of her father were aroused by some accident which cannot now be known: the plot was unravelled, the daughter effectually secured, and the unfortunate negotiator dismissed and discarded.

Upon this sad *denouement,* the kinswoman came hastily towards London, to acquaint the disappointed lover with the failure of his cause. He went to her on this occasion to hear the relation of the whole circumstance, when a result most unforeseen and unexpected arose from the visit. He applauded her zeal for his welfare, the hazard which she had incurred for him, and compassionated the calamity which had befallen her on his account; and which was still more grateful and generous, and the more extraordinary for a man of his aspiring character, he proposed, as some satisfaction for her misfortunes, that she should be a substitute for her rich relation; in a word, that she should be his wife.

There are persons who, if an obnoxious character should by chance perform a kind office, are nevertheless quite ready to attribute his benevolence to some interested motive, or to neutralise the good bearing of it by some subtle insinuation; in the minds of such, this conduct on the part of the young advocate would naturally give rise to much conjecture, and, considering the future conduct of the man, would provoke an unfavourable interpretation if there were any room for it. But it is worthy of consideration, that amongst all the faults with which this judge has been charged, whatever may have been his anxiety to grasp large possessions, whatever his eagerness to feed his own ambition at the expense of others;—a want of generosity, independently of that ambition, has never been attributed to him, but rather a habit of prodigality; and there is not any reason why censures of a new kind should be laid upon one who has been already the object of so many. This was certainly one

of those bursts of good feeling which spring
occasionally from the darkest of men,—a bright
gleam of sunshine amidst a world of mist.

On the 23d of May, 1667, he married, at All-
hallows Church, Barking, Sarah, the daughter
of Thomas Neesham, A. M. And it was by no
means a discreditable alliance : he had espoused
the daughter of a clergyman; and although
she could not be said to be mistress of thousands,
it seems that she brought her husband three
hundred pounds. And he had not erred in
judgment, if he foresaw that his partner had
possessions of much greater price than the pit-
tance of money which he received with her,
since she proved an excellent wife;—a very
great acquisition to one of his careless and dis-
solute manners. By this lady he had several
children, of whom we shall have occasion to
speak hereafter.

As the tide of Jeffreys's fortune set in first at
Guildhall, it is no wonder that we soon find him
wedded to the luxuries and jovialities of the
great city. His chief object was to make an
interest for himself in London; and by the
carelessness of his disposition, and his love for
social hours, he succeeded in gaining the affections of many opulent merchants. There

were, indeed, two aldermen of the same name with himself about this time;[1] and although it does not seem to be agreed whether they were in any way related to him, there being assertions on both sides;—one of them, a great smoker, took a vast fancy to his namesake, and very soon determined to push his fortune with all the strength of his purse and connection, which was far from being inconsiderable.

Accordingly, young as he was, scarcely indeed twenty-three, on the resignation or surrender of Sir Richard Browne, Bart., he was made common serjeant.

This elevation took place March 17, 1670-71.

[1] John Jeffreys elected sheriff of London, and alderman of Bread-street, in 1661; but discharged from both offices on paying fines.

Robert Jeffreys, sheriff in 1674, and knighted. He was elected alderman of Cordwainer's ward in 1676, and lord mayor in 1686, died in 1704. An hospital was erected in Kingsland Road in 1712, pursuant to his will, for as many of the founder's relations as should apply for the charity; and in default thereof, for fifty-six poor members of the company. He was buried at St. Dionis' Backchurch, where there is a stately monument to his memory.

Jeffery Jeffreys, knt. sheriff in 1700, alderman of Portsoken 1701, died at Roehampton in 1709, and was buried at St. Andrew Undershaft.

One of these, probably Robert, was called, by way of distinction ($\kappa\alpha\tau'$ $\epsilon\xi o\chi\eta\nu$), "the great smoker."

But he was not yet a servile favourite; for either presuming upon the good-will which he had secured by his address among the citizens, or impelled by that confidence which so often accompanies success, he was accustomed to set the authority of the mayor and aldermen at defiance, and, in fact, he never rested until he had placed the city entirely at his devotion. How he conducted himself with respect to the orphanage dues, with which he was concerned by virtue of his office,* we are not informed : had there, however, been any cause of complaint against him on this ground, posterity would probably, through the zeal of some enemy, have been made acquainted with it. Yet, as far as interest would avail, the following story will show that he could control the application of the funds, even when recorder.

A country gentleman married a city orphan, and demanded her fortune, about £1100, but could not procure it. At length, all friends failing, he betook himself to Mr. Recorder with ten guineas in hand, which the learned officer received, and informed his visitor that the court of aldermen would sit on a certain day, na-

* See Bohun's Privilegia Londini, 1723, p. 329, where the business of the common serjeant with these orphans' portions is described.

ming it. The gentleman attended it. " Sirrah! what's your business?" quoth Jeffreys. The application was made in form. Had he asked the consent of the court of aldermen? To which the suitor replied in the negative. Jeffreys complimented him forthwith with the terms rogue and rascal, and told him he should have asked leave of the court for such a marriage. The gentleman asked pardon, and pleaded ignorance of the city customs, but this did not save him from fresh abuse. Nevertheless, there soon appeared a note from the great man, authorizing the receipt of the money; and all the blustering was ascribed to an anxiety on the part of Mr. Recorder that the court should not peer into the bribe.

We shall now have occasion to speak of an entire revolution in the political prospects of our wary common serjeant. The reader has been apprised of the subtlety and address with which he became acquainted with the secrets of a faction, as well as of the outward regard which he professed for his disaffected friends; and it has been no secret, that of all the men who ever thirsted for preferment, Jeffreys was the most eager. Some, who have in view the prospect of considerable good which they cannot reach without a sacrifice of their ancient friendships, will withdraw themselves with a gradual and quiet backsliding from their associates; and while they forswear the inconsistent intercourse, will hold the confidence inviolate which has been reposed in them. Others again, advancing a little farther on the same ground, although they have gained sufficient boldness to betray the counsels which have been entrusted to them, have yet abstained from grosser acts of hostility, and have patiently anticipated the fruits of their apostacy. But we have now a character before us, who would have held this proficiency in changing sides as merely trifling; he had not only the nerve to desert his confederates, and to expose their secrets, but to harrass them with furious persecution; and if he met with any in after life, to treat them " not only as if they were his greatest enemies, but as if they were the common enemies of mankind."

Well may a reason be demanded for this most singular proceeding: we have none to give as it respects his friends, for it seems that they had given him no provocation; but as it respects his preferment, when we come to detail the result, it would be weakness to say otherwise than that reasoning on the subject must be superfluous.

The court party had become triumphant, and

places and honours, which flowed abundantly from them, were the rewards of a pliant favourite and an easy conscience. Comparatively obscure as the common serjeant might be, nature had never denied him a yielding and careless demeanour; so that in these respects he was a fitting candidate for the favour of those in high office. He had, moreover, the sense to know that employments were never bestowed upon the factious, unless they gave strong proof of their regeneration, and by some bold stroke confirmed their apostate acts. He had held his present situation for some years, was in a vast career of forensic business, and, which weighed still more with him, the recorder, Sir John Howel,' was spoken of as likely to quit his place. Now, although the gradual ascent from the one of these offices to the other was not, as at present, by any means common, it could not fail to strike Jeffreys, that, if he showed a bold disposition to serve the court, he might be made recorder; and that there could not be a more favourable conjuncture for a turn in his politics than one which promised a vacancy he could so faithfully

' Howel presided at the trial of the celebrated William Penn for a tumultuous assembly, and treated his prisoners with a ferocity which Jeffreys could not have excelled. In the State Trials he is called Thomas Howel, Recorder.

supply, for just then the city was on very fair terms with the government.

He soon decided, changed at once, made no secret of his treachery, and bade defiance to the revenge of those whom he had thus abandoned.[1]

But reason suggests that we should seek a better cause for the kind reception of this man by the court, than his being a sudden renegade from a discontented and defeated party; since, whatever might have been his flexibility, whatever the nature of his disclosures, he could scarcely have expected impunity, much less promotion, by virtue of this tergiversation. One writer[2] attributes this result to a successful ambition on the part of Jeffreys for advancement; another[3] speaks of his accumulating profits and connection; but Mr. North, in his Life of Lord Guilford, seems to throw much more light upon the subject by giving a note of the Lord Keeper

[1] Well, quoth Sir G. the whigs may think me rude,
   Or brand me guilty of ingratitude;
   At my preferment they (poor fools!) may grudg,
   And think me fit for hangman more than judg;
   But though they fret, and bite their nails, and brawl,
   He'll slight them, and go kiss dear Nelly Wall.[*]
                                   Midsummer Moon.
[2] The Author of his life and character, 1725.
[3] The Author of the Bloody Assizes.

[*] Nell Gwyn.

himself regarding this affair.' After introducing
the celebrated royal page Chiffinch² as a com-

¹ We give the quotation at length, being in itself highly
interesting: "Then being acquainted with Will. Chiffinch
(the trusty page of the back stairs), struck in, and was
made recorder." This Mr. Chiffinch was a true secretary as
well as page; for he had a lodging at the back stairs, which
might have been properly termed the spy office, where the
king spoke with particular persons about intrigues of all
kinds; and all little informers, projectors, &c. were carried
to Chiffinch's lodging. He was a most impetuous drinker,
and, in that capacity, an admirable spy; for he let none part
from him sober, if it were possible to get them drunk; and his
great artifice was pushing idolatrous healths of his good
master, and being always in haste, for the *king is coming*,
which was his word. Nor, to make sure work, would he
scruple to put his master's salutiferous drops (which were
called the King's, of the nature of Goddard's,) into the
glasses; and being an Hercules, well breathed at the sport
himself, he commonly had the better, and so fished out many
secrets, and discovered men's characters, which the king
could never have obtained the knowledge of by any other
means. It is likely that Jeffreys, being a pretender to main-
feats with the citizens, might forward himself, and be entertained by Will. Chiffinch; and that, which at first was
mere spying, turn to acquaintance, if not friendship, such as
is apt to grow up between immane drinkers; and from thence
might spring recommendations of him to the king, as the
most useful man that could be found to serve his Majesty in
London, where was need enough of good magistrates, and,
such as would not be, as divers were, accounted no better
than traitors.—8vo. ed. vol. ii. pp. 98, 99.

² There were two Chiffinchs, both closet-keepers to King

plete court spy, and a most incorrigible wine-bibber, he tells us that Jeffreys was in the habit of keeping company with this trusty servant, and that something like regard sprang up between them; whence it happened that a strong recommendation of Chiffinch's guest went forth to his Majesty, as a person likely to do good service.

It seems that the era of this entertainment and confidence was that in which the young lawyer was immersing himself in faction, kneeling at one table to drink King Charles as " the god of his idolatry," at another, to pledge confusion to his reign.

A conclusion almost irresistible results from this inquiry; so that we are tempted to consider

---

Charles, perhaps father and son, but the latter is the most notorious character. The former is mentioned by Evelyn, and by Pepys in his Diary, who says that he died in 1666. The latter, therefore, must have been the companion of Jeffreys. This man was the royal pimp, and used to find cons.ant employment in discovering new faces for his master. He lived much with Nell Gwyn at Filberd's, which was a favourite seat of the king in Berkshire; and it was his duty to see t.at every accommodation was provided for the fair courtezans. It was Chiffinch who introduced the priest Hudleston to the king's dying bed, when the bishops were requested to withdraw for a season, little dreaming that their sovereign was on better terms with the Pope than with the followers of Luther.

Jeffreys, during much of this interval, as a spy of the court, pledged deep by Chiffinch on one side and paid by the foes to royalty on the other; that he was playing his game like a general, who is prepared to act on the offensive when occasion offers; that he would have held to the mal-contents if the crown had been vanquished, as he deserted them when the city honours were blossoming within his grasp. It is probable also, that about this time, he became acquainted with the celebrated Duchess of Portsmouth through this channel of favouritism: certain it is, that allusion was made in the ballads of those times to Her Grace as an enemy to Monmouth, and no mean friend to our recorder.

> Monmouth's tamer, Jeffery's advance,
> Foe to England, spy to France,
> False and foolish, proud and bold,
> Ugly, as you see, and old.
> *Duchess of Portsmouth's Picture.*

La fin couronne les œuvres. Sept. 14, 1677, he was knighted; and on the resignation of Sir William Dolben,' who was made a judge of the

---

' William Dolben was recorder of London, after the cession of Sir John Howel. He was made judge of the King's Bench in October, 1678; but removed from that place in

c

King's Bench, was elected Oct. 22, 1678, recorder of London; or, as he himself termed it,
the "mouth-piece of the city;" thus attaining
to be capital judge of the Guildhall, in which
he first began his prosperous pleading. There
were three other candidates, Mr. Richardson,
a judge of the Sheriff's Court; Mr. Turner, of
Gray's Inn; and Mr. Roger Belwood,' a barrister of the Middle Temple; and Nicholls, in
his History of Leicestershire, has furnished a note
extracted from the city records, from whence it
appears that Sir George was "freely and unanimously elected by scrutiny."

1683 to make room for Wythens, who scrupled less to fulfil
the measures of the new court-party. However, as soon as
the Prince of Orange came in, he was restored to his seat
again, and died in 1693. There have been some great men
of this name: John Dolben, archbishop of York, and the
late Sir William Dolben, Bart. and LL.D. whose knowledge of church history was so much distinguished during
some recent debates on the Test Act.

' Roger Belwood was engaged in many of the state prosecutions during the latter part of King Charles's reign. He
was afterwards a serjeant, and died about 1691. His library
was extremely choice, and some rare tracts and manuscripts
were sold by auction after his decease.—See *Bibliotheca
Belwoodiana.*

CHAP. III.

THE new recorder became a widower shortly
before his elevation, for Lady Jeffreys had died
on the fourteenth of the preceding February :[1]

[1] She was buried on the 18th, in the vault at Aldermanbury church.

upon this, he lost no time in repairing the domestic breach; and while he had proved that
his first marriage had been an effusion of generosity, he showed by his second choice that he
was not unwilling to unite attachment with interest. He, accordingly, made his advances to
the widow of a Montgomeryshire gentleman,[1]
a daughter of Sir Thomas Bludworth,[2] who had
been lord mayor, and for many years one of
the city representatives, and he very soon succeeded in his wishes, for the citizens of London
were always ready at that time to match their
children with favoured courtiers.[3]

He married this lady about May, 1678, not
more than three months from the death of the
former; and by her also had several children,
whom we shall mention at a future time. The
assertion of several writers, that his first wife
lived to see him chief justice of England,—is
therefore clearly ill-founded, though the mistake
might have arisen from the register of burials in

[1] Mr. Jones.

[2] An account of this knight is given in a subsequent page.

[3] A proof of this is the earnestness with which Sir John
Lawrence, the city broker, desired the union of one of his
daughters with Mr. Solicitor-general North.—See *Life of
Lord Guilford*, 4to. p. 79.

St. Mary, Aldermanbury, where the lady *Sarah* Jeffreys is stated to have died in 1703; whereas his second wife, Lady Ann, certainly died in that year.

It was indeed time that Mrs. Jones should again enter into the legitimate state of marriage, for she certainly was brought to bed of a son much too early for a common calculator to say otherwise than that there had been a mistake somewhere. And Jeffreys was once very uncomfortably reminded of this precipitancy by a lady who was giving her evidence pretty sharply in a cause which he was advocating. "Madam, you are very quick in your answers!" cries the counsel. "As quick as I am, Sir George, I was not so quick as your lady."[1]

We cannot forbear to insert here that very curious copy of verses, called—

A Westminster Wedding, or the Town Mouth;[2] *alias, the Recorder of London and his Lady: Feb. 17, 1679.*

> 'Tis said when George did dragon slay,
> He saved a maid from cruel fray:
> But this Sir George, whom knaves do brag on,
> Mist of the maid, and caught the dragon;

[1] There were reasons, therefore, for Jeffreys's second marriage so soon after the death of his wife.

[2] " Mouth-piece of the city."—*Jeffreys.*

Since which, the furious beast so fell,
Stares, roars, and yawns like mouth of hell:
He raves and tears, his bad condition
Distracts his mind, as late petition.
Peace man, or beast (or both) to please ye,
A parliament will surely ease ye.
Marriage and hanging both do go
By destiny; Sir George, if so,
You stand as fairly both to have,
As ever yet did fool or knave:
The first your wife hath help'd ye to;
The other as a rogue's your due:
No other way is left to tame ye;
And if you have it not, then blame me.
But ere it comes, and things are fitting,
Judge of his merit by his getting:
He's got a ven'mous heart, and tongue
With vipers, snakes, and adders hung,
By which, in court he plays the fury,
Hectors complainant, law, and jury:
His impudence hath all laws broken,
(To the judges honour be it spoken,)
For which he got a name that stinks
Worse than the common jakes or sinks:
But to allay the scent so hot,
George from the court has knighthood got
Bestow'd upon him for his bawling,—
A royal mark for caterwauling:
But certain, George must never boast on't,
'Cause traitors, cheats, and pimps have most on't.
Now rogue enough he got in favour,
To bind good men to worse behaviour,

And bark aloud they will deceive ye,
In that he matches tribe of Levi;
Who now with Pope bear all before 'em,
Priests made just-asses of the quorum.
Faith make 'em judges too, most fine-o,
And then they'll preach it all Divino.
There's somewhat more that George has got,
(For Trevor[1] left him, who knows what)
A teeming lady-wife * * *
 *   *   *   *   *   *   *
 *   *   *   *   *   *   *
 *   *   *   *   *   *   *

But one thing more I can't let pass,
When George with Clodpate[2] feasted last,
(I must say Clodpate was a sinner,
To jerk his brother so at dinner,)
He by his almanack did discover,
His wife scarce thirty weeks went over,
Ere she (poor thing!) in pieces fell,
Which made Mouth stare and bawl like hell.
What then, you fool! some wives miscarry,
And reckon June for January.
This Clodpate did assert as true,
Which he by old experience knew,
But all his canting would not do.
George put him to 't upon denial,
Which set him hard as Wakeman's trial:
They rail'd, and bawl'd, and kept a pother,
And like two curs did bite each other,

[1] Sir John Trevor, said to be his lady's gallant in the time of her widowhood, &c.—*Note to the poem.* Of this Trevor we shall speak hereafter.
[2] Scroggs, lord chief justice of the King's Bench.

Which brought some sport, but no repentance ;
So off they went to Harris' sentence,
Which soon they pass'd against all laws,
To glut their rage and popish cause :
For which injustice, knaves ! we hope
You 'll end together in the rope :
And when the gallows shall you swallow,
We 'll throw up caps, and once more holloa.
If this we wish from private grudge,
Or as their merit, England 's judge :
Who seek the nation to enthrall
Are treacherous slaves and villains all.
And when confusion such does follow,
We 'll throw up caps, and once more holloa,
   That 's their exit,
   Tho' they rex-it,
   We shall grex-it.

Some persons about this time had printed a
Psalter, which they called " The King's Psalter,"
expecting to shelter themselves under the authority of so high a name from being called to
account for their piracy, for they had invaded
the rights of the Stationers' Company ; but this
subterfuge did not avail them, since the Company
immediately brought the matter before the Privy
Council, and being desirous of retaining a resolute advocate, they took the new recorder
with them in that capacity. Sir George thought

 ' Benjamin Harris, the bookseller.—*Note to the poem.*

this an admirable opportunity for him to attract
the notice of royalty; and he therefore, in opening the stationers' title to the property which
had been invaded, ventured upon a very bold
speech which had almost ruined any other man.
" They," meaning the literary pirates, " have
teemed," said he, " with a spurious brat, which
being clandestinely midwived into the world,
the better to cover the imposture, they lay it
at Your Majesty's door." Perhaps the King
might have been flattered (for much depended
upon his humour at particular times) with this
public proclamation of his gallantries; doubtless,
he thought it a most impudent address on the
part of his loyal recorder; but so far from re-
senting it, he turned to one of the lords who sat
next to him, and said, "This is a bold fellow, I'll
warrant him!" and he, probably, was so much
tickled with it, as to recollect very shortly afterwards, that no one could better befriend the
crest-fallen government, than he who had ha-
zarded so free a reflection upon the royal person.
The stationers had a decree in their favour.

The new magistrate was not destined to be long
inactive. Every one knows, that the furious
fanaticism against the Catholics burst forth
about this time, and that the Duke of York's
imprudent valour, in demanding an investiga-

tion of matters which very few at that time
knew or cared any thing for, kindled the em-
bers, which were just expiring, into a flame.
That which neither Dr. Tongue's hypocrisy, nor
Oates's quackery could effect, was most fully
accomplished by the royal Head of those who
were so soon to undergo the most wicked and
unmerited persecution.

And as though no incitement should be wanting to embroil the nation in civil tumult, Sir
Edmondbury Godfrey, who had taken informations against some of the accused papists, a man
naturally given to vapours and melancholy, was
found with the marks of strangulation upon him
in a ditch, and with a sword in his body. His
spleen is by some considered as sufficient to
brand him with the crime of suicide; but there
is equal reason to believe, that by some dark
contrivance of those who afterwards reaped such
immense harvests, he was made a victim to the
clamour of the day; the announcement of his
fate being a tocsin against the miserable followers
of popery. At first the people were comparatively passive, and seemed contented with a
few sacrifices; and during these early scenes of
blood, the recorder made his appearance, sometimes as counsel for the crown, sometimes as
judge to pass sentence of death upon the male-

factors. We shall see presently how the times
changed on a rumour that the plot was to be
stifled, and how Jeffreys was affected by the alteration.

He has been charged with violence throughout
the whole of his professional and judicial career,
and no doubt he was an overbearing advocate
and an intemperate judge; but he lived in a
day when all men of any spirit were vehement,
and when nearly all judges ' were given to rude
language: the marvel would have been, if he had
shown kindness, when fashion and prejudice ran
so strongly to the contrary: there could be none
to find him striking in with the confirmed mad-
ness of the age.² If it be once admitted that

' There must be an exception in favour of Sir Francis
North, and perhaps one or two others; but North had encouraged a very wary and fox-like demeanour during the whole
of his life.

² We do not by any means intend to justify the judge's
conduct upon this occasion; the chief object of the biographer
being to reveal every feeling of human nature in its clearest
light. But that which is held to be a crime in our age, might
have been esteemed a virtue in another; and it certainly was
not for a successful recorder, under the crooked policy of
Charles, to foresee these most liberal days, when every judicial movement is criticised with the utmost rigour. Had
the present improvements of the home secretary been suggested, it might be said, even twenty years since, they certainly
had been treated as chimerical, or at least marvellous in the

he was not worse than his contemporaries,' posterity will the more readily do him justice in
respect of any good qualities which he might
have possessed ; and these again will be displayed in a more favourable light, if virulent
and unlicensed invective can be silenced, though
it be but for a moment.

The first state prosecution against the supposed popish conspirators, was the case of
Coleman ; and if the account of those proceedings, as detailed in the state-trials, be carefully

extreme; *we* regard them, beyond a doubt, as proofs of an
enlightened legislation. We condemn those who have loaded
our statute-book with capital punishments ; but we do not give
them credit for that degree of information which has sprung
up since their day. Whatever might have been the asperity
of Jeffreys, it certainly was not exceeded by that of Rains-
ford, Scroggs, Pemberton, or Sanders ; and we must therefore
be content (laying aside all mention of his subsequent conduct)
to class him with those whose examples he was imitating ;
neither exaggerating his roughness, nor palliating it, by ap-
plauding the excesses of which he was guilty.

' He certainly could not have shown more jocoseness at a
capital trial than Sir William Dolben, who was a judge after
the Revolution. Thwing and another were indicted for high
treason at York ; and in the course of his challenges, Thwing
said,—" My lord, I shall willingly stand to the other jury."
—Justice Dolben. " What jury?"—Thwing. " My Lady
Tempest's jury."—Justice Dolben. " Oh, your servant ! you
are either very foolish, or take me to be so."

examined, it will be made evident, that however busy the recorder might have been as counsel for the crown, his conduct was mildness itself when compared with the harshness of the judges and serjeants towards the accused. And it is worthy of remark, that his anxiety for a regular system of evidence, which he was always ready to promote when on the bench, appeared upon this trial. Counsel were constantly in the habit of interrupting the witnesses, and that license was frequently allowed to the prisoner; but Jeffreys begged that the court would suffer Oates to go on without any interposition to the end of his story, which the chief justice promised, but soon interfered himself as briskly as any one. Ireland, Pickering, and Grove, were tried next; and notwithstanding the shrewd suspicions which we may entertain at this day of the recorder's sincerity, when he affected pity for these poor people, he went not one step farther in his denunciation of their religion and customs than other judges, who were occasionally called upon to give judgment of death upon the papists. The following specimen of his seeming commiseration, mixed with reflections on the superstitious ceremonies of the Catholics, is curious. "Thus I speak to you, gentlemen, not vauntingly; 'tis against my nature to insult upon

persons in your sad condition : God forgive you
for what you have done ; and I do heartily beg it,
though you don't desire I should : for, poor men !
you may believe that your interest in the world
to come is secured to you by your masses, but
do not well consider that vast eternity you must
ere long enter into, and that great tribunal you
must appear before, where his masses (speaking
to Pickering) will not signify so many groats to
him ; no, not one farthing. And I must say it,
for the sake of these silly people whom you have
imposed upon with such fallacies, that the
masses can no more save thee from a future
damnation, than they do from a present condemnation." He was next counsel on the trial
of Green, Berry, and Hill, for the murder of Sir
Edmondbury Godfrey ; and seems again to have
exercised great caution in abstaining from leading
the witnesses with questions, and eliciting their
testimony in a general manner, which varies but
little from the practice now followed. Here he
exhibited a strong sense of humanity and justice.
A tipstaff had deprived the prisoners of their
clothes as soon as they had been committed,
pretending that they were his fee; on which the
recorder, previously to his praying judgment,
complained openly to the court, and obtained an
order that the property should be restored ; a

barbarous custom having been set up in favour
of this plunder, but disallowed by the judges.

Shortly afterwards Langhorn and the Jesuits
were condemned, and it fell again to the recorder's lot to pronounce the judgment of death,
which he did with much apparent humanity,
regretting that one of his own brethren of the
bar had brought himself to a fate so untimely,
and giving express orders that the unfortunate
persons should receive every comfort, and enjoy
the company of their friends at all convenient
seasons. More tenderness could not now be
shown to prisoners in that unhappy situation,
saving, perhaps, the absence of abuse which
was then bestowed upon the unfashionable
creed.

The recorder, however, was certainly an object of terror to the Romish party, and they
used every effort to mollify him when they came
before him for judgment, but rarely with good
success; for he never was at a loss for some
sarcasm upon their religious opinions.

Yet it is curious to observe how pliant he
seemed when the names of the great and powerful were mentioned, especially if any high person had expressed himself favourably towards
the accused. As where Starkey, a condemned
priest, having been overruled on all the legal

objections which he had started, happened to plead the very gracious reception which he had received some years before from the King, the Duke of York, the Chancellor Hyde, and the Bishop of London, to whom he had unravelled some conspiracy;—Jeffreys softened directly, spoke of the King as a fountain of mercy, promised to relate every extenuating circumstance to His Majesty, and intimated in conclusion the excellent opportunity which the prisoner then had of enlightening the government on the subject of the plot. It is evident that he had been treated hitherto more as the tool than the confidant of the ministry; for they were then lying in wait for a convenient handle to brand the whole narration with imposture, though they dared not as yet brave the infatuation of the parliament and the populace. However, he in reality was never friendly to the Catholics, even when King James filled the throne, and it became his interest to patronize them. This is confirmed by an anecdote related by Sir John Reresby, which he received from the Rev. Mr. Gosling of Canterbury, and which he gives entire as it was communicated to him.

" One day, while he was chancellor, he invited my father home with him from the King's Chapel, and inquired whether there were not a

building at Canterbury called the Sermon-
house, and what use was made of it. My father said it was the old Chapter-house, where
the dean, or his representatives, might convene
the choir once a fortnight, and hear the chan-
ter's account how well the duty had been attended in that time. 'This,' said he, 'will not
do;' and explained himself by saying, that the
presbyterians had then a petition before the
king and council, asking it, *as a thing of no
use,* for their meeting-house. On this, my father
told him, that if it were made a chapel for the
early prayers, and the choir reserved purely for
cathedral service, this would be a great convenience, and the Sermon-house would be in
daily use. 'This will do,' said the chancellor:
'pray let the dean and chapter know as soon as
possible, that I advise them to put it to this use
without delay;' adding, 'if the presbyterians
do not get a grant of it, others perhaps will,
whom you may like still worse.' His advice
was taken; and it has been the morning-prayer
chapel ever since."

It is not our province to weary the reader
with a description of all the state prosecutions
which arose out of the pretended popish or
presbyterian conspiracies; the recorder was
engaged in all, save one or two; and as the con-

D

victions multiplied, he grew bolder in his as-
sumptions, and more elated with his victories.
He was singularly resolute in propping up the
character of Dangerfield, a man who had been
disgraced in every possible way, and who came
branded and pilloried into court for the purpose
of convicting Lord Castlemaine and the persecuted Mrs. Cellier.   When the record of this
man's conviction for uttering counterfeit guineas,
and of his subsequent punishment in the pillory
was read, Jeffreys directly replied, that he was
not the same person, which, however, turned
out a bad defence.   He then combated the objection to the witness's competency, which was,
that an attainted felon could not be restored to
his capacity of witness by a pardon.   And this
he did successfully, though, after all, the true
reason for admitting the testimony came from
the Court of Common Pleas, whither Mr. Justice
Raymond ' went to learn the opinions of the

' Sir Thomas Raymond was the author of some reports in
the common law courts.   He was made serjeant, Oct. 26,
1677, and a baron of the Exchequer, May 5, 1679, though
much against his will ; for he tells us, that he laboured, not
without great reason, to prevent it.   Feb. 7, 1680, he became
judge of the Common Pleas ; and on the 29th of the following April, judge of the King's Bench, in which situation he
died soon afterwards.   He was the father of Robert Lord
Raymond, Baron Raymond of Abbott's Langley, in the

judges there. It probably came from that great lawyer, Lord Chief Justice North; and it was because the offender, having been burnt in the hand, had expiated his crime by the punishment, which is conformable to the doctrine entertained at this day.

In the prosecutions for libel also, which were frequent about this time, the city advocate was very sanguine, sometimes threatening, sometimes coaxing the defendants to confess; though in the case of Sir William Scroggs's [1] libellers their

county of Herts, some time solicitor and attorney-general, a judge of the King's Bench, and chief justice of that court. Lord Raymond, also an author of reports, died in 1732, and was interred at Abbott's Langley, where a magnificent monument was erected to his memory. The title became extinct in 1753.

[1] William Scroggs was born at Dedington, Oxon, and became a commoner of Oriel in 1639, at the age of sixteen, although some have held him to be the son of a one-eyed butcher near Smithfield-bars, and a big fat woman with a red nose like an alewife. [*] He afterwards went to Pembroke College, and proceeded M. A. in 1643. His father had intended him for the church, and had procured him the reversion of a good living, but he took arms for the king, and was captain of a foot company, which entirely changed his fortune. He then entered at Gray's Inn, and in 1669 was made serjeant, and knighted, and soon after became king's

[*] This was said by Sir William Dugdale, Garter, because Scroggs refused his knighthood-fees, and must therefore be taken cum grano.

submission availed them little, since, although
they had been assured by the insinuating coun-

serjeant. May 31, 1678, being at the time a judge of the
Common Pleas, he was promoted to the chief seat in the
King's Bench through the Earl of Danby, and there ensured
many convictions of the supposed popish conspirators.
However, in the full belief that the sway of parliament was
all-powerful, and that Shaftesbury was guiding the destinies
of the state, he one day asked a lord of the privy council,
if the lord president (Shaftesbury) really had that influence
with the king which he seemed to have? The reply was,
" No; no more than your footman hath with you." Scroggs
was converted, and threw cold water on the plot, for which
he was impeached; but he escaped on the dissolution of parliament, and retired to Weald-hall, near Burntwood, in
Essex, with the loss, however, of his place. He died of a
polypus in the heart in 1683, * having survived his wife, a
daughter of Matthew Blucke, Esq., some time. This judge
was a great lover of good living; and Sir Matthew Hale,
whose taste was quite different, refused Scroggs the privilege
of a serjeant when he was arrested, which made a great talk
at the time. His son and heir, Sir William Scroggs, sold
his estate to Alderman Erasmus Smith. No man was more
smartly lampooned by the wits of the day than this turncoat
chief justice. Beneath are extracts from some of the squibs
which were let off against him :—

Justice in Masquerade, or Scroggs upon Scroggs.

A butcher's son 's judg capital,
Poor Protestants for to enthral,

* Some say he died in Essex-street, but surely this must be a blunder
for Essex.

sel that they would find mercy at his hands, he
nearly, if not quite, ruined some of them by his

And England to enslave, sirs:
Lose both our laws and lives we must,
When to do justice we entrust
    So known an errant knave, sirs.

Some hungry priests he once did fell
With mighty strokes, and them to hell
    Sent presently away, sirs:
Would you know why? the reason's plain;
They had no English nor French coin
    To make a longer stay, sirs.

His father once exempted was
Out of all juries: why? because
    He was a man of blood, sirs:
And why the butcherly son (forsooth!)
Shou'd now be judg and jury both,
    Cannot be understood, sirs.

The good old man, with knife and knocks,
Made harmless sheep and stubborn ox
    Stoop to him in his fury:
But the brib'd son, like greasy oaph,
Kneels down and worships golden calf,
    And so do's all the jury.

On the same.

Since Justice Scroggs Pepys and Dean did bail,
Upon the good cause did turn his tail,
For two thousand pounds to buy tent and ale,
        Which nobody can deny.

strict exaction of justice. It must have been with great complacency that Sir George echoed the chief justice's expressions in Carr's affair, who was indicted for publishing " The Weekly Packet of Advice from Rome ;" a trial in which the bias of the government against the plot was

---

Scroggs was at first a man of the blade,
And with his father followed the butcherly trade,
But 'twas the Peter-pence made him a jade,
　　　　　Which nobody, &c.

He'd stand by the protestant cause he said,
And lift up his eyes, and cry'd, we're betray'd ;
But then the pettifogger was in a masquerade,
　　　　　Which nobody, &c.

When Danby mentioned to the king his name,
He said he had neither honesty nor shame,
And would play any sort of roguish game,
　　　　　Which nobody, &c.

He swears he'd confound Beddlow and Oates,
And prove the papists sheep, and the protestants goats,
And that he 's a tool that on property dotes,
　　　　　Which nobody, &c.

The Wolf Justice.

VERSES FIXT UPON HIS CHAMBER-DOOR.

Here lives the Wolf Justice, a butcherly knave,
Likes protestants' goods, but the papists' do's save, &c.

See also the " Westminster Wedding," which we have inserted, and in which he is called " Clodpate."

pretty strongly manifested: when the verdict was given, after the interruptions of a tumultuous crowd of people, which considerably annoyed Scroggs, he said, " You have done like honest men." To which the recorder very joyfully added, " They have done like honest men."

The recorder, indeed, was always very severe upon libellers; but, even on this subject, he sometimes spoke very good sense; and his opinion, with regard to the proof of malice which he expressed in Sir Samuel Barnardiston's case, has been mentioned with much approbation. " Certainly," said he, (at this time he was chief justice) " the law supplies the proof, if the thing itself speaks malice and sedition. As it is in murder; we say always in the indictment, he did it by the instigation of the devil: can the jury, if they find the fact, find he did it not by such instigation? no, that does necessarily attend the very nature of such an action or thing. So, in informations for offences of this nature, we say, he did it falsely, maliciously, and seditiously, which are the formal words; but if the nature of the thing be such as necessarily imports malice, reproach, and scandal to the government, there needs no proof but of the fact done; the law supplies the rest."

And had he lived in these days, the vengeance of the public press would have fallen on him as a subject for condign punishment; for when recorder, he was guilty of promulging this singular heresy:

Sir G. Jeffries, Recorder.

" All the judges of England having met together to know whether any person whatsoever may expose to the public knowledge any matter of intelligence, or any matter whatsoever that concerns the public, they give it as their resolution, 'that no person whatsoever could expose to the public knowledge any thing that concerned the affairs of the public, without licence from the king, or from such persons as he thought fit to intrust with that power.'"

Observing upon this, says Lord Camden, " Can the twelve judges extra-judicially make a thing law to bind the kingdom by a declaration, that such is their opinion.—I say no; it is a matter of impeachment for any judge to affirm it."

Mr. Recorder Jeffreys was, conformably with his creed, very severe upon a poor bookseller named Francis Smith. This person had been so indiscreet as to publish a book against the expenses of mayors and sheriffs, in which there were declamations against feasting and wine worthy of

a Spartan. " Debauchery is come to that
height," said the writer, " that the fifth part of
the charge of a shrievalty is in wine, the growth
of another country." However, the grand jury,
who (although they might have liked wine exceedingly well) could not persuade themselves
that these general censures of expense were
libellous, thought fit to indorse that obnoxious
word to court ears, "ignoramus," upon the bill
of indictment; and this was an unanimous
ejectment of the charge. However, somebody
scraped out the ignoramus, and next sessions
the bill came forth again, upon which it was resolved with one voice to renew the ignoramus,
and thus the bill was returned. Jeffreys flew
into immense choler, and sent back the bill a
third time. But the jury stuck to their favourite ignoramus, and again tendered the disgraced writing to the incensed recorder, who
might well have thought that all his interest
with mayor and sheriffs would fleet away, if this
heretical proscription were suffered. " God
bless me from such jurymen!" vociferated the
city advocate; " I will see the face of every one
of them, and let others see them also." And so
he ordered the bar to be cleared, that the citizens who had thus acted might be laid open to
the public gaze. But in vain :—

Non vultus instantis tyranni
Mente quatit solidâ.

One by one, *seriatim*, as lawyers say, did the
jury, seventeen in number, utter ignoramus; and
in a moment, blasphemy and perjury were
thundered out in their ears: they had committed a sin which God would never pardon.
It was the apotheosis, the anathema maranatha
of Mr. Recorder. Still the jury say nothing.
Utterly inefficient, when a firm body of men,
sheltered by the imperishable constitution of
their ancestors, had decided on a matter which
belonged solely to their jurisdiction, Sir George
was driven from his high position, and instantly
betook himself to a land of gins and snares.
He doffed the lion's hide, and hid himself in
the soft sleek coat of the fox. " Come, Mr.
Smith!" and he beckoned the crest-fallen bookseller, who knew that he was on very slippery
ground; " there are two other persons besides
you whom this jury have brought in ignoramus;
but they have been ingenuous enough to confess,
and I cannot think to fine them little enough;
they shall be fined but two-pence a-piece for their
ingenuity in confessing. Well come, Mr. Smith,
we know who hath owned both printing and
publishing this book formerly." Most probably Smith had been in the trap before, and had

probably escaped with some severe injury, as a mouse does who loses the greater part of his tail; and so, says he, "Sir, my ingenuity hath sufficiently experienced the reward of your severity already formerly; and besides, I know no law commands me to accuse myself, neither shall I; and the jury have done like true Englishmen and worthy citizens; and blessed be God for such a just jury!" Then Jeffreys foamed again; and the bookseller found his way into Newgate, and was compelled to give bail. We shall just give the sequel. He asked for a copy of his indictment, which even Scroggs said he was entitled to; but Jeffreys put it off from time to time, under pretence that his private house was not a court, and that he could not meddle with ordering any thing there. At last Smith got a nice compact charge of seventeen sheets against him; but it gives us pleasure to say, that he ultimately got clear of that charge, and indeed of another, at the expense of a small fine. This is his winding-up of the matter:—"From such a judge, and such a recorder of London, and such judgment, good Lord deliver me! and may every true citizen and right Englishman say, Amen."

It was now time that this persevering zealot should receive some token of favour from those

whose dictates he had so faithfully obeyed.
And, indeed, when he had once planted himself
in the track of preferment, he moved on with a
speed which has seldom been equalled, for the
court would have been puzzled to have found
another so exactly fitted to their service—one
who scrupled so little, and did so much.

He was called serjeant, Feb. 17, 1680: on
which occasion he gave rings with the motto—
A Deo rex; a rege lex:[*] and became a Welsh
judge about that time, when his brother preached
an assize-sermon before him. On the 30th of
the following April, he had succeeded in de-
spoiling Sir Job Charlton of the chief justiceship
of Chester, which he secured for himself. He
was made king's serjeant on the 12th of May,
in the same year; and Nov. 17, 1681, was
created a baronet. This chief justiceship was
given him in consideration of his loyalty and
good services; and the dignity of one of his majesty's counsel at Ludlow, with a permission to
retain the office of recorder, was joined with it.

Sir Job was an old man, and was most unwilling to give up his office, for he had a considerable estate in Wales; but finding the matter determined against him, he took it to heart,

---

[*] The king from God; the law from the king.

and going to Whitehall, placed himself so that
the king could not avoid seeing him on his return from St. James's Park, and " set him down
like hermit poor."¹ But King Charles espied
him at a distance, and knowing too well the
burden of his speech, could not bear to pass
him; but turned short off, and went another
way. Sir Job was sorry for his master, but
never sought another interview. He was constituted judge of the Common Pleas, where he
brought with him much dignity and learning.
However, it is pleasing to reflect, that in the
reign of James II., the old judge had his
quietus in Westminster-hall, and was restored
to his much-loved station in the principality.²

Some time before this, Sir George had gained

¹ North's Lives.
² Sir Job Charlton was not the only chief justice of
Chester who loved his place. We are told that Sir Eardley
Wilmot very anxiously longed for that situation by way of
retirement, and was only prevented from filling it by Mr.
Morton, who could not be prevailed on to give it up. This
was previous to the elevation of Sir Eardley to the chief
justiceship of the Common Pleas.—*Life of Wilmot, by his
son.* The real reason of the removing of Sir Job was his
refusal to concede the king's dispensing power; but he was
doubtless glad to occupy his old seat again, which, on petition,
was granted him.

a firmer footing at court by his introduction as
solicitor-general to the Duke of York.

On the ripening of the popish persecutions,
history acquaints us, that the Duke retired to
Brussels, in conformity with his brother's advice
and request, but not without having obtained an
explicit declaration of Monmouth's illegitimacy.
His solicitor was very active during this season
of trouble; for although no one was more violent
than he, when the accused came to the bar, he
promoted in secret every design which could be
imagined for sheltering his master, removing the
stigma of the plot from him, and foiling the obnoxious Exclusion bill. And hence it was, that
he held so long and powerful a dominion over
the mind of that prince, though he had possibly
sunk at last, if the religion of the country had
changed, since, it admits of little doubt, that
bigotry will forswear the warmest friendships.

It may not be amiss to relate an affair in this
place connected with the post-office, because
though it will carry us forward to the year
1682, it entirely arose from Jeffreys's management of the Duke's property. By a statute
passed in the early part of King Charles's reign,[1]

---

[1] 15 Car. 2. chap. 14.

the post-office was settled upon the Duke of York and his heirs male. William Dockra, a merchant, in a subsequent part of the reign, invented a penny-post, which he completely arranged, and directed for a considerable time with the approbation of the inhabitants of London. But the Duke, being the general grantee of revenues acquired in this manner, it occurred to his solicitor, that he was entitled to those also which Mr. Dockra was enjoying; and finding the project capable of high improvement, he filed an information on the post act against that person, and obtained a conviction against him in the King's Bench.

Had Dockra been a wise man, it seems, that he might have received for his life the place of commissioner for the management of this post, yet he would not submit himself, but continued his fruitless complaints, while the crown at length became possessed of the benefit, which has remained in the same hands ever since.[1] How-

[1] About 1776, a penny-post was set up in Edinburgh, by Mr. Williamson, unconnected with the general post-office. It met with but indifferent encouragement for some years, doubts being entertained as to its punctuality in delivering the letters; by degrees, however, it seemed to be advancing in estimation and was more frequently employed. Twenty years after, the general post-office, by virtue of the act of

ever, the disappointed merchant made another
attempt at the Revolution to gain some repara-
tion for his loss by memorialising the House of
Commons, and printing an appeal to the public
in the shape of an advertisement.[1] Here, he
complains of the injustice done him by the then
late king, who had, under colour of law, deprived him of his rights, without any manner of
recompense, and states the progress of his petition to Parliament, which was adjourned before
his case was heard. He tells us also, that there
had been an "Answer to Mr. Dockra's case concerning the Penny-post;" to which he wrote a
reply, but did not print it. If we may believe his
account, he had a wife and eight children, and
had spent many thousand pounds upon the
concern.[2]

And now, the new Welsh chief justice increased in haughtiness every day, and his vanity

parliament, prohibiting the conveyance of letters by any but
those employed under the postmaster-general, took the penny-
post entirely into its own hands; and *Mr. Williamson was
allowed an annuity during life, equal to what his private
establishment yielded.*

[1] An advertisement on the behalf of William Dockra,
merchant, concerning the penny-post.

[2] He had a small pension at last. He is praised for the
ingenuity of his discovery, in the State Poems, vol. iii.
p. 246.

advanced in an equal ratio with his preferments and favour. But some of the judges would not brook this torrent of conceit, and he received a very severe lesson from Mr. Baron Weston' at the Kingston Midsummer assizes for 1679. Being counsel there in some cause at *Nisi Prius*, he took on himself to ask all the questions, and tried to browbeat the other side in their examination of witnesses, when the judge bade him hold his tongue. Some words passed, in the course of which he told the baron that he was not treated like a counsellor, being curbed in the management of his brief. "Ha!" fiercely

' There have been four Westons judges of our courts: Richard Weston, of the Common Pleas, in the reign of Elizabeth; Richard Weston, a baron of the Exchequer, in the time of Charles I.; James Weston, a baron, in the same reign; and Richard Weston, to whom allusion has been made in the text. The two barons of Charles the First's reign were celebrated for their courage; and this Sir Richard in no wise came behind them in resolution: for, being impeached for some words he had let drop in a charge on the circuit, he, unlike to Scroggs and Jones, who had incurred the same displeasure, and were much troubled at it, was "gay and debonair as at a wedding." Indeed, he desired nothing so much as a great balk with the Commons; in the course of which he intended to set up Magna Charta, the *judicium parium*, and his lawful challenges—in fact, to dispute every inch of ground. But the prosecution was dropped. He died March 23, 1681.

E

returned the judge : " since the King has thrust
his favours upon you, in making you chief justice
of Chester, you think to run down every body :
if you find yourself aggrieved, make your complaint; here's nobody cares for it." The counsel
said, he had not been used to make complaints,
but rather to stop those that were made; but
the judge again enjoined him silence. Jeffreys
sat down, and wept with anger.

Lord Delamere, afterwards Earl of Warrington,
in a speech which he delivered on the corruption of judges, was very severe upon the new
chief justice of the County Palatine. He spoke
thus upon that point :—" The county for which
I serve is Cheshire, which is a County Palatine,
and we have two judges peculiarly assigned us
by His Majesty : our puisne judge I have nothing
to say against him, for he is a very honest man
for ought I know; but I cannot be silent as to
our chief judge, and I will name him, because
what I have to say will appear more probable :
his name is Sir George Jeffreys, who I must
say behaved himself more like a jack-pudding,
than with that gravity which beseems a judge :
he was mighty witty upon the prisoners at the
bar; he was very full of his jokes upon people
that came to give evidence, not suffering them
to declare what they had to say in their own

way and method, but would interrupt them, because they behaved themselves with more gravity than he; and in truth, the people were
strangely perplexed when they were to give in
their evidence; but I do not insist upon this,
nor upon the late hours he kept up and down
our city: it's said he was every night drinking
till two o'clock, or beyond that time, and that
he went to his chamber drunk; but this I have
only by common fame, for I was not in his company: I bless God I am not a man of his principles or behaviour:' but in the mornings he
appeared with the symptoms of a man that over
night had taken a large cup.   But that which I
have to say is the complaint of every man, especially of them who had any law-suits. Our chief
justice has a very arbitrary power, in appointing
the assize when he pleases; and this man has
strained it to the highest point: for whereas we
were accustomed to have two assizes; the first
about April or May, the latter about September;
it was this year the middle (as I remember) of
August before we had any assize; and then he
dispatched business so well, that he left half the
causes untried; and to help the matter, has re-

' This savours very much of " I thank God I am not as
other men are," &c.

solved that we shall have no more assizes this
year."

While George was thus climbing the slippery
summits of ambition, his brethren were pros-
pering at home, partly by their own merits,
partly by the assistance of their eminent kinsman. His eldest brother, John, was high-she-
riff of Denbighshire in 1680; and James, another brother, preached the assize-sermon in
the same year, when Sir George rode his first
circuit as chief judge. Dr. James Jeffreys
was of Jesus College, Oxford, and took his degrees thus; M.A. 1672, B.D. 1679, D.D. 1683.
Through the same influence he was installed a
prebendary of Canterbury, Nov. 9, 1682: he
was canon of the ninth stall. Pennant tells
us, that one brother was Dean of Rochester,
(and his account must clearly be referred to
James,) and that he died on the road to visit
his brother, when under confinement in the
Tower. But there has not been any dean
of that name in Rochester cathedral;' and Dr.
Jeffreys died on the 4th of September, 1689,
some months after the chancellor's decease,

' John Castilion, canon of Canterbury, was dean from
1676 till October 21, 1688; and Simon Lowth from December, 1688, till the Revolution.

which disproves the latter statement. His epitaph
is in Canterbury cathedral, as follows:—

Sub hoc marmore depositæ sunt reliquiæ JACOBI JEF-
FERIES S. T. P. hujus ecclesiæ canonici, qui obiit 4 Sep-
tembris, Anno Domini 1689. Ætatis suæ 40.

Thomas, another brother, was knighted at
Windsor Castle, July 11, 1680. He was a
knight of Alcantara,¹ and resided much among
the Spaniards, who greatly admired his an-
cestry,² as consul at Alicant and Madrid. He
had so far conciliated the esteem of the Spanish
ministry, as to be recommended for Lord Lans-
down's successor, as British envoy in Spain;
but this good fortune was arrested by the Revolution. When Pennant wrote, there was a full-
length picture of him by Kneller in Acton-
house, with a long white cloak over his coat,
and the cross of the order upon it.

A storm, which had been gathering for some
time, was now ready to burst on the heads of
the court favourites; and it fell not only upon
the underlings of the ministry, but even on the

¹ A religious order, instituted in 1170 by Fernan Gomès,
under the pontificate of Alexander III.
² From Tudor Trevor, earl of Hereford, who was himself
descended from Kynric ap Rhiwellon.

ministers themselves : it was not likely, therefore, that upon any serious change in the
posture of affairs, so noted a stickler for government as Sir George Jeffreys should escape.
Ostensibly, the country party had taken great
umbrage at a supposed attempt by the administration to stifle the plot; and in pursuance of
this, they instituted prosecutions against some
persons, who, however honestly, had expressed
themselves indiscreetly on the subject of that
bugbear; and the King, with equal dissimulation, professed himself friendly to these proceedings. But the plot was a mere pretence : the
old arm of faction was not yet withered : the
sprightly and gallant Duke of Monmouth had
gained much upon the affections of the people;
and the Catholic religion, with the heir-presump-
tive as its patron, was unpopular, both within
and without the walls of parliament. The ex-
clusionists, by pressing their obnoxious bill,[1]
were at length visited by the black rod; and the
parliament was prorogued from time to time, in
spite of the earnest desire of the opposition to

---

[1] Although the bill was thrown out in the House of Peers
by a considerable majority, the violence of the Commons
continued; and their desire to renew it, with their threat
against such as had advised its rejection, produced a proro-
gation.

persecute the abhorrers, and to question the King's proclamation against tumultuous petitioning. In order to compel King Charles to summon his parliament, the most violent addresses were got up; and to counteract them, the court contrived that anti-petitions, expressing an abhorrence of this clamorous proceeding, should be prepared and presented; whence it was, that the term, *abhorrer*, was derived. Money, however, was wanting for the exigencies of the state, and thus the country faction at length prevailed : the session began, and a furious punishment was menaced against all those who had dared to violate the subject's liberty, by suppressing the voice of petition. After expelling two of their members, and sending one to the Tower, they let loose their wrath against the recorder. He had fallen under their displeasure on more accounts than one; for not only had he opposed their petitioning to the utmost, but he had of late become quite lukewarm in the prosecution of their beloved popish plot. When this " Genesis of abhorrences," as a certain writer styles it, began, the King sent for the mayor and aldermen in council, hoping that through their high authority an early check might be imposed on the hostile petitions which were coming forth. Jeffreys attended as their

spokesman. The lord mayor was one of the
factious; and when it was required of him to
punish the undue practices that were complained of, he answered, "that he knew of no
course to suppress the inconvenience, for that
the people took it as a right in them to petition
upon any grievance they were sensible of."
Then Jeffreys, hoping to shift from the city to
the council the responsibility of this check,
moved, That his Majesty would issue a proclamation, prohibiting the framing and presenting
any such petitions, and commanding all magistrates to punish such as should act to the contrary. But few approved of this, as being too
positive ; and North, the chief justice, like a true
statesman, took exception to the recorder's motion ; and though he admitted that a proclamation on the subject matter might be beneficial,
yet objected to one according to the proposed
tenor as rather prejudicial, and capable of a
captious construction. And then his lordship
recommended the proclamation to be directed
against seditious and tumultuous petitioning
only ; and that it should not by any means be
supposed to condemn the undoubted privilege
of the people. The King highly approved of
this, and the recorder pleased neither party.
Soon afterwards, he, nevertheless, got up an

anti-petition in the name of the loyal citizens of London, in which they declared this method of petitioning to be the method of forty-one,[1] and likely to bring His Majesty to the block, as his father was brought;—all which doings they abhorred.

These were the offences which the House of Commons remembered against Sir George when they recovered their temporary power, and lifted up their voice of censure; accordingly they proceeded to several votes against him, which are recorded in the journals, and are here copied.

Sabbati, 13° *die Novembris,* 1680.

Mr. Trenchard reports from the committee, to whom the petition of divers citizens of London against Sir George Jeffreys, recorder of the said city, was referred;—that the said committee had taken the same into consideration, and had heard the evidence of the petitioners, and of the said Sir George Jeffreys, &c.

" Resolved, That Sir George Jeffreys, re-corder of the city of London, by traducing and

[1] Serjeant Maynard, who was a popular man, was whispering something, not very pleasing, to Gadbury, a witness on Elizabeth Cellier's trial, when the man said, " Mr. Serjeant, I was none of the tribe of forty-one."

obstructing petitioning for the sitting of this
Parliament, hath destroyed the right of the
subject.

"Ordered, That an humble address be made
to His Majesty, to remove Sir George Jeffreys
out of all public offices.

"Ordered, That the members of this House,
that serve for the City of London, do commu-
nicate the vote of this House relating to Sir
George Jeffreys, together with their resolutions
thereupon, to the court of aldermen for the said
city."

To this address the King replied, "that he
would consider of it."

Had this gentleman stood upon his right, and
refused to give up the office of recorder, (for the
principal object of the country party was to
substitute Sir George Treby for him in the city
of London) he had probably continued the
"mouth-piece of the city" as long as he desired. The course which must have been pursued for the purpose of compelling him to deliver up the corporation writings, would have
been by mandamus; and the cause which the
parties asking for it must have alleged, might
probably have been held insufficient by the
judges then in office; but he, who had so long
acted the terrorist towards others, was himself

considerably alarmed upon this occasion, and, in the end, was imposed upon by a trick adopted by the adverse faction. He had a reprimand upon his knees at the bar of the House; and on condition that he should remain unmolested for his crime of abhorring, surrendered his situation quietly to that eminent lawyer, Sir George Treby, afterwards chief justice of the Common Pleas. Some discourse that was held out to him about taking heads off, probably hastened this pusillanimous decision. He certainly played a very weak part at this crisis, for he begged and importuned the King to allow the vacating of his place, which the Monarch was not by any means willing to concede, on account of the influence which the former had with the citizens, added to his fierce and intractable carriage towards His Majesty's enemies. He gained his point, however, at last, but lost his credit, for King Charles facetiously observed, " that he was not parliament-proof;' and some

* King Charles seems to have been parliament-proof. He sold Dunkirk to the French when he thought his Commons parsimonious; he demanded a repeal of the triennial act; shut up the exchequer against the bankers without fear of being questioned for it; and when the House became clamorous and turbulent, he would very quietly send his black rod to tap at their door, and warn them all home. His natural sense was

pretend, that he was never afterwards held in esteem by that sovereign, for his timid behaviour; and, indeed, Mr. North tells us, that Jeffreys was "none of the intrepids." However, Burnet says, that they [the House of Commons,] "fell on Sir George Jeffreys, a furious declaimer at the bar; but that he was raised by that, as well as by this prosecution:" and this is certainly true; for although he might have been under a cloud for a season, the sequel will show, that he soon regained his ground, and triumphed more surely than before.

Some have said, that he lost his recordership by vote, but this is clearly a mistake; and there is yet another account of this matter, which is as follows:—The King, having recovered from a very dangerous indisposition, was greeted on his going abroad by an address of congratulation from the mayor and aldermen, upon which

very strong and good; and it is probable that the little cultivation he allowed his mind was greatly assisted by the advice of such great men as Sir William Temple, of whom too much cannot be said in panegyric, and the calm, calculating, sure, lord-keeper, North. However, this Monarch knew that he could not affront his parliament beyond a certain pitch, and therefore once facetiously observed to his brother James, who wanted him to do some extraordinary act, not warranted by the constitution, " Brother, I have no mind to go upon my travels again; you may, if you please."

the recorder proposed that they should wait upon the Duke of York, who had not long returned from Flanders, with a like courtesy. This motion not being relished, he stayed behind with his father-in-law to gain access to the Duke; at which the city took offence, imagining (and indeed not without some colour,) that he was espousing a cause not exactly coinciding with their interests; and thence it was determined in the council-chamber, that he should be requested to deliver back the papers and writings with which he had been entrusted as their officer, and so give up his place. This he did without delay.

Both these relations may be correct; for the latter only describes the feelings of the parliament expressed through the court at Guildhall; and there is nothing unreasonable in the supposition that both parties, the city and the parliament, had been displeased with his manœuvring. However, he was not turned out in absolute disgrace, as will appear from the proceedings on the subject, which we subjoin.

Court of Aldermen, Nov. 23, 1680.

" This day the members that serve for this city in parliament came to the court, and brought down the votes and resolves of the honourable

House of Commons, in reference to Sir George
Jeffreys, that he will forthwith surrender to this
court his said place of recorder. Ordered, That
Sir Henry Tulse, and Sir James Smyth, knights
and aldermen, with the town clerk, do speedily
acquaint Mr. Recorder herewith, and desire
him to be present at the next court.

" Ordered, That the town clerk deliver a
copy of the court's proceedings in reference to
Sir George Jeffreys to Sir Robert Clayton,
knt. and alderman, one of the city members,
to be by him communicated to the House of
Commons, if the same should be required."

" On the second of December Sir George Jeffreys, knt. serjeant-at-law, recorder of the city,
here present, did freely surrender up unto the
court his place of recorder, and all his right
and interest therein; of which surrender the
court did accept and allow. George Treby,¹ of

¹ Of Plympton, Devon. He entered himself a commoner
of Exeter College in June, 1660, and afterwards became a
fellow-commoner. He was of the Middle Temple, and sat
for his native town in 1678 and 1679. In the beginning of
October, 1683, he lost his recordership, on the bursting of the
fanatical plot, but was restored to it on the approach of the
Prince of Orange, and again sat for Plympton. In the following March he became solicitor-general, and when Pollexfen was made chief of the Common Pleas, rose to be
attorney. In 1692 Pollexfen died, and Sir George Treby

the Middle Temple, London, Esq. was elected the same day, and sworn in December 3rd. At the same time, it having been noticed that the sum of £200 remained unpaid, which had been voted to Sir George Jeffreys on the 22nd of October, for his good services performed to the city, it was ordered that Mr. Chamberlain do pay the same. And a committee was also appointed to take into consideration the great sums of money disbursed by the late recorder, in fitting up his dwelling-house in Alderman-bury, which he held of the city."¹

The mob generally take part against a falling favourite, and this misfortune of Jeffreys afforded them great amusement; for when the pope was burnt in effigy at Temple Bar, on Queen Elizabeth's birth-day, the wags of the day had a figure of a man set on horseback with his face to the tail, and a paper on his back, " I am an Ab-horrer." Indeed, he was no favourite with the

was named for his successor. He died December 13, 1700. He was the author of several pamphlets which made a great noise at that time of day, and is supposed to have written the annotations in the margin of Lord Chief Justice Dyer's Reports.

¹ Elkanah Settle, who composed a panegyric in verse upon Jeffreys, ascribes his removal from the recordership to the influence of Shaftesbury.

populace either in this or the following reign,
and he went shares with poor Sir Roger
L'Estrange in the general odium. L'Estrange
was burnt in effigy with the pope,[1] and Jeffreys
with the devil.

A curious circumstance happened about this
time respecting one Verdon, a Norfolk attorney,
which is not unworthy of a place here by way
of digression. A petition had been presented to
the House of Commons against this man by the
inhabitants of his county, for undue practices in
returning knights of the shire, and other misde-
meanours;[2] and an order was made that he

---

[1] L'Estrange had given great offence by his ridicule of the
popish plot, in a narrative which he published in derision of
Titus Oates's " Narrative." " There was a consult," says
Sir Roger, " of three or four booksellers over a bottle of
wine, what subject a man might venture upon at that time,
for a selling copy. One of the company was of opinion that
a book of the fires would make a smart touch, and so they
all agreed upon't, and propounded to get some of the King's
witnesses' hands to it; naming first one, and then another,
they came at length to a resolution, and pitcht upon *Trap
ad crucem*, and the History of the Fires, &c." It was " A
Narrative and Impartial Discovery of the Horrid Popish
Plot, carry'd on for the Burning and Destroying of the
Cities of London and Westminster, with their Suburbs, &c.
And Dedicated to the Surviving Citizens of London ruin'd
by Fire, &c."

[2] He once helped off a fellow attorney on a charge of

should be sent for in custody of the serjeant-at-
arms. But Verdon was not so easily taken; he
shifted about from place to place, and so eluded
the search after him for some time, although he
offered a composition in money for his fees, and
agreed to surrender upon those terms; to which
the serjeant replied, that he could not sell the
justice of the House. However, after a fruitless
attempt to reach him in London, the messengers
went down to Norwich, and there he struggled
and battled with them considerably; he would
neither mount or dismount from his horse, but
made the officers put him on and lift him off,
while his clerks were taking notes all the time,
and marking the various assaults, for each of
which the attorney proposed to bring a distinct
action of battery. But as soon as they had come
on about midway between London and Norwich, the parliament was prorogued, and Verdon said, that the subsequent custody was a
false imprisonment, upon which he sued the
parties in the Exchequer. William Williams,
the speaker, who had signed the warrant,

murder by returning a favourable jury; and the consequence
was, that his acquitted friend committed an assault on the
persons who were sent to arrest him by order of the parliament upon this occasion.—See the Journals of the House of
Commons for 1680, p. 678.

F

led for the defendants, and Jeffreys was employed for Verdon. Williams alleged, that
the men could not have known of the pro-
rogation, and said much to excuse them upon
that ground. Verdon then stepped forth, and
said, " My lord, if Sir William Williams will
here own his hand to the warrant, I will
straight discharge these men." Roger North,
who tells this story, then adds, that " Jeffreys
was so highly pleased with this gasconade of his
client, that he loved him ever after, of which
Verdon felt the good effects, when his learned
counsel came that circuit as chief justice; for
although many complaints were intended against
him, and such as were thought well enough
grounded, yet he came off scot-free." Jeffreys
hated Williams, because he had received a censure on his knees at the bar of the House from
that gentleman, when speaker, and as North
says, " they were both Welshmen ; "[1] so that
when the former got uppermost, he prosecuted
his quondam lecturer.

[1] Sir George seemed not to be ashamed of his country, or
its peculiarities. He was indulging himself one day with a
very common amusement, that of bullying a witness, and
thus addressed him : " Look thee, if thou can'st not compre-
hend what I mean, I will repeat it again, for thou shalt see
what countryman I am, by my telling my story over twice :
therefore I ask thee once again."

CHAP. IV.

Situation and new prospects of Jeffreys—He refuses to admit
dissenters on the grand jury—Trial of Fitzharris—Colledge,
the joiner, tried—Witticisms of Jeffreys—Election of the city
sheriffs—Dudley North elected—Account of Sir Edmund
Sanders—Judge Jones—The *quo warranto* judgment—Trial of
Pilkington for a riot—Anecdote of Dare, the petitioner—Some
account of Sir Thomas Bludworth, and the fire of London—The
Rye-house Plot—Sir Francis Pemberton—Conduct of Jeffreys
on the trial of Lord William Russel.

For this sudden veering of the compass Jeffreys was but ill prepared; he had submitted to
the disgrace of apostacy with the full expectation of a reward so secure and permanent as to
make him ample amends. Now, on a sudden,
he was driven forth an outcast from the city
magistracy, publicly denounced by the Commons, and jeered at by his royal master for a
want of common resolution. To secure his own
fortunes, let the means or consequences be as
they might, was the utmost he had any care
for, but the difficulty lay in discerning the best
political game for accomplishing those ends. He
was, indeed, possessed of a valuable judgeship,

and was invested with very high honour amongst
his coifed brotherhood; but the court interest
had sunk to an ebb so low, as to give a probable earnest of some instant and fatal revolution
in the state. Then it was that he bethought
him of his old companions, many of whom were
careering with the triumphant party: a seat in
parliament, and a clamorous disapprobation of
all government measures, seemed to him the
best things in prospect; nothing remained but
to seek a reconciliation; and to obtain this, he
would, probably, have stooped to any sacrifice.
But his conduct had been so despicable, that,
audacious as he was, there were many whom
he could not approach with any degree of assurance; and from those to whom he ventured the
hint, (for it seems he actually made some endeavours,) he met with a reception so unfavourable,
as to determine him at once to live and die
under the royal banner.

And it happened, that notwithstanding all
these rebuffs, he maintained a considerable influence both at court and in the city; so that
when the Southwark petition was carried up in
the next year to Hampton Court, he was invited
to dinner by the King with his wife's father, Sir
Thomas Bludworth, and was particularly noticed; whilst the lord mayor, aldermen, and com-

mons were sent away with a reprimand. He
continued also an active member of the lieu-
tenancy, and appeared among them girded with
his sword; and, on the whole, we may say of
him, as Waller did of the Protestant faith in the
reign of James the Second, "This falling church
has got a trick of rising again."

Having had a little time for consideration,
Jeffreys bethought himself how to avenge his
disgrace upon those who had been instrumental
in annoying him, and he, at last, fixed upon
the dissenters as the party who had influenced
the court of aldermen to turn him out; and,
ever after, he directed his especial malice against
these persons. It was no slight pleasure to him,
for the gratification of this hostility, to find himself appointed chairman of Hickes's-hall, though
he lost some portion of his practice through it;
and here he soon embroiled himself with his new
enemies. He would allow no dissenters to serve
on the grand jury, and ordered the under-sheriff
to return a new panel, purged of the secta-
rians; but this was refused, on which he ordered the sheriffs to attend on him the next day.
However, instead of them, came the recorder,
fraught with the opinion of the court of aldermen, that the privilege of the city exempted
the sheriffs from coming to Hickes's-hall, and

that the service of the under-sheriff was sufficient. On this, the court fined the sheriff 100*l.*,
and declared, that the judges should be made
acquainted with the matter. Accordingly, the
discussion was renewed before ten judges at the
Old Bailey, where the sheriffs attended; and
after considerable demur, they consented to re-
form the panel.

Lucky, indeed, was it for our King's serjeant,
that he had not succeeded in appeasing the
offended brotherhood of his early days: the sense
of shame, or conquering dread which assailed
him when he thought of them, most indisputably
averted the wreck of his fortunes. The King,
actuated by wise advice, had the firmness to
retrench his expenses, and dispense with his
unruly parliament; and the government rallied
irresistibly against its opposers, and was soon
in a condition to crush them utterly. Fitzharris,
an Irish gentleman, who had thrown himself in
an odd way at the mercy of some eaves-droppers,
was the first on whom the ministers retaliated
the insults which had been offered them; he
was ostensibly sacrificed to the old popish plot
mania, but, in truth, fell a victim to the furious
jealousy which raged between the crown and the
parliament. Jeffreys roared prodigiously against
this unfortunate and indiscreet spy; he insisted

that the prisoner had condemned himself by disparaging his own witnesses; and he further told the jury, that if they acquitted Fitzharris, they could neither have respect to their credit, nor to their consciences. He delivered, moreover, a speech of extraordinary ability; and one who wrote shortly after those days, has not scrupled to affirm, that this rhetoric weighed mainly with the jury, who were in some doubt as to their verdict. However, the court before whom he was tried, the chief of whom[*] was a moderate man, highly approved of the decision; and the government no less exulted in ridding themselves of one who had been a rallying post for faction: yet, notwithstanding all this, Fitzharris died a martyr to violence and prejudice, for he was clearly in the Duchess of Portsmouth's confidence, although it pleased Her Grace to forget every thing of the kind in a moment of political convenience; and those were days in which a culprit's witnesses could not be subjected to the test of an oath. The serjeant, elated by success, rather increased in his roughness at the trial of the titular archbishop, Plunket; so that Sawyer, attorney-general, was obliged to interfere, and to beg that the prisoner might have fair play to ask his

[*] Sir Francis Pemberton.

questions. He gave the court another speech;
at the end of which, as usual, he held that all the
treasons were punctually and precisely proved.
But it was in the following August, at the trial
of Colledge, the London joiner, that he suffered
his temper to break fully forth; not only essay-
ing to overrule the opinion of the court, but
scattering abroad his untimely jests even against
the accused, and thus giving somewhat of a
foretaste of the chief justice who was to come.
In fact, this was the first trial of the court party,
to signalize their triumph over those of the country; and Jeffreys could hardly contain himself
for joy to think that his ship had righted again,
and that he should sail on now with all his
colours flying. He fell first on North, who was
the presiding judge, and who felt disposed to let
the prisoner have some papers which had been
taken from him, to which the advocate objected,
till the King's counsel had seen them :—" Look
you, brother!" says the chief, " we will have
nothing of heat till the trial be over: when that
is over, if there be any thing that requires our
examination, it will be proper for us to enter
into the consideration of it; but in the meanwhile what hurt is there, if the papers be put
into some trusty hands, that the prisoner may
make the best use of them he can, and yet they

remain ready to be produced on occasion?"—
Serj. Jeffreys. "With submission, my lord, that
is assigning him counsel with a witness." And,
at length, the papers were retained by the court,
on the ground of their being scandalous. Sir
George could hardly allow the attorney-general
and the other leading counsel to examine the
crown witnesses, so anxious was he to gain a
conviction; but the prisoner's trade of a carpenter afforded him excellent opportunities of showing his wit. A libel, called Rary-Show, was
produced with cuts: "I suppose 'tis his own cut-
ting," said Jeffreys.—Again Jeffreys. "Do you
know that he had any pistols in his holsters at
Oxford?"—Dugdale. "Yes, he had."—Jeffreys.
"I think a chisel might have been more proper
for a joiner."

Sometimes he would affect great coolness.
—Colledge. "Is it probable I should talk to an
Irishman who does not understand sense?"
—Haynes. "It is better to be an honest Irishman
than an English rogue." Jeffreys (to Haynes
the witness)—"He does it but to put you in a
heat; don't be passionate with him." Colledge's
mother-in-law came forward to say, that he
always carried himself like a gentleman, and
scorned any thing unhandsome. "Pray, how
came you by this witness?" said Jeffreys; "have

you any more of them?" However, some of the
witnesses indulged themselves with a sharp hit
upon the counsel, and upon his sorest part, and
he would yet give them their answer in turn.[*]
One John Lun was called to throw a discredit
upon a crown witness, and he, of course, en-
countered Jeffreys, to whom the attorney and
solicitor-general seemed to have left all the
rough work.—Lun. " I will take the sacrament
upon it, what I say is true."—Mr. S. Jeff.
" We know you, Mr. Lun; we only ask questions about you, that the jury may know you
too, as well as we. We remember what you
once swore about an army." Colledge was
frightened at this, for he said, " I don't know
him," meaning the witness.—Mr. Lun. " I
don't come here to give evidence of any thing
but the truth; *I was never upon my knees before
the parliament for any thing.*"—Jeffreys. " *Nor I
neither for much;* but yet—once *you* were, when
you cried, Scatter them, good Lord !" Now this

---

[*] This is not unlike Johnson's description of Foote :

Boswell—" Sir, the ostler would have answered him;
would have given him as good as he brought, as the saying
is."

Johnson—" Yes, sir; and Foote would have answered
the ostler."

Boswell's Johnson, 4to. Vol. ii. p. 491.

Lun had been a drawer at the Devil Tavern, and was " gifted like an army saint." He was once heard praying against the cavaliers, and was crying out, Scatter 'em, scatter 'em; which gained him the nickname of Scatter 'em. The next rub came from Titus Oates, who appeared for Colledge, to show subornation against the Protestants. The doctor was appealing to Sir George as to his knowledge of Alderman Wilcox. The very name of an alderman could not have failed to have tickled the lawyer rather unpleasantly; and so he said, " Sir George Jeffreys does not intend to be an evidence, I assure you."—Dr. Oates. " I do not desire Sir George Jeffreys to be an evidence for me; I had credit in parliaments, and Sir George had disgrace in one of them."—Mr. Serjeant. " Your servant, doctor; you are a witty man and a philosopher."[1]

[1] The wit of this word " philosopher " here may be explained by looking to a subsequent cross-examination of Oates's brother. Wilcox gave Dr. Oates a dinner, where were several persons; and Colledge had examined the brother, who was one of the company, to show that no treasonable words had been uttered there. Serj. Jeffreys. " Hark you, sir, were there no disputations in divinity?"—Ans. " Not at all."—Jeff. " Nor of philosophy?"—Ans. " No."—Jeff. " Why, pray, sir, did not Dr. Oates and Mr. Savage talk very pleasantly of two great questions in divinity—the being of God, and the immortality of the soul?"

A day of retribution was at hand for Oates, and
Jeffreys was his judge.

It is not a little amusing to read the account
of Jeffreys setting the evidence of such men as
Oates and Dugdale against each other; though
we regard with very different feelings the perpetual comparison which he was making before
the jury between the testimony of Dugdale, as
being on oath, and so highly credible, and that
of Oates, unprotected by such sanction, and so
worth nothing. Nevertheless, he showed even
on this trial a strong partiality for the strict rules
of evidence: for when the witness Everard was
discoursing of what one Justice Warcup wanted
him to swear, Jeffreys interrupted him, saying,
" We have nothing to do with what you and Justice Warcup talked of: for example's sake, my
lord, let us have no discourses that concern third
persons brought in here." He kept up his ani-
mosity against the prisoner throughout a very
long trial; and though Colledge was noted for his
zeal against popery, the serjeant, in summing
up part of the evidence, (which he did with
many canting expressions,) told the jury, that
they would trip up the heels of all the evidence
and discovery of the plot, unless they believed
Dugdale, Smith, and Turbervile, the principal
witnesses. The prisoner was convicted and

executed, and died firmly in the Protestant faith.

In the following November, Serjeant Jeffreys appeared against Lord Grey of Werk, who had deflowered the Lady Henrietta Berkeley; and, although he occasionally indulged in a slight stroke of satire, he behaved very much like a man of the world in this affair. However, when that lady came to deliver her testimony in favour of the noble defendant, the serjeant could not help his accustomed slight upon witnesses against his own case; and so, when he found that the court had overruled the attorney-general's objection to her being sworn, he drily added, " Truly, my lord, we would prevent perjury if we could."

And now we come to speak of the troubles which befel the city of London in 1682 and 1683, in consequence of the unconquerable predilection of the members of the common-hall for choosing their own sheriffs. In forwarding their punishment, Jeffreys was a great political engine : he had been fortunate enough to bring two discomfited adversaries within his grasp— the city and the dissenters; and whatever were his good qualities (for such he certainly had), forbearance and forgetfulness of affronts were never numbered amongst them.

It had been a custom for the lord mayor to choose one sheriff, and for the commonalty to elect the other. At the Bridge-house feast, which was a few days before the 24th of June, the day for electing sheriffs, the mayor used to drink out of a large gilt cup to some person, naming him, by the title of sheriff of London and Middlesex for the year ensuing. If the favoured citizen were not there, the cup, being placed in the great coach, was carried in state to his house by the sword-bearer and other officers, and presented to him there; upon which he was saluted my lord mayor's sheriff, and shortly after summoned before the mayor and aldermen, when he either gave bond or fined. This drinking and fining was very often a well-concerted finesse for the benefit of the corporation; for if the party declined, the gilt cup went travelling again, and so continued, till some one would pledge, and hold; and this was called " going a birding for sheriffs." In 1641, the factious party having got the ascendency, my lord mayor's choice was set aside, and the livery selected both. Now the court being much vexed at this time with the ignoramus by which Shaftesbury was let loose, and chagrined indeed by the want of pliability which the city had shown respecting the popish plot, by the peti-

tioning assemblies, and the treatment of the Duke
of York,—was determined to revive the old
usage; and having got a mayor, Sir John Moor,[1]
who would drink, they cast their eyes around for a
fitting sheriff to be drunk unto. After some delay,
Jeffreys, who was at the bottom of all the transactions, hinted, that Dudley North, the chief
justice's brother, a rich Turkey merchant, would
be a creditable man for the ministers to pitch
upon for a recommendation to the city. This was
a good device on the part of Jeffreys; for if the
chief justice had objected to this nomination, he
had possibly embroiled himself with the King,
and so made room for another; and if he made
no scruple, as it happened, then the crown was
served equally well by this insinuation. Sir
John drank to Mr. North, and sent him the gilt
cup in full parade, which the merchant boldly
accepted, amidst all the fury and menaces of the

[1] " Nor was it without cause that the news of his being
chosen mayor was entertained with so much joy and triumph
at Holyrood-house; for some behind the curtain had un-
doubtedly laid the project of serving themselves in this, if not
other considerable matters, by him."—Modest Inquiry concerning the Election of Sheriffs of London, 1682. However,
when Moor came to be examined in parliament after the
Revolution, he denied that any one had instructed him; and
Dudley North said the same thing, though Secretary Jenkins
was a likely man to have done something of that kind.

opposite faction, who held out the penalties of
hanging, parliament, beating brains out, and
even of something worse after death, against
any one who should dare stand against their
will. And for a time they so far gained the
day, that North was the victim of pamphleteers
and tongues from every quarter: " the whole
country rang with his name; and wherever he
went, people started out of the way, and cried
out, ' That's he !'"   However, after a conversation or two with his brother, the judge, who
promised to advance him 1000*l.* towards making
up his account, he cared very little for the clamours which flew about his ears, for he was a
jolly, red-faced, good-humoured man; and, as
Roger North says, " he thought no more of the
adventure or consequence, than he did in shifting a bale of cloth."   At last came " the tug of
war;" the 24th of June arrived, and brought with
it, as far as the factions were concerned, " A
Midsummer Day's Dream."

The chief justice North went to Sir George
Jeffreys, (who, though not a chief actor, was
present at the hustings,) and stayed at his house
during the election; for Sir George was working
all his interest to promote the new sheriff; and
the presence of these great men might, besides,
assist the spirits of the chief magistrate, lest

they should droop in the tumult. On the other side went forth the Lord Grey of Werk, and the green ribbon council,[1] and the floor of the Guildhall was soon crowded. After an immensity of wrangling, the livery refused to confirm North's appointment;[2] on which a warm discussion arose, which ended in a long argument by counsel, whether the hall could be dissolved. The attorney-general was flat to the point, that the mayor was head of the corporation, and so, that nothing could be done without him: on which he plucked up a remarkable spirit, rose unexpectedly, and bade the officer take up the

[1] Many clubs and associations were formed at this time in different quarters of the city. The most celebrated was the green ribbon club, which consisted of two hundred persons devoted to opposition and the bill of exclusion. Sir Robert Payton, who incurred the censure of the House of Commons for having made his peace with the Duke of York, being questioned by the House, informed them that the Duke of York said to him, " You have been against me, Sir Robert; you was a member of the green ribbon club."—*Somerville's Political Transactions*, p. 101. and Ib. p. 10.

[2] " The dissenters, who were much the greater number, instead of holding up hands, screwed their faces into numberless variety of No's, in such a sour way, and with so much noise, that any one would have thought all of them had, in the same instant of time, been possessed with some malign spirit that convulsed their visages in that manner."—*North's Examen*, p. 605.

G

sword, saying, as he went off, " If I die, I die."
He then took his seat upon the hustings, and
directed Crispe, the common serjeant, to adjourn
the hall. Sir John Moor intended that the case
should have been argued by counsel, and he
fixed on Mr. Sanders (afterwards the chief justice), together with Sir George Jeffreys, for that
purpose; but " upon receiving a letter from a
certain minister, his lordship came down, and
dismissed the court." [1]

In the end, the court prevailed; and North,
with one Sir Peter Rich, a citizen-courtier,
were sworn for the ensuing year. But Jeffreys,
although not permitted to interfere with these
proceedings on account of his deprivation, was
not without full employment in this affair soon
afterwards. For, doubting perhaps the firmness
of the crown, the old sheriffs, Pilkington and
Shute, were so indiscreet as to set up a poll in
the common-hall after the adjournment; for
which, on information and oath made, they
were forthwith arrested, and obliged to put in
bail, and in the following May took their trial
with several others for a riot.

Upon this occasion the serjeant appeared in

[1] See " The Rights of the City further unfolded, and the
manifold Miscarriages of my Lord Mayor, &c. displayed and
laid open," 1682.

all his glory. There was some objection in the outset as to swearing the jury; in the legal phrase, it was attempted to challenge the array. " Pray, gentlemen," said the good-natured chief justice Sanders, " don't put these things upon me : you would not have done this before another judge; you would not have done it if Sir Matthew Hale had been here. This is only to tickle the people." And Jeffreys exclaimed, when the challenge was read, " Here's a tale of a tub, indeed !"

This Sir Edmund Sanders was a most remarkable character : he was derived from the meanest origin, a mere beggar-boy, and " courted the attorneys' clerks for scraps." But he contrived to make himself in due time a very expert special pleader; and being conversant with all the traps and snares of the law, very often baffled his superiors, (Maynard* among

* This very considerable man was the eldest son of Alexander Maynard, Esq. of Tavistock, Devon, and was born about 1602. At the age of sixteen he was entered of Exeter College, Oxford; and, previous to his taking the degree of A. B., was admitted a student of the Middle Temple. He was a friend of Mr. Attorney Noy, and was contemporary with Selden, Rolle, and other great lawyers of the day, whose custom was to converse very unreservedly together, and thus cement their various stocks of knowledge. Maynard soon had great practice, which he managed to retain to the

the rest,) and had certain business which none
but himself could do.   Hale had no great fancy

end of his forensic career : for whether there was a monarchy
or a commonwealth, he equally prospered ; and was concerned
in the state persecutions which distinguish the reign of the
second Charles.   His knowledge of law was exquisite, and
Jeffreys was often glad to avail himself of a hint from the
old serjeant, which he would greedily swallow, and crow
over the other counsel with the new information he had
gained.   One day, however, he unguardedly broke loose
upon his instructor, and told Maynard, who was then quite
mellow with age, that he had grown so old as to forget the
law.   " 'Tis true, Sir George, I have forgotten more law
than ever you knew," was the punishing retort.   In 1640,
this lawyer sat for Totness, and soon after was employed
against the Earl of Strafford and Archbishop Laud.   In 1647,
he was so eminent as to get 700l. in one circuit : " more,"
says Whitelock, " than was ever got before in that way:"
and in 1653, the Protector made him his serjeant.   There were
some points, however, which this stout advocate would not
submit to yield ; and he so conducted himself in the famous
case of Cony, (who was imprisoned by Cromwell without
process of law for refusing to pay taxes,) as to be sent to the
Tower, from whence, however, he soon got out by submission.   At the Restoration he was fox enough to be made
serjeant ; and very soon after, King's serjeant, with the honour
of knighthood, at which time he was appointed a judge,* but
made his excuses, probably because that post was held only
during the King's pleasure.   In 1661, he was returned for

* This refutes what is somewhere sneeringly said, that Maynard contrived to be made King's serjeant at the Restoration, but could get no further.

for him, for he was quite besotted with ale and brandy; so much so, that in summer his brethren of the bar suffered a kind of martyrdom in being obliged to stand near him, for intemperance had given him rather an unwholesome carcase. However, he passed off all their grumbling with a jest, and used to be so merry and facetious, and withal so loyal, that he had no enemies; and having had the settlement of the pleadings in the great *quo warranto* case against the city, (for he was the government devil ' of those times,) came quietly upon the cushion of the King's Bench, where his science soon reconciled the lawyers to him.

We return to Pilkington's affair, where Sir

Beeralston, Devon, and sat throughout the two reigns in the House of Commons. He was a member of the Convention, and was very vigorous and able in managing the conference between the Lords and Commons. At the age of 87, he was promoted to be first commissioner of the great seal, and the year after was chosen member for Plymouth, but resigned his seat in Chancery soon afterwards. He died at Gunnersbury, near Ealing, on the 9th of October, 1690, and was buried in the church there. Every one knows his celebrated reply to King William, who told him that he had outlived all the men of the law of his time. "He had like to have outlived the law itself," he answered, " if His Highness had not come over."

' An eminent counsel who settles pleadings for government.

George was exercising his *grossièretès* in perfect freedom. The counsel for the defendants were pressing their challenge: " Pray tell me, Robin Hood upon Greendale stood," quoth the serjeant, " therefore you must not demur." And in the course of the trial he rose into a towering passion, rebuked the advocates on the other side with considerable violence, and, in fact, carried the verdict by storm. He was the more annoyed, because of the frequent allusions which were made to his having held office in the city, and he himself was obliged incidentally to mention circumstances which had happened in his time there. Nevertheless, he evinced great acumen in fixing the guilt of this riot on the respective prisoners whom he found he could convict; and there was, indeed, some need of his blustering amidst the din and clamour which disturbed the court during the trial.

And now he was able to requite some of his enemies; for in estimating the amount of fines, and the abilities of the defendants to pay them, recourse was had to his advice, which he so gave as to bring down a heavy penalty upon their heads. This judgment was reversed in parliament on the coming in of King William. Soon afterwards, it fell to the lot of Sir Patience Ward to be tried for perjury; in which inquiry

Jeffreys was concerned, but exhibited nothing remarkable, if we except the precision with which he detected the inaccuracy of some short-hand notes.

Yet his most signal victory over the city par-tizans was certainly the *quo warranto* judgment. Secretly he had urged this measure as a punish-ment for the perpetual rebellion which the citi-zens had been waging against the ministry; and he succeeded not only in overturning their pri-vileges, but in reducing them to beg for favour at his hands. The same man had complimented the King and the Duke of York on the removal of a similar proceeding in 1680; but he was not at that time an ex-recorder.

This pulling down of so great a charter as that of the Londoners was a bright example for one so fond of power and terror as Sir George Jeffreys: so that as soon as he became chief justice, he went the northern circuit, in the plenitude of authority to save or annul the cor-porate privileges of those parts at his pleasure:

Diruit, ædificat, mutat.

There was in truth a northern, as well as a western campaign. Having plotted, that the King should give him some token of acceptance in respect of these services, on the morning of

his expedition he had a ring fresh from the royal
finger.   And so he went forth, a mighty legate,
while all the charters, " like the walls of Je-
richo,"[1] fell down at his feet; and he returned
" laden with surrenders, the spoils of towns."
This ring was called the *blood-stone;* and when
the King gave it, he is reported to have said,
that now the judge was going his circuit, " as
the weather was hot, he had better not drink
too much."

It is well known, that Judge Jones gave the
opinion of the court upon the *quo warranto;*
and it is probable, that he was rewarded with
the chief seat in the Common Pleas for this
eminent service.   Jones was of Welsh extrac-
tion, and was brought up at Shrewsbury free-
school.   Like his countrymen, he was given
to occasional heats; and these were shown, says
the author of the Examen, " in a rubor of countenance set off by his grey hairs."   He was the
judge who punished the famous Mr. Dare for
seditious words.   It is a well-known story, that
this Dare presented one of the violent petitions
to the King, and that when his Majesty asked
him, how he dared present it, " Sir," said the
man, "my name is Dare." However, Jones would

---

[1] North's Examen, 4to. p. 606.

have been supplanted if Sir George might have had his will, for it seems that he pressed very hard for the place, and it might have been only a promise that he should be the next King's Bench premier that quieted him, particularly as Sanders was ill, and the place was one of greater power, though indeed, at that time, of less emolument. This was a second effort to outstrip another, though not so successful as the ejectment of poor Sir Job Charlton.

Sir John Reresby tells us,[1] that, when the chief justice Jones[2] was dispensed with by James II. Mr. Jones, his son, said, that his father had observed to the King, that he was by no means sorry he was laid aside, old and worn out as he was in his service, but concerned that His Majesty should expect such a construction of the law from him, as he could not honestly give; and that none but indigent, ignorant, or ambitious men would give their judgment as he expected; and that to this His Majesty made

[1] Memoirs, p. 233.

[2] He was choleric, but, on the whole, a very tolerable judge for those times. The greatest stain upon his character seems to be the violence which he used towards the unhappy Mrs. Gaunt. He was made judge of the King's Bench, April 13, 1676, and chief justice of the Common Pleas, September 29, 1683.

answer, "It was necessary his judges should
be all of one mind." Jones replied, "Twelve
judges you may possibly find, sir, but hardly
twelve lawyers."

"Sir Thomas Bludworth, the father of Lady
Jeffreys, died about this time. He was sheriff
in 1663, and lord mayor of London in 1666, and
he represented the city from the restoration
until the thirtieth year of Charles II.'s reign,
the year of his daughter's marriage. Pepys
falls very foul upon him in his Diary, repeat-
edly characterizing him as a weak and inefficient man; for which some proof is certainly
adduced. He suffered the impressment of some
respectable persons who had not been accustomed to a sea-faring life, and neglected to
give them the bounty money, which Mr. Pepys
says, he was obliged to furnish from his own
pocket.[1] The account which that journalist
gives of Sir Thomas's pusillanimity during the
great fire, is as follows : " At last, met my lord
mayor in Canning-street, like a man spent,
with a handkercher about his neck. To the
King's message,'[2] he cried, like a fainting woman, 'Lord! what can I do? I am spent: people will not obey me. I have been pulling down

[1] Diary, Vol. i. p. 425.
[2] That houses should be pulled down.

houses, but the fire overtakes us faster than we can do it.' That he needed no more soldiers; and that, for himself, he must go and refresh himself, having been up all night. So he left me, and I him, &c."

Something that came out on Rosewell's trial, which we shall mention by and by, seems to confirm this supineness of the lord mayor. A witness, named Smith, stated that the prisoner had preached to this effect :—"There was a certain great man that lived at the upper end of

' Vol. i. p. 446. Pepys seems afterwards to have been on good terms with Jeffreys, as appears from a letter printed among the correspondence subjoined to the Diary :—

Lord Chancellor Jeffreys to Mr. Pepys.

Bulstrode, July ye 7th, 1687.

My most honrd. Friend,

The bearer, Capt. Wren, came to mee this evening, with a strong fancy that a recommendation of myne might at least entitle him to your favourable reception : his civillities to my brother, and his relation to honest Will. Wren, (and you know who else,) emboldens me to offer my request on his behalfe. I hope he has served our Mr. well, and is capable of being an object of the King's favour in his request : however, I am sure I shall be excused for this impertinency, because I will gladly in my way embrace all opportunities wherein I may manifest myself to be what I here assure you I am, Sir, your most entirely

Affectionate friend and servant,

JEFFREYS, C.

Gracechurch-street, about this time eighteen
years agone; I name nobody, you all know him
whom I mean. And there came a certain poor
man to him; he was not a poor man neither, but
a carpenter by trade;—one that wrought for his
living, a labouring man; and told that great
man, if he would take his advice, he would tell
him how to quench the fire; but he pish'd at
it, and made light of it, and would not take his
advice. Which if it had not been for that great
man, and the lord mayors and sheriffs that have
been since,—nor the fire at Wapping, nor the
fire at Southwark, had gone so far, or come to
what they did." Then said the chief justice,
"There was a great man that lived at the
end of Gracechurch-street? who did him
mean by that?" As if Jeffreys did not know
that his own father-in-law lived there!—Mr.
Recorder. "He meant, we suppose, Sir Thomas Bludworth, that was lord mayor at the
fire time."

However, Dr. Freeman, the rector of St.
Ann's, Aldersgate, who had the task of performing his funeral sermon, indulged in most lavish
praise of the knight. "He had the unhappiness
to live in an age that's full of uncharitable censures. He was an excellent father and husband, feared God and loved his church, and

died without an expression of discontent.". The reverend doctor could not have said more if the mitre had been descending upon his head.

There was another Sir Thomas, probably the son of the lord mayor, who, among others, strenuously opposed a bill for charging the chancellor's estates in Leicestershire, after his decease, with 14600*l.*, and interest, for the payment of his debts. By calling in the assistance of counsel, the property was saved to the heir, the bill being lost.

The Rye-house Plot, a real substantial conspiracy, was now discovered, in which many persons of high blood were deeply implicated; and we should not do justice to the character of Jeffreys were we to pass over the details of it in silence. The king's counsel were on the alert, and Sir George had precedence next to the attorney-general, (Sawyer,) and the solicitor, Mr. Finch.' The judge was Pemberton, who had been

' Mr. Finch was the second son of Heneage, Earl of Nottingham, Lord High Chancellor of England. He was sent to Christ Church at the age of fifteen, in 1664, and went thence without a degree to the Inner Temple. At the age of twenty-nine, being then solicitor-general, he was chosen member for Oxford University, which honourable trust he held for many years. Sir Francis Winnington having displeased the ministry, Finch took the place of solicitor-general in the room of that lawyer in 1678, but was

removed to the Common Pleas, a very self-suf-
ficient, but acute lawyer, whose bias was not
how he should please the one party or the other,
but how he might best administer to his own
fancy and opinion. He used to boast that in
making law he had outdone kings, lords, and
commons. He had not been of Sir Matthew
Hale's school as to morals, for he began to prac-
tise in gaol, after he had spent all his money,
and there made himself so busy, that he came
out sleek and sharp with his gains. This is a
specimen of his judicial opinion, after summing
up the evidence in a case of treason : " Look
you, gentlemen of the jury, you hear a plain
case of a barbarous murder designed upon the
King, one of the horridest treasons that hath
been heard of in the world ;—to have shot the
King and the Duke of York in their coaches as
they were coming upon the road. You have had

obliged, in his turn, to give way in 1686 to Powis. In 1685
he was returned for Guildford. He was one of the counsel
for the seven bishops in 1688, and in the reign of Queen
Anne was created a peer, with the title of Baron Guernsey.
George the First made him Earl of Aylesford, and in 1714
he was constituted chancellor of the duchy of Lancaster,
which office he held only two years, and died in 1719, three
years after he had resigned. He is supposed to have written
some pamphlets on the Rye-house Plot, and the *quo warranto* against the city of London.

full evidence of this man's being one of them, and, therefore, I am of opinion, that you must find him guilty." And so the jury found him guilty. It is said that this judge was removed for taking bribes, but Burnet attributes his quietus to the leniency which he showed Lord Russel.

After Walcot and Hone had been convicted, Lord William Russel came before the court; and however careful Jeffreys might have been to avoid irregular evidence on former trials, it seemed, upon this, as though he were endeavouring to establish the fullest doctrine of hearsay. Thus, when he asked Sheppard whether he remembered any writings or papers read; the witness said, " None that I saw."—" Or that you heard of?" continued the serjeant. And, indeed, the chief justice was compelled to interfere, with a declaration, that a great part of the evidence was such as the chief witness, Lord Howard, had heard from others; observing, at the same time, that the prisoner should not be affected by it, while Jeffreys was assuming the whole of this fallacious testimony for sworn facts.

The most pointed question put during the whole business was by the shrewd serjeant, who had sense enough to perceive that the case

was mainly deficient, for want of clear proof
that Lord Russel had assented to the plans of
the conspirators : wherefore it was, that he asked
very earnestly of the Lord Howard this : " But
he did consent ?"—Lord Howard. " We did not
put it to the vote, but it went without contradiction ; and I took it, that all those gave their
consent." The prisoner had been in the habit
of associating with the persons who were said to
have formed a treasonable council on this occasion, and so far the evidence was against him ;
but it was indispensable to a just conviction that
he should have participated in some overt act ;
and had not Pemberton, in the conclusion of this
summing up, fallen upon the design to seize the
King's guards, which he interpreted as a design
to seize the person of the King, the matter had
gone lame indeed to the jury. Nevertheless,
Jeffreys manifested a bravado which must have
been perfectly astonishing ; he told the jury that
the King's counsel had raked no gaols for their
witnesses ; that it was not likely that two men
should damn their own souls to take away the
prisoner's life ; that the religion of the country
ought to be preserved ; that they should not forget the horrid murder of that pious prince, King
Charles the First ; and that they should not be
corrupted by the greatness of any man. An

anonymous writer [1] tells us, that this speech had
great influence on the jury, and that it was delivered from a pique against the nobleman accused, because he had been in parliament when
the orator was brought down upon his knees
there: and there may be some colour for this,
since the address of the judge must be considered as containing an intimation that the jury
might acquit, if they dared.

Sanders, the chief justice, was now dead by
apoplexy; an admirable lawyer, and one who
has left behind him a very bible for special
pleaders; but a man of careless morals, and a
bigot to the ale-cask. In his room came Sir
George Jeffreys, who was made on the 29th of
September, 1683, and soon afterwards sworn of
the privy council.[2]

[1] The Bloody Assizes, p. 10.
[2] Somerville says, that he was first a puisne judge; but
this is incorrect: *Pemberton* had been a puisne before his
elevation.

H

CHAP. V.

THIS promotion, it may be well imagined,
could hardly be denied to Jeffreys; always
busy in the intrigues and politics of the court,
from a mere adventurer in state manœuvres, he
at length became a chief engine in working

them, and in the course of a few months he was admitted into the cabinet. There hardly needs any speculation as to the immediate cause of this elevation, when we consider the immensity of service which he had rendered the crown; the abundance of convictions he had procured; the unhesitating and devoted servility which he had displayed : yet it has been said, that his promise to bail the popish lords helped materially to lift him up, that he showed much irresolution and deceitfulness about the matter, and, in the writer's own words, "failed at the touch." Certain it is, that Danby and the three others (for Stafford had suffered death) applied by petition to be bailed ; but their request was refused on the first application, although means were found afterwards to renew it with better success.

There was now another victim to be sacrificed, and the ministers knew their new judge too well not to prefer him to Pemberton. It was one of Jeffreys's first judicial employments to preside at the trial of that considerable man, Algernon Sidney. He began very fairly, for he openly reprobated the practice of whispering to the jury. " Let us have no remarks," said he, " but a fair trial, in God's name !" Sir John

Dalrymple has observed in his Memoirs,' that
when the court would have persuaded Sidney
to make a step in law, which he suspected was
meant to hurt him, he said, " I desire you
would not try me, and make me to run on dark
and slippery places, I don't see my way;" as
though the judges wished to lead him into a
trap. In justice to the chief of the court, who
has been so much censured for his deportment
here, let us hear the caution which he distinctly
gave the prisoner :—

Lord Chief Justice. " Put in what plea you
shall be advised; but if you put in a special
plea, and Mr. Attorney demurs, you may have
judgment of death, and by that you wave the
fact." And again, " I am sure there is no gentleman of the long robe would put any such
thing into your head. There was never any
such thing done in capital matters." The deep
blemish upon this trial was, that the unfortunate
colonel was found guilty upon inadmissible evidence, and a misrepresentation of the law by
Jeffreys. A witness was suffered to give evidence that he knew Sidney's hand-writing,
because he had seen him write once, and had
met with indorsements upon bills in the same

' Vol. i. p. 35.

hand-writing; and another was allowed to speak from his experience of those indorsements only: and the judge would have mere writing to be an overt act of treason. Whereas, the men ought to have testified to Sidney's hand of their own knowledge, without consulting any other papers; and the doctrine, *scribere est agere*, ought never to have been entertained in a court of justice, unless a publication were proved.

But there is no colour for saying, as some have done, that the court refused to hear the prisoner, and give him the benefit of his defence. The report of the proceedings bears ample proof that great patience was shown, even by Jeffreys, and that he pointed out the advantage which would be gained by throwing a discredit on Lord Howard's statement, who was a principal witness against the prisoner. It was not until questions were demanded by Sidney at their hands, that he was interrupted by the judges, and with regard to some suggestions by the chief, that irrelevant discourses should not be indulged;—in this, our own enlightened day, if an accused person strays far from the point, it is rarely indeed that he will not be minded by the judge of the true course material to his defence. Sir John Dalrymple brings a further

charge against the chief justice for endeavouring to ensnare the colonel into an avowal of the
seditious writing attributed to him. We will
give the passage from the State Trials at length,
always premising that Jeffreys had such an
overbearing tendency in his composition, as to
reveal any artifice he might have been desirous
of employing by the very violence of his method.

Mr. Att. Gen.—So much we shall make use
of; if the colonel please to have any other part
read to explain it, he may.—[Then the sheets
were shown to Colonel Sidney.]

Col. Sidney.—I do not know what to make
of it; I can read it.

Lord Ch. Just.—Ay, no doubt of it! better
than any man here. Fix on any part you have a
mind to have read.

Col. Sidney.—I do not know what to say to
it, to read it in pieces thus.

Lord Ch. Just.—I perceive you have disposed
them under certain heads : to what heads would
you have read?

Col. Sidney.—*My lord, let him give an account
of it that did it.*

And then the King's counsel went on with
their evidence.

Can it be denied, that, at this day, if the
publication of a libel be proved, it may be pro-

posed to the defendant, without offence, to read any detached parts of it? a proposal which may come from the court, if they see fit, for his benefit. The papers produced had been found in Sidney's study; and there could hardly be a question but that he had been the author. If Jeffreys intended the address he made for artifice, he was most deplorably off his guard; for the most natural reply which a prisoner would make, when told that he knew all about a matter with which he might be charged, would be, " My lord, I know nothing at all about it."

Nor would an assumption by the judge that he had done any particular act, in any wise alter his course; for having determined to deny the thing itself, he would be brought to the very point of denial by being challenged so publicly as the author. If it be intended to applaud the skill of the conspirator, Sidney, it may be agreed, without difficulty, that he opposed craft infinitely superior to that exercised against him, admitting a design to entrap him. This last reply is justly celebrated : he would give no ground to his prosecutors; and, at the last, would have had his writ of error, but for the dissent of the attorney-general. Just before judgment, he exclaimed, " I must appeal to God and the world, I am not heard ; " and after sen-

tence pronounced, he firmly uttered his appeal
to God, that inquisition for his blood might be
made only against those who maliciously persecuted him for righteousness' sake. Jeffreys, as
well he might, on hearing this, started from his
seat, and lost his temper. " I pray God," cried
he, " work in you a temper fit to go unto the
other world, for I see you are not fit for this."
—Col. Sidney. "My lord, feel my pulse (holding out his hand), and see if I am disordered; I
bless God, I never was in better temper than I
am now." Sidney's solicitor entertained a very
different feeling: far from participating in the
prisoner's philosophical calmness, he could not
help declaring, that the jury were a loggerheaded
jury, for which he was immediately committed.
It is said also, that the chief justice was seen to
speak with the jury; but the maxim, *de mortuis nil
nisi bonum*, has never been of the least advantage
to poor Jeffreys, whose character is destined to
bear every curse which the fierce imagination of
men can devise.

The attainder was reversed, because the
law had been improperly expounded; and
the friends of Russel and Sidney would, of
course, combine to blacken the judge who
had deprived them of their associates, when
they themselves rose in power at the Revolu-

tion. Jeffreys had grossly erred; but must be
held acquitted upon this occasion of that vast
brutality and artifice with which writers have
loaded him : for, excepting Hale and Pemberton,
all his predecessors in that reign were accustomed to language and manners quite as arbitrary, and occasionally even more unpolished.

However, this conduct plainly showed that
he would go all lengths for the attainment of
rank; or, as one writer says, " so as he rode on
horseback, he cared not whom he rode over."
And the truth was, that people in general were
seriously frightened when they found this man
seated on so high a throne :[1] they were preju-
diced against him; and, no doubt, regarded every
thing which fell from him with much less allowance than the words of other contemporary
judges, although no less violent when it suited
their purposes. Burnet is outrageous upon the
subject : " Jeffreys was scandalously vicious,"
says he, " and was drunk every day, besides a
drunkenness of fury in his temper that looked
like enthusiasm." He then launches out against
the partiality and declamation which Sir George
displayed on the bench, the indecency which
he yielded to on his post; and abuses his elo-

[1] Evelyn says, " Sir George Jefferies was advanced, reputed the most ignorant, but most daring."

quence as "viciously copious, and neither correct nor agreeable." It was very proper that a
clergyman should feel scandalized at a character, who was frequently not only *ebrius*, but
ebriolus; but it does not follow from all this
tirade, that Jeffreys was drunk every day; and
the future bishop could not be complimented
upon his choice of companions, if he had any
actual proof of such indulgences : the fact was,
that men of that day had adopted a system of
mutual abuse and recrimination. Treby, who
never left the bottle while there was a man to
stand by it, comes out of the furnace a most
respectable judge ; and Jeffreys, as though he
were a perpetual firebrand.[1]

His private life at this time is described much
in the same manner by North, who had no
great love for him, because he was for ever
thwarting his brother, the lord keeper. He
used to drink and talk with " good fellows and
humourists:" and so he would unbend himself
in " drinking, laughing, singing, kissing, and

[1] Bevil Higgons, in his Review of Burnet's History, has
observations upon this subject nearly similar: " If my Lord
Jefferies," said he, " exceeded the bounds of temperance now
and then in an evening, it does not follow that he was drunk
on the bench and in council." There are several other remarks which may be found in Higgons's Historical Works,
Vol. ii. p. 263.

every extravagance of the bottle." But the
writer is driven to confess, that when this judge
was in temper, and had an indifferent matter
before him, he became a seat of justice better
than any other. And then he had a set of ban-
terers, as North calls them, but who were most
probably parasites suffered to live upon his hospitalities; and when they all sat down together,
there was a general flow of abuse and scandal,
which regaled the chief justice amazingly. Some
of these hangers-on were at the bar; and although our author acquaints us that there was
no friendship which he would not use ill, we
cannot help chuckling at the idea, that he
would fall upon these minions without mercy
when he was pleased to do so, even in public;
and this he called giving " a lick with the rough
side of his tongue." Who can condemn the
host for lashing such guests as these on occasion? He kept up the dignity of the bar by it;
for he said as much as that, although such men
might be his boon companions, he did not consider them as deserving of the least favour.
And truly he was equally impartial, as far as
relates to any preference of his friends when he
got into the chancery, for there he lectured all
the counsel round. From this we gather at
once the secret of his violating friendship when

he arrived at promotion; for none except abandoned characters would stoop to be his co-mates,
and he had ample sense enough to know that
they were never worth consideration. He met,
however, occasionally, with more respectable
men, amongst others with Evelyn. Very soon
after Sidney's trial, at most a day or two, he
went to a grand wedding of one Mrs. Castle,
where the lord mayor and several of the city
quality were present—Judge Wilkins and Evelyn were there. Jeffreys and his brother judge
danced with the bride, and were very merry.
The party spent the afternoon, till eleven at
night, in drinking healths, taking tobacco, and
" talking," says the author of Sylva, " much
beneath the gravity of judges that had but a
day or two before condemned Mr. Algernon
Sidney." Yet every one knows that judges
must unbend as well as other people; and the
customs of times much later than those have
warranted the pledging healths and cracking
bottles even unto the peep of the day succeeding the bridal night.

Some violences of his temper at this period
may be accounted for, from the severe fits of
the stone which intemperance had bestowed on
him. It must have been one of these which
prompted his severity to Armstrong. Sir Tho-

mas demanded the benefit of the law. Lord Chief Justice. "That you shall have, by the grace of God! see that execution be done on Friday next, according to law: you shall have the full benefit of the law." This looks like brutality; but Sir Thomas had almost infuriated the judge, by telling him that he had been robbed and stripped of his clothes; and therefore, as lawyers would not plead without money, that he could not fee them; and he half hinted, that the court knew of his being plundered.

When Armstrong found that nothing he could say would prevail, he exclaimed aloud against the chief, saying, "My blood be upon your head!"—"Let it, let it; I am clamour-proof," returned Jeffreys. After the great change of 1689, an attempt was made to procure 5000*l.* for the Lady Armstrong and her children, from the estates of Sir Thomas's judges and prosecutors; but, like many others of the same kind, the bill failed, and the attainder remained in force for some years, when it was reversed, but without the compensation clause.

Fierce as he was, our chief justice did not always escape the sting of a repartee. He went a country assize once where an old man with a great beard came to give evidence, but had not the good fortune to please the judge: so he quarrelled with the beard, and said, " If your conscience is as large as your beard, you'll swear any thing." The old blade was nettled, and briskly returned, " My lord, if you go about to measure consciences by beards, your lordship has none." He had a strange remembrance of slights. There was a certain jury at Guildhall, with one Best among them, who acquitted a man for publishing a pamphlet much against the recorder's will (who was Jeffreys), and he did not scruple to upbraid the twelve with perjury. The jury were so much irritated, that they moved the Old Bailey court for leave to indict him, and Mr. Best was very active in the business. Scroggs, the judge, said, that they had better defer their charge, for the sessions were nearly ended, and it could not be tried until the next; and that he did not like to leave so high a man as the recorder under an imputation so long. The matter dropped, because Treby came in recorder before the next sessions; but there was one who recollected Mr. Best very keenly for it. This man afterwards drank a health to the pious memory of Stephen Colledge, for which he was convicted, but absconded to avoid the fine. However, he met the chief justice on horseback, some time afterwards, going the circuit; and on being told

who he was, cheated perhaps by some roman-
tic idea that great men forget the injuries done
them in their inferior stations, was so silly as to
tell his name, and desire his service to his lordship. He little dreamt that he should be immediately fetched back, sent off to York gaol,
and thence brought to the King's Bench a prisoner, for a fine of £500. And Williams, the
speaker, shared the same fate: he had undergone
the task of lecturing the present head of his court
at the bar of the House of Commons, and was now
sued to the utmost for publishing Dangerfield's
Narrative of the Popish Plot, although in his capacity as speaker; for which he paid no less a sum
than £8000, as a fine for his ministerial conduct.

To notice all the state prosecutions in which
this judge figured, would be a long task, and
inconsistent with the duty which we owe a
kind and patient reader. He was, of course,
the presiding magistrate on the principal of
these occasions; and though sometimes most
unjustifiably rough, would generally keep the
counsel in good order, confining them to the
point in issue, and was a tolerably good guardian of such rules of evidence as were then understood. Some remarkable passages, while he
sat on the common law bench, cannot be passed

over: one of which is a stormy conversation which he had with Mr. Ward, afterwards lord chief baron,' in an action against an ex-sheriff for arresting the lord mayor. The counsel was alluding to the trial of Pilkington and others for a riot, which he coloured over by calling it a matter of right and election: " No, Mr. Ward, that was not the question determined there," interrupted my lord chief justice.—Mr. Ward. " My lord, I humbly conceive the issue of that cause did determine the question."—" No, no, I tell you it was not the question."—" I must submit it to your lordship."—" I perceive you do not understand the question that was then, nor the question that is now. You have made a long speech here, and nothing at all to the purpose; you do not understand what you are about: I tell you it was no such question:—no," continued the chief justice, " it was not the question; but the defendants there were tried for a notorious offence, and disorderly tumultuous assembly. Do not make such excursions, *ad captandum populum*, with your flourishes. I will none of your enamel, nor your garniture."

' Edward Ward was attorney-general to King William in 1693; made chief baron in 1695; and died July 16, 1714, in office.

And then, after a few more words *pro* and *con*,—
" Indeed, Mr. Ward, you do not understand the
question at all, but launch out into an ocean of
discourse, that is wholly wide from the mark."
—" Will your lordship please to hear me?"—
"If you would speak to the purpose; come to
the question, man! I see you do not understand
what you are about."—" My lord—"—" Nay,
be as angry as you will, Mr. Ward," &c.—[Then
there was a little hiss begun.] Lord chief justice. " Who is that? What, in the name of God!
I hope we are now past that time of day, that
humming and hissing shall be used in courts of
justice; but I would fain know that fellow that
dare to hum and hiss while I sit here; I'll assure him, be he who he will, I'll lay him by the
heels, and make an example of him. Indeed, I
knew the time when causes were to be carried
according as the mobile hiss'd or humm'd; and
I do not question but they have as good a will
to it now. Come, Mr. Ward, pray let us have
none of your fragrancies, and fine rhetorical
flowers, to take the people with." There was a
little more blustering, but great civility on the
part of Ward, when Serjeant Maynard got up,
and stated the law, which the chief justice
adopted in a moment, and all went on quietly.
He had also a habit of scolding the popular ad-

I

vocates of those noisy times, if they happened to displease him; and this he would do with great severity. Williams, the speaker, his old enemy, who was afterwards solicitor-general,[1] and Mr. Wallop, came in for a full share of this punishment.

In the trial of Braddon and Speke, for publishing a statement that the Earl of Essex had been murdered in the Tower, the latter counsel was especially visited with an effusion of this kind. He had asked some question which the chief by no means approved of, and on his persisting,—" Nay, Mr. Wallop," exclaimed his lordship, " you shan't hector the court out of their understandings."—Mr. Wallop. " I refer myself to all that hear me, if I attempted any such thing as to hector the court."—Lord chief justice. " Refer yourself to all that hear you? refer yourself to the court : 'tis a reflection upon the government, I tell you, your question is, and

[1] William Williams, sometime recorder of Chester and speaker of the House of Commons, was solicitor-general with Powis, attorney, during the latter part of James the Second's reign, and was made a baronet in July, 1688. He was, nevertheless, one of King William's learned counsel, and is famed for introducing the Treating Act. His wife was the daughter and co-heiress of Watkin Kiffin, Esq. He died July 11, 1700. Sir Watkin Williams Wynn, that munificent lord of Wales, is his great-grandson.

you shan't do any such thing while I sit here,
by the grace of God, if I can help it."—Mr.
Wallop. " I am sorry for that; I never intended
any such thing, my lord."—Lord chief justice.
" Pray behave yourself as you ought, Mr. Wallop; you must not think to huff or swagger here."
And afterwards he said, amongst other things,
" We have got such strange kind of notions,
now-a-days, that forsooth men think they may
say any thing, because they are counsel." With
a little more coarseness of the same kind, he
contrived at last to lay the spirit of Mr. Wallop.
He fell very foul upon Mr. Stanhope on the
trial of Sacheverell for a riot. There was a
quarrel about the mayor's mace, and the counsel
thought there was no great sauciness in demanding the ensign of office. He was mistaken. " I
say it was saucy," cries Jeffreys; " and I tell
you, you had been saucy if you had done it; for
every man that meddles out of his province is
saucy. Every little prick-eared fellow, I warrant you, must go to dispose of the government!"
Stanhope was sulky, and he replied, " It may
be I should have known better than to have
gone on such an errand."—Lord chief justice.
" So you would have done well to do; and you
should know better than to ask such insignifi-
cant, impertinent questions as you do," &c.

Serjeant Bigland was laid hold of in the same
trial. He was recorder of Nottingham, and
swore in the sham mayor. When he came to be
sworn, he told the court, that he had asked the
mayor, whether he desired his advice as recorder,
or how? Jeffreys took him up: " But what authority had you to swear him? I reckon it to be
worse in those people that understand the law,
than in others, that they should be present at
such things. *Do you ask me as recorder, or as
counsel?* But they would have done well to
advise people to meddle with their own business;
let my brother take that along with him."[1]

It is difficult to say, why he should have been
so grossly accused of partiality: the following
instance will show that the crown counsel had
no more mercy than the rest, when they ventured beyond the rules of evidence. In Titus
Oates's case, when he was indicted for perjury,
Jeffreys would not suffer the attorney-general
to prove the narrative of the popish plot, delivered to the House of Commons by Oates, till
he had distinctly satisfied the court of its

[1] Roger North says, that in Sacheverell's trial, the lord
chief justice sided with him, and reproved the attorney-general: but how can this be? for the attorney-general was not
there, and the chief justice was clearly against the defendants.

having been made on oath in the Lords' House.
And when Sir Robert Sawyer put a witness into
the box, and asked him, whether what he swore
at a former trial was true, the judge burst forth
against the King's counsel : " That is very nau-
seous and fulsome, Mr. Attorney," said he, " methinks, in a court of justice."—Mr. Attorney-general. " 'Tis not the first time by twenty that
such evidences have been given."—Lord chief
justice. " I hate such precedents at all times,
let it be done never so often. Shall I believe a
villain one word he says, when he owns that he
forswore himself?"—Attorney-general. " Pray,
my lord, give me leave; I must pursue my Master's interest." Then the solicitor-general tried
to persuade Sir George, but in vain ; and when
Mr. North was beginning, he was stopped with,
" Look ye, sir, when the court have delivered
their opinion, the counsel should sit down, and
not dispute it any further." And so it ended.

However, nothing could exceed the treatment
which a reluctant witness would experience
from this judge. He fastened himself on such a
person at the trial of Lady Lisle ; and he was
Dunne, the messenger who carried on a correspondence between the prisoner and Hicks,
the person she was charged with harbouring :
but the witness bore the attack for some time

with great adroitness, for he seemed to have
made a resolve that his mistress should never
suffer through his testimony. However, Jeffreys
grew quite mad; he lectured the witness, menaced him with hell-fire, then persuaded him,
and uttered the most savage exclamations; but
all in vain. At one time he thought of his old
witticisms, and asked the man what trade he
followed. "My lord, I am a baker by trade."
—"And wilt thou bake thy bread at such easy
rates?" The witness had said, that he travelled a great many miles, and had only a piece
of cake and cheese for it. "I assure thee, thy
bread is very light weight, it will scarce pass
the balance here." He got out a name with all
the acumen of the most wire-drawing advocate.—
"Now must I know that man's name."—"The
man's name that I went to at Marton, my lord?"
—Lord chief justice. "Yes; and look to it, it
may be I know the man already; and tell at
what end of the town the man lives too."—
Dunne. "My lord, I cannot tell his name presently."—Lord chief justice. "Oh! pray now,
do not say so; you must tell us, indeed you must
think of his name a little."—Dunne. "My lord,
if I can mind it, I will."—Lord chief justice.
"Prithee do."—Dunne. "His name, truly, my
lord, I cannot rightly tell for the present."—

Lord chief justice. " Prithee recollect thyself; indeed thou canst tell us if thou wilt."—Dunne. " My lord, I can go to the house again, if I were at liberty."—Lord chief justice. " I believe it, and so could I; but really neither you nor I can be spared at present; therefore, prithee do us the kindness now to tell us his name."— Dunne. " Truly, my lord, I cannot mind his name at present."—Lord chief justice. " Alack-a-day! We must needs have it! Come, refresh your memory a little." And then it came out.

Dunne made a few trips, but was very cool at first: " How came you to be so impudent," cried the judge, " as to tell me a lie?"—" I beg your pardon, my lord."—Lord chief justice. " You beg my pardon! That is not because you told me a lie, but because I have found you in a lie. I hope, gentlemen of the jury, you take notice of the strange and horrible carriage of this fellow." The worst was yet to come for poor Dunne: he was again at issue about some fact which Jeffreys wished to get from him, and which he was by no means desirous of giving, when the judge struck upon a new plan, saying, " Dost thou think, that after all this pains that I have been at to get an answer to my question, that thou canst banter me with such sham stuff

as this? Hold the candle to his face, that we
may see his brazen face." The witness declared
that he was cluttered out of his senses, and that
he would say whatever the court desired. And
soon afterwards they held the candle nearer to
his nose, but then he would tell nothing, except
that he was robbed of his senses. Jeffreys had
long since summed up his character; " Thou art
a strange, prevaricating, shuffling, snivelling,
lying rascal," said my lord.[1]

We come now to September, 1684, when Sir
George Jeffreys was summoned to the cabinet.
No act in the King's reign could have annoyed
Lord Guilford more than an introduction of
this kind; and in truth it was something like the
letting a bear loose into a garden. The lord
keeper had been brought up with the old school
of Charles the Second's better days; he was a
staid, sober, thinking counsellor, rather stiff in
his demeanour, but loyal to a proverb. It was,
in spite of this, his misfortune to come under the
denomination of a trimmer, a class of people
whom Jeffreys maligned and persecuted without
example. These persons were a subdivision of

[1] The whole of the very long examination of this man is
well worth the reading. It is to be found in the State Trials,
fol. vol. iv. pp. 108—122.

the Tory party who would not go along with all the high-flown measures of the court. Yet we shall see that the hatred which Sir George bore them ultimately cost him his life.

The venerable sages who have kept the great seal of England, seem generally to have regarded such as have approached their dominion with much jealousy: Lord Ellesmere could never reconcile himself with Coke; and North felt an uneasiness whilst he had the seal, which must be mainly attributed to his proximity with Jeffreys. In a word, whatever the one proposed, the other thwarted; and as Sir George was fully in the Duke of York's confidence, who influenced the King's mind very greatly during the last period of his life, it was no marvel to find the young man of thirty-six gaining a frequent victory much to the mortification of the veteran. However, when they came to contest a matter of business, the man of real metal prevailed. As soon as the new cabinet minister had returned from his northern expedition against the corporations, the lord keeper was addressed by the Duke of York on a Sunday morning, and requested to aid a motion to be made on that evening to His Majesty.

All the great men were shy as foxes; and it soon appeared, that a great secret was on the

point of development. The lord keeper came
to the cabinet, ignorant of the whole, and the
King took his seat, when up rose Jeffreys with
the recusant rolls before him, and made a speech
as follows: " Sir, I have a business to lay before your Majesty, which I took notice of in the
north, and which will deserve your Majesty's
royal commiseration. It is the case of numberless numbers of your good subjects that are imprisoned for recusancy. I have the list of them
here, to justify what I say. They are so many,
that the great gaols cannot hold them without
their lying one upon another." When he had
spoken, he laid his papers and rolls on the
table; but no one answered him for some time,
contrary to North's expectation, who concluded
that some Protestant lord would take up the
matter. At length the Lord Guilford addressed
the King: " I humbly entreat your Majesty,"
said he, " that my lord chief justice may declare, whether all the persons named in these
rolls were actually in the prisons or not." The
chief justice hastily replied, " that all the gaols
in England could not hold them; all certainly
were not actual prisoners, but they were liable
to prosecution if any peevish sheriff chose to enforce the law." On this, the lord keeper turned
to the King, and boldly said, " he thought that

there was no reason to grant such a motion
then; that all these persons were not Roman
Catholics, but that there were many sectaries
amongst them; that they were a turbulent and
seditious people; and that if it pleased the King
to pardon any Roman Catholic, he might issue
a particular and express immunity in favour of
the persons intended to receive grace." The
King was very attentive, and the matter dropped
for that time. It had not escaped the lord
keeper that it would have been his province to
affix the seal to the proposed general pardon.
As soon as the great man returned home, he
exclaimed, "Are they all stark mad?" And
then he noted it down thus:

> Motion, cui solus obstiti.
> Motion, which I alone opposed.'

However, in the next year, the royal compassion was extended to some particular cases.

This was a bold proceeding for a Protestant
chief justice, and savoured highly of that be-
nighted bigotry on the part of James, which led
him so soon afterwards to brave the indignation
of his subjects.

Whether this judge had any religion of his

' North's Lives.

own, it is difficult indeed to say: he was ostensibly a Protestant, and it is affirmed, that he
declined in favour at court through his reluc-
tance to countenance the new religion. Nevertheless, Lady Russel, in a letter to Dr. Fitz-
william, (April 1, 1687,) tells him, that Lord
Peterborough was declared a Roman Catholic,
and that two more, the *chancellor* and the lord
president (Sunderland), were reported as forthcoming papists on the following Sunday: yet,
fortunately, as it happens upon many occasions,
report is one thing—fact another; and from the
best authorities we now have of the bearing of
Jeffreys towards either faith, he certainly did
the most acts for the support of the Protestant
establishment. Sir John Dalrymple also affirms,
that the chancellor regretted his having yielded
so much to the King's inclination for popery;
that he " hesitated, repented, trembled." The
choice of his chaplain, Luke Beaulieu[1] of Christ
Church, confirms the surmise of his attachment
to the reformed faith. He was divinity reader
in St. George's Chapel at Windsor, and pub-

---

[1] This divine was born in France, and educated at the
university of Saumur. He came over to England, where he
was naturalized, and became a student at Oxford for the
sake of the public library. He was rector of Whitchurch,
Oxon, in the year 1685.

lished several things against popery; and Wood
says, that he asserted the rights of His Majesty
and the Church very usefully. Another of his
chaplains was Thomas Spark.[1] When the brief
allowed by the King for the benefit of the distressed Protestant refugees was put in operation,
Jeffreys (who at first refused to affix the seal
to it[2]) was so strict as to the qualifications of
the relieved persons, that it was believed he

[1] Spark, student of Christ Church, anno 1672, aged seventeen, was the son of Archibald Spark, of Northop, in Flintshire. He was indebted to Lord Jeffreys for much advancement. He died in 1692, rector of Ewehurst, near Guildford,
Surrey; of Norton, or Hog's Norton, near Bosworth, Leicestershire; prebendary of Lichfield and of Rochester, D.D.
By his excesses, and too much agitation in obtaining spiritu-
alities, he brought himself into an ill disposition of body,
which, contrary to his expectations, brought him in the prime
of his years to the grave.—*Wood.*

[2] Lady Russel tells something which shows that the chancellor had some good points which he would occasionally
develope. In one of her letters, she says, " I am unwilling
to shake off all hopes about the brief, though I know them
that went to the chancellor since the refusal, and his answer
does not encourage one's hopes. But he is not a lover of
smooth language; so that in that respect we may not so soon
despair."—*Letters,* p. 55. Dr., afterwards Bishop Beve-
ridge, objected to the reading the brief in the cathedral of
Canterbury, as contrary to the rubric. Tillotson replied,
" Doctor, doctor, Charity is above rubrics."—*Note to the
above.*

admitted no one to receive the alms, who would
not take the sacrament from his own chaplain.
And the remarkable passage which occurred at
his death when he sent for Scot, another divine
and author against popery, to give him consola-
tion, confirms still more his secret regard for
protestantism.' When a man comes to die, the
true feelings of his heart are apt to burst forth;
and the main argument to prove King Charles
II. a Catholic, is, that he had Hudleston, a
priest, smuggled, as it were, into his apartment, which was in general the rendezvous of
Protestant bishops; and having succeeded in
obtaining his priest, confessed, and died a true
Catholic.²

¹ This will be related hereafter.

² Extract from Dalrymple's Memoirs, Appendix, part i.
p. 96, *et seq.* :—" What the Duke of York said was not
heard; but the King of England said from time to time very
loud, ' Yes, with all my heart.'—' The King wills that every
body should retire except the Earls of Bath and Feversham.'
The physicians went into a closet, the door of which was
immediately closed, and Chiffins brought Mr. Hudleston in.
The Duke of York, in presenting him, said, ' Sir, here is a
man who has saved your life, * and is now come to save your
soul.' The King answered, ' He is welcome.' He afterwards confessed himself with great sentiments of devotion
and repentance."

* After the battle of Worcester.

In November, 1684, Mr. Rosewell, a dissenting minister, a gentleman of sufficient consequence to be panegyrized by a funeral sermon,[1]
came within the grasp of the chief justice, and
by a good fortune quite remarkable for those
times, ultimately escaped. He was taken in his
own house, and carried by water to a coffee-
house near Aldermanbury, where Jeffreys lived.
Jeffreys received him " like a roaring lion, or a
raging bear;" and, amongst other questions,
asked him where he preached on such a day,
naming it. Rosewell answered in Latin, that
he hoped his lordship would not insist upon his
answering that question, as he might thereby
accuse himself. The judge, in a passion, said,
he supposed the prisoner could not speak another sentence in Latin to save his neck. The
parson thought it civil to try another language,
and so he spoke in Greek. Jeffreys was astonished at this, but soon ordered him to be taken
away; and at night there came a warrant for
committing him to the Gate-house on a charge
of treason. The next morning his wife begged
admittance to him; but meeting with a refusal,
she petitioned the great man for an interview,
who loaded her husband with the most severe
invectives, calling him a great knave, a great

---

[1] By Mead, 1692.

villain, and so on, and bade her petition the
King.¹ This she did, and the King read her request, the chief justice standing near him ; upon
which leave was given that she should visit the
prison at the discretion of my lord chief justice,
who, nevertheless, huffed very much when he
heard of His Majesty's kind speech, and kept
her from her husband for several days afterwards. Roger North, always railing at those
to whom he was politically opposed, informs us,
that Rosewell had made his peace with the
chief justice, whence some corrupt motive is
drawn as a natural inference. He would make
us believe, that a bribe was taken in this affair ;
but confesses, in another place, that when Jeffreys was pleased to be impartial, no one became
a seat of justice better. We shall presently see
that there is no ground for imputing corruption ;
though it may be very true, as North asserts,
that the judge was " tickled with mirth and
laughter at the King's counsel," and " openly
rejoiced at the accident." This accident was a
flaw in the indictment. When Sir George came
upon the bench, he seemed to have sat down

¹ When Mrs. Rosewell discovered some uneasiness at this
abuse of her husband, " Mind him not," said the friend to
whom she was speaking, " you'll be able to hold up your
head with comfort, when he will look down with shame."

with the most impartial resolutions, and seeing
Mr. Wallop, an advocate, always obnoxious to
him because he was retained for the dissenters,
he asked him what business he had there. Wallop alleged a curiosity to hear the trial, and
moved a short distance from the bar. But
Jeffreys declared that the trial should not proceed whilst he was in court, and so he was
obliged to retreat. He was afterwards employed to argue in arrest of judgment on Rosewell's behalf. As the case proceeded, the
dreadful magistrate was softened, and gave the
accused a very fair and patient hearing; but,
notwithstanding, the jury pronounced him
guilty. Jeffreys behaved with more gentlemanly
manner to this jury, who were persons of very
good station, than he was accustomed, and evidently repressed the coarseness so familiar to
him. The fact was, that the principal witnesses against the minister were three women
of infamous character, common informers against
conventicles; one of whom was convicted of
perjury, and pilloried in the next reign, and
another whipped at the cart's tail for some bad
behaviour.

Rosewell made a very admirable defence;
and, happily for him, there was present a baronet, Sir John Talbot, who though not friendly

K

to dissenters, highly appreciated what he had
said, and thought the verdict wrong. From
the trial he posted away to the King, and declared, that he had seen the life of a person,
who appeared to be a gentleman and a scholar,
in danger upon such evidence as he would not
hang his dog on; and, " Sir," says he, " if your
Majesty suffers this man to die, we are none of
us safe in our houses." This address had a full
influence upon the royal ear; and whilst it was
operating, in came Jeffreys, overjoyed, and
vaunted of the signal service which he and the
Surrey jury had done;[1] when to his utter confusion the monarch replied, under a strong feeling
of sympathy, that the prisoner must not die,
and that he, Jeffreys, must find out some way
to bring him off. In due time judgment was
moved for against the preacher by Sir Thomas
Jenner, the recorder, to whom Rosewell attributes his persecution; and the attorney-general,[2]

[1] Rosewell was tried at Kingston-upon-Thames.
[2] Sir Robert Sawyer. He conducted the court prosecutions with sufficient violence; but was turned out by James
the Second for his objections to the dispensing power, by
which James proposed to introduce the Catholic religion. He
was an old friend of Mr. Pepys, who expresses himself very
much pleased on one or two occasions to find his old chamber acquaintance in such good practice at the bar. Sir Robert's daughter was married to a son of Lord Pembroke.

who was present, could not have had any pre-
sentiment of the coming scene. The convict
did what was very common, but almost always
unsuccessful in those times—he moved to arrest
the judgment. The King's counsel of course
expected a fierce reply from the chief, overturning all the objections without scruple, and the
usual submissive nod from the puisne judges;
but instead—"What say you to it, brother Jenner,* and the King's counsel?" inquired the
judge. "I cannot see," doled forth Mr. Serjeant
Jenner,* the recorder, "that he has alleged any

* Thomas Jenner, made a baron of the Exchequer in 1686,
when honest Gregory was turned out; and judge of the Common Pleas in 1688. He was the judge who punned upon
Dr. Hough's name, during the famous controversy between
the King and Magdalen College respecting the election of a
president. "Sir," said Jenner to the Doctor, "you must
not think to *huff* us." Hough was afterwards Bishop of
Worcester. This Baron Jenner was a mere tool of the court,
and was afterwards excepted out of King William's bill of
indemnity. There is reason to believe that he was one of the
judges who tried the Duke of Monmouth's adherents in the
west.

From Sir Thomas Jenner's Speech to his Wife and Children.

A wise learned serjeant-at-law I was made,
And a fine dainty coif was put on my head,
Which is heavier by far than an hundred of lead,
This it is to be learned and witty.

objection, which here requires an answer from
any of us that are of counsel for the King." Ho-
garth, or some such genius, could alone have represented to us the countenance of the person thus
addressed, when he archly and drily returned,
" Yes, brother, methinks he does." And again,
after some words from the attorney-general,
there was the same tenderness. " But if I
take the gentleman right, (for I tell you before-
hand justice must be done to all people impartially. The crime is a very great crime that
he stands accused of; and the jury have found
him guilty of the crime laid in the indictment.
But if I take him aright,)" &c. The attorney
was thunder-struck, he had never dreamed

But soon after this I was made the recorder,
To keep the worshipful rabble in order,
And wore a red gown with long sleeves and border.
                    This it is, &c.

By great James I was raised to the Common Pleas
    bench,
'Cause he saw I had exquisite politic sense,
Which his wisdom perceived in the future tense.
                    This it is, &c.

At Sarum five hundred pounds have I gotten,
To save malefactors from swinging in cotton,
For which they were hang'd, and are now almost rotten.
                    This it is, &c.

of such a human kindness, nevertheless he mustered up courage to say, "All this, my lord, is only in delay."—" Mr. Attorney ! *De vitâ hominis nulla est cunctatio longa.*"[1] Rosewell, finding how the tide had set in, exclaimed, " I pray God to bless your lordship!"—Lord chief justice. " Nay, you have no need to thank me; for I desire to do justice to all men." And then he thundered against conventiclers, concluding : " I could not forbear giving that hint that I did, that this might be a warning to people, how they trangress the law in going to such meetings."

Rosewell was afterwards pardoned ; the court inclining strongly in favour of his objections.

The struggle respecting the recusants was not the only contest between Lord Guilford, the chief of the trimmers, and the lord chief justice, the managing tool of the high party. In reality, it seems to have been understood that Jeffreys was to have the seals as soon as the lord keeper could be displaced; and death, which overtook that great man shortly afterwards, probably saved them the odium, and him the mortification of delivering them to his rival. The promotion of Bedingfield,[2] who became chief justice of the Common Pleas in James the Second's

[1] We can't linger too long, when a man's life is at stake.

[2] This chief justice died suddenly whilst he was receiving the sacrament, in 1687.

time on the removal of poor honest Jones, gave
Sir George an opportunity of trying his strength
against the old statesman. The lord keeper
wished to make this man a judge, and he told
him of such his intention. With a thousand
acknowledgments, the serjeant bowed down,
and poured forth what is common when a great
man speaks, adding, that he should own his
preferment from that quarter, and no other, as
long as he lived. Now the serjeant had a brother, a woollen-draper in London, who was one
of the chief's companions. No sooner had Jeffreys discovered the channel through which the
pliant counsellor was to reach the bench, than
he sent for this draper, and plainly told him,
that his brother must be judge through my lord
chief justice's interest, or not at all; for that he
should be opposed if he presumed to owe his
elevation to any other. North tells us, that
Bedingfield was glad to compound for his promotion in any way rather than affront the powerful favourite, and the lord keeper had the generosity to overlook this want of resolution; so that
the serjeant had his place in due time, though
not during the life of Lord Guilford, whom he
avoided ever after this incident.'

' He got his place in the Common Pleas, Feb. 13, 1686,
and was made chief justice, April 21, in the same year.

Another story of the same kind belongs to the history of Chief Justice Wright.[1] When this person was a serjeant, he brought himself, through a prodigal style of living, into a state of the deepest distress; so that, as he declared, unless he were made a judge, his ruin was sealed. But he was not nice about trifles, and had the particular good fortune to have made Sir George Jeffreys acquainted with his easy character, which led to as much friendship as Sir George was capable of. On a vacancy, therefore, Wright was to be judge. But all powerful as his patron was at court, another person must be consulted— the lord keeper; and with this upright man he had little hope from the following circumstance:—

[1] Sir Robert Wright was descended from a good family at Thetford, in Norfolk, and bore a character for extravagance and licentiousness. He was " of a handsome person, voluble tongue, and plausible behaviour;" which ensured him some very fair practice, although he seems to have been but superficial in his profession : for he frequently came to his friend North, when he had an opinion to give, got his advice, and then wrote it down as his own. When North was in town, he contrived the business by post, and meanwhile, put his clients off on pretence of more serious consideration. He married a daughter of Dr. Wren, Bishop of Ely, which set him going on the Norfolk circuit. He died at last miserably in Newgate, in the beginning of King William's reign, being charged with an endeavour to subvert the government.

When they both went the Norfolk circuit together, they became very intimate; and the serjeant finding his purse empty, availed himself
of his brother North's friendship, by borrowing
his money. These loans became at last so considerable, as to induce North to take a mortgage
of his friend's estate, which he charged with
1500*l*. However, it was not long before the
serjeant desired some more money, and bor-
rowed 500*l*. accordingly from Sir Walter Plummer on the same estate, *making an affidavit that
it was free from all incumbrances*. Plummer
brought the affidavit to Sir Francis North, while
he held the original mortgage, but he said
nothing on the subject, and the serjeant had his
pockets filled a second time out of the estate.
When the King asked his lord keeper whether
this gentleman was not a proper person to be a
judge, the case assumed a very different fea-
ture; his lordship said, " he knew him but too
well : he was satisfied that he was the most unfit
person in the world to be judge."—" Then," said
the King, " it must not be." But then came
the influence of Jeffreys. Again and again the
King pressed the lord keeper, saying, " Why
may not Wright be a judge ?" And, at length,
Lord Guilford told His Majesty every thing,
the perjury not excepted; and it was very cre-

ditable that he would not speak ill of his old
acquaintance till his duty overpowered him.
" And now," said he, " I have done my duty to
your Majesty, and am ready to obey your Majesty's commands, in case it be your pleasure
that this man shall be a judge."—" My lord,"
said the King, " I thank you :" and went away.
Soon after came the warrant, and the keeper
sealed it.'

Such events as these may be called the victories of the chief justice over the head of the
Chancery; and it had been well if the former
could have been content with his triumph, and
had not chequered it with the blemish of arrogance. Vain and upstart, he shook forth his
new plumage for the public wonder; and, decked
with the bewitching influences of a court favourite, stalked out supreme. This was one
way by which he vented himself. There was
formerly a side bar below in Westminster-hall,
where the King's Bench judges used to robe;
while the court of Chancery sat a little above,
but within view of the judges. Jeffreys saw
Wright walking in the hall, his promotion being
determined on, and beckoned him. The serjeant approached very humbly; on which the

* See North's Lives, 4to. pp. 246, 247, 248.

chief took him by the shoulders, whispered in
his ear, and flung him off, holding out his arms
at the same time, and leaning over the bar in
the sight of Lord Guilford, who observed the
motion, and was hurt at it. It was as much as
to say, says North, that in spite of that man
there, Wright should be a judge.

One instance more of his hatred to this eminent individual, and we have done. There happened to be a dispute between the Duke of
Norfolk and his brother, which was heard in
Chancery. The chief justices, of whom North
was one, and the chief baron, were asked for
their opinions, which they gave; but Lord Nottingham, the chancellor, decreed the contrary,
without canvassing their reasons. When North
became lord keeper he reversed this decree, on
which an appeal went up to the House of Lords;
and Jeffreys, chief justice, indulged himself with
a formal abuse of this latter opinion, which he
loaded with every censure, and hesitated not to
affront his lordship himself, which was a rude-
ness quite unheard of in that august assembly.
He procured, however, the keeper's decree to
be reversed, for a papist was affected by it; and
just then it was the interest of court suitors to
support popery.

This heedless judge would come down to the

council sometimes quite drunk, and inveigh
against trimmers. The justices of Stepney and
Wapping once fell out, and by the violence of
two parties, headed by Smith and Bailey, the
sessions were disturbed. One of these factions,
that of Smith, was patronised by Sir George;
and he came to the board quite furious, telling
the King, that he had trimmers in his court,
and would never be happy while trimmers were
there. The lord keeper drily answered, (for he
knew that all this outrage was levelled at him,
the principal trimmer,) that the chief justice
seemed so well informed on the subject of these
quarrels, it would be advisable to refer the whole
matter to his arbitration. This was agreed to; but
the fracas continued for some time, till Bailey's
party was overturned. It was so ordered, says
North. This fertile and lively writer lets fly
another arrow at our chief justice for helping off
one Hayes with the jury, who was tried for treason
about this time, adding, " upon what terms who
knows?" Hayes came to his trial towards the
close of the year 1684, and certainly was acquitted; but on examining the report in the
State Trials, it appears, that the judge rather
leaned against him when the evidence was
summed up: so easy is it to entertain and

create a prejudice against men who have become obnoxious.

In February, 1685, the King died; it was at
a very critical moment, for measures had been
adopted for reconciling him with his son, the
Duke of Monmouth, and his brother was about
to visit Scotland by the royal command. It
was the policy of Charles to keep himself un-
shackled, and that of his brother to spread such
toils round the monarch as should secure him
from the approach of those he in reality loved
the most. The parliament, the cabal, even the
fair chamber counsel, had failed to enchain this
master of dissimulation; but his heart had one
avenue open, and there natural affection lived
and throve. Very important were the changes
which ensued upon his decease; and favourably
so, according to the probability of all human
events, for Jeffreys. Had the liberal party,
with Monmouth at their head, been blessed
with the royal countenance, the day of retribution had sooner overtaken the judge who had
robbed them of their best associates, and gibed
at their love for freedom : as Providence willed
it, there was for him a change from suspense
to a triumphant certainty; from the prospect of
a headsman and axe, to the stillest whisperings

of the royal closet. The Duke of York was King, and Jeffreys his prime minister.

On the 15th of May, 1685, the honours of the peerage were conferred upon the ambitious favourite : it was the second instance of ennobling a chief justice which we find in our history.' Probably, as Mr. Nichols suggests, he composed or dictated the preamble to his own patent ; and as it tends to illustrate the intention of parties at that time, the original and translation are here given :—

ORIGINAL.	TRANSLATION.
Quum nihil magis regium sit, quam eos, qui se vel in togâ vel in armis claros et insignes reddiderunt tum premiis augere tum honoribus illustrare ; quumque predilectus et perquam fidelis consiliarius noster Georgius Jeffreys, eques auratus et baronettus, per omnes jurisprudentiæ gradus, eâ industriâ et felicitate processerit, ut nos,	Since nothing can be more worthy of a king, than to enrich with rewards and dignify with honours such as have distinguished themselves in civil and military achievements; and since our much loved and right faithful counsellor George Jeffreys, knight and baronet, hath advanced through the degrees of jurisprudence with such diligence and success, as that, when we were Duke of York, we

¹ Hubert de Burgh, a very considerable judge in the reign of Henry the Third, was the first who attained to the honour.

ORIGINAL.

TRANSLATION.

cum dux Eboracensis esse-	chose him to be our solicitor-
mus, eum pro solicitatore	general, and held his fidelity
nostro generali elegerimus,	and courage undoubted in all
ejusque fidem et fortitudi-	things which touched our person
nem in omnibus quæ vel	or our affairs, especially at that
personam vel res nostras	time, when by the wicked insti-
spectârunt semper explora-	gation of some factious persons,
tam habuerimus, illo præ-	we were torn from our most
sertim tempore cum pravâ	illustrious brother, our Lord,
quorundam malevolorum	Charles the Second, late of
instigatione nos a præcla-	Great Britain, Scotland, &c.
rissimo fratre nostro domino	against his will, and scarcely
Carolo secundo, nuper	less than banished from his most
Magnæ Britanniæ, Scotiæ,	kindly presence, first into Flan-
&c. ipso licet invitissimo,	ders, then into Scotland; duly
avulsi fuimus, et a suavis-	considering all which, and de-
simâ ipsius præsentiâ, pri-	sirous in some way of acknow-
mum in Flandriam, postea	ledging the merits of the said
in Scotiam, tantum non re-	George Jeffreys, our most be-
legati; quæ omnia perpen-	loved brother raised him to the
dens frater noster amantis-	highest judicial benches; first to
simus, et singularia Georgii	be chief justice of Chester, then
Jeffreys' merita aliquo mo-	chief justice of the King's Bench
do agnoscere cupiens, eum	at Westminster, where he even
ad summa juris dicundi tri-	now sits, resolutely and faith-
bunalia evexit, unde primô	fully administering justice and
capitalis Cestriæ justicia-	protection to our subjects ac-
rius evasit, deinde capitalis	cording to the law: in conside-
justiciarius Regii Banci a-	ration of whose merits, and
pud Westmonasterium, ubi	which our brother above men-

¹ " Dicti " should have been here.

ORIGINAL.	TRANSLATION.
etiamnum sedet, justitiam et tutelam subditis nostris ad normam legis intrepide et fideliter administrans: quarum ejus virtutum intuitu, id quod supra memoratus frater noster, dum adhuc viveret, in animo habuit; nos jam sponte nostrâ, et pro eâ quâ dictum Georgium Jeffreys benevolentiâ prosequimur, eum inter pares hujus regni cooptandum esse censuimus. Sciatis igitur, &c. &c.[1]	tioned intended, whilst he lived, we, of our own will, and from that regard which we bear the said George Jeffreys, are of opinion that he should be admitted amongst the peers of this realm. Know therefore, &c. &c.

He was created Baron Jeffreys of Wem, in the county of Salop. This title was derived from his property in that county. He held the barony of Wem, and the manors of Wem and Loppington, besides other lands and tenements in those parts. Evelyn, who seems to have been on pretty good terms with every one, wished him joy on his creation; and he says, that the new peer was very civil upon the occasion.

Whatever may be the real secret of the "horrid popish plot;" whether a real conspiracy to be

[1] From the original in the possession of James Bindley, Esq., F.A.S., given in Nichols's Leicestershire, Vol. ii. part 1. p. 116.

executed with screwed guns and silver bullets;
(by the way, the management was most clum-
sy; at one time the assassins had their flints
loose, at another they charged their screwed
guns with all bullets and no powder, then with
no powder in the pan, and again with all powder and no bullets;) or whether it was a mere
treasonable bauble to dazzle the eyes of the
populace,—we of this day care very little : but
it becomes our duty to mention Oates,[1] the
great hero of the piece, in this place, since the
day for expiating his unlucky jest upon Jeffreys
was come : he stood at the King's Bench bar
charged with perjury, the prince on the throne
against whom he had whetted his tongue, and
the judge on the bench whom he had stung
with his untimely wit ; a judge too not given to
be very impartial when he viewed his prisoner
through the mirror of political hostility.   However, an appearance of indifference and fairness
was evinced by the court, till they found that

[1] Oates, Bedlow, Dugdale, Prance, whose breath alone,
  Cou'd almost states subvert, and kings dethrone !
  To sculp their shadow 's in the pow'r of art :
  Ink may be black enough to act that part.
  Drawn to the life would you their souls behold,
  That work requires a more infernal mould.
              Memoirs of Titus Oates, 1683.

Oates was resolute and stubborn in his defence; and even then the rules of evidence were respected, and there was a little fracas between the chief and the King's counsel respecting them. But Jeffreys became very turbulent occasionally, and once his temper broke out beyond all discretion. Oates wished to know Lord Castlemaine's religion, and Sir George said, that every one knew that. But Oates would have it told in court, and, said he, "That's not the point, my lord; I must have it declared in evidence."

Ld. Ch. Just.—I wonder to see any man that has the face of a man, carry it at this rate, when he has such an evidence brought in against him.

Oates.—I wonder that Mr. Attorney will offer to bring this evidence; men that must have malice against me.

Ld. Ch. Just.—Hold your tongue; you are a shame to mankind.

Oates.—No, my lord, I am neither a shame to myself or mankind. What I have sworn is true, and I will stand by it to my last breath, and seal it, if occasion be, with my blood.

Ld. Ch. Just.—*'T were pity but that it were to be done by thy blood.*

A very sanguinary speech! but Oates did not

L

regard it; he went on wrangling for some time afterwards.

The doctor (but Jeffreys could not endure that he should be called so) was convicted upon two indictments, and was visited with such floggings as might have made him wish himself most cordially within the pale of the Roman church with all her penance and stripes: he had such a punishment as should have chased perjury from England for a century afterwards, from the mere dread of it.

1st. He was to pay a thousand marks upon each indictment.

2nd. To be stripped of all his canonical habits (a sentence which belongs only to the courts ecclesiastical).

3rd. He was to stand twice in the pillory.

4th. To be whipped from Aldgate to Newgate one day, and two days afterwards from Newgate to Tyburn.

And 5th. He was to stand in the pillory on five days in every year as long as he lived.

Yet, notwithstanding this, (and the sentence was executed with great severity,) " there are thousands," says his biographer in 1685, " of those unthinking, unconverted animals, that have that veneration still for their darling Titus, that they pay him even a wild Indian adoration,

and make a god of the devil himself." An unsuccessful attempt was made to reverse this cruel
judgment; but he was pardoned at the Revolution, and lived to publish several things afterwards. It is not a little singular that so slight
a mention has been made of the harsh conduct of
other judges during these times, whilst many of
the chiefs, and Jeffreys among the number, have
been set down for monsters, though all their
brethren were doing the same thing. No doubt
they cannot be excused ; but the plea of *commu-
nis error* will avail much, when it is considered
that an age of faction is never remarkable for
delicacy. In the trial which has been mentioned, Sir Francis Wythens,' a puisne judge,
was full of these indecent railleries against the
prisoner, and the close of his speech on passing
sentence is very memorable :—" And I must
tell you plainly, if it had been in my power to
have carried it further, I should not have been

' He was of no great value. Being called before the
House of Commons to answer for his courtly opposition to
petitioning, (for he was an abhorrer,) he cringed and sneaked,
and said he knew he had done wrong, but feared to offend
the king ; on which, North tells us that even his own friends
voted with the country party against him, and so he was
unanimously kicked out of the House. He was also excepted out of King William's act of indemnity.

unwilling to have given judgment of death upon
you, for I am sure you deserve it." This Wythens was perpetually indulging in levities and
humour at the expense of prisoners. When
Fernley was tried for treason, there was a specimen of this judge's propensity. A witness was
called for the prisoner. Officer. " He is a great
whig."—Judge Wythens. " If he be a whig, he
can't be a little one."—Witness. " I formerly
knew the man; he was a barber, and used to
trim me. I always looked upon him to be a good
sober man."—Wythens. " A Wapping man!
a sober Wapping man!" Soon after he found
room for a pun upon Trimmers. The prisoner's
witnesses were asked if they went to church.
Wythens. " There were a parcel of them that
went constantly to church *trimmingly.*" Even
Chief Justice Jones, who, by comparison is
highly estimated, was harsh on occasion; and
on the trial of Alderman Cornish will be found
not to have treated him too tenderly.

About this time Crispe, the common-serjeant,
who, we may remember, dissolved the tumultuous common-hall by order of the court lord
mayor, had the misfortune to displease Lord
Jeffreys, and, though the particular nature of
his offence has not been communicated to us,

he fell under some censure, though he found means to withstand the prejudice against him, and to continue in office until his death.[1] He is spoken of with high praise by North.

Hitherto we have abstained from speaking of the subject of this memoir as a judge in civil matters; yet it has not been from a fear of exhibiting him in that capacity; since, however he might have been denied the reputation of legal knowledge by the furious and successful whigs of the revolution, it seems now pretty well agreed that he brought a considerable share of experience, and a very rare acuteness, to the Nisi Prius Bench. Indeed, through the diligence and fidelity of those learned and laborious men, who from time to time oblige us with the arguments and judgments which take place in our courts, the members of the law are enabled to form a fair estimate of the proficiency which the judges of Nisi Prius have attained in the science. As far as relates to Jeffreys, we must have recourse to the reports of Sir Bartholomew Shower,[2] and Mr. Skinner,[3] who wrote

[1] About the year 1700.

[2] Bartholomew Shower, brother to John Shower, an eminent divine, attained to considerable practice at the bar. He was constituted recorder of London in 1687, in the room of Mr. Tate, who succeeded Sir John Holt. He was

while he presided in the King's Bench; and
to some parts of the " Modern Reports." Sir
Bartholomew was recorder of London; and if
Sir Robert Wright, the chief justice when the
seven bishops were tried, is to have credit, the
learned gentleman was very fond of a speech,
the judges at the same time not being over
partial to too much oratory. Several counsel
had been already heard in the case of the
bishops, (a pruriency which perhaps will now
receive a check in the Court of Chancery, if the
new act be passed,)[4] when the recorder rose to

obliged to yield his place, in 1688, to Sir George Treby,
when the city charter was restored; and Wood says that he
stood in competition for the recordership, in 1691, with Sir
John Hawles, who lost it. But the fact was, that as soon
as Treby became chief justice of the Common Pleas, Sir
Sathaliel Lovell, afterwards a baron of the Exchequer, succeeded to the city honours; and thus both must have been
disappointed. He was Sir John Fenwick's counsel, and
pleaded vehemently against the bill of attainder. In 1701
he died, and was buried at Harrow-on-the-hill. His publi-
cations were law reports and pamphlets.

[3] Robert Skinner, father of Matthew Skinner, King's
ancient serjeant, and chief justice of Chester, in 1742, who
died in 1749.

[4] An act to amend the practice of the Court of Chancery,
introduced at the end of the session of 1826 into the House
of Commons.

We cannot forbear inserting Lord Nottingham's elegant

speak to some point which had been started. Ld. Ch. Just. " What again? Well, go on, Sir Bartholomew Shower, if we must have a speech." However, the learned counsel gave way; but soon after, there being a pause till some one arrived who was to give evidence, the judge began his raillery again:—"Sir Bartholomew Shower, now we have time to hear your speech, if you will." Soon afterwards a great many more speeches were delivered, and Sir Bartholomew grew restive again; " Will your lordship be pleased to spare me one word ?"— Ld. Ch. Just. " I hope we shall have done by and by."—Mr. Recorder. " If your lordship don't think fit, I can sit down."—Ld. Ch. Just. No, no; go on, Sir Bartholomew Shower, you'll say I have spoiled a good speech." Then Ser-

compliment to Mr. Somers, afterwards the chancellor. Six or seven counsel had been heard to what was understood to be motion of course, when Mr. Somers rose, and said, " that he was of the same side ; but that so much had been already said, that he had no room to add any thing ; that therefore he would not presume to take up his lordship's time, by repeating what had been so well urged by the gentlemen that went before him." " Sir," said the chancellor, " pray go on ; I sit here to hear every body. You never repeat, nor will you take up my time ; and therefore I shall hear you with pleasure." It often happened in those days, that six, eight, or even ten advocates on a side were heard in the Court of Chancery.

jeant Trinder began, "My lord, I have but one word."—Ld. Ch. Just. How unreasonable is this now, that we must have so many speeches at this time of day! But we must hear it; go on, brother!

But to return to Jeffreys. The reader need not be apprehensive that we are going to inflict a critical disquisition on this judge's legal merits upon him; no one doubts them at this day, as Serjeant Davy, of facetious memory, said on the trial of Elizabeth Canning. "The chief justice, with all his faults, has ever been esteemed a great lawyer."

Two very remarkable occasions presented themselves whilst he remained on the common law bench, which gave him opportunities of displaying his learning and shrewdness to great advantage. The first is styled, *par excellence*, " the great case of monopolies:" the next was Lady Ivy's monstrous attempt to possess herself of valuable property in Shadwell, through the medium of false writings. In the latter case some little incidents happened, which we shall also give, as they tend to prove Jeffreys's near acquaintance with the world in small things.

The East India Company quarrelled with Thomas Sandys for invading their exclusive right of trade; he said, that the sea was open for all merchants to pass with their merchandizes where they pleased, whereupon the company were pleased to demur, as it is technically called; that is to say, they would not allow Mr. Sandys's plea to be a sufficient answer in point of law to their action, and they referred the decision to the Court of King's Bench. Jeffreys delivered a very elaborate judgment. He made two points: 1st. Was the grant good, which licensed the company to trade to the Indies to the exclusion of others? Then, Was the action maintainable? He began by complimenting the King for his condescension in allowing his prerogative to be debated in Westminster-hall, thereby following the example of Lord Chief Baron Fleming. All things had their commencement by royal grant, so that an artificer in the city of London could not use two trades; a carpenter could not be a joiner, nor a bricklayer a plasterer, &c., and yet there was more liberty for inland than foreign trade. For the law merchant prevailed in most matters of merchandize, especially when the goods were upon the high seas; so that even by the allowance of the common law, a great difference was observable between the customs and rights of traders, and those of ordinary persons. Beyond question, it was a just measure of the prerogative to restrain foreign trade. Welwood's Epistle had

been quoted, who spoke of vindicating the con-
servancy of the seas in favour of all loyal traders: Westminster-hall was not the place for
quoting epistles or authorities; but Welwood
doubtless little dreamed of interlopers, when he
spoke of loyal subjects. Foreign trade being
introduced by the laws of nations, ought to be
governed and adjudged by those laws; whence
springs the Court of Admiralty. Therefore, as
the restraint of such trade was ever reckoned
inter jura regalia, and uncontrolled by any act of
parliament, and as it was agreeable to the law of
nations, the royal prerogative was clearly effi-
cient in the case at bar. Again, with regard to
an injurious monopoly, which had been insisted
on by the defendant's counsel, such would not
be the case, for an exclusive privilege would
only be granted upon good cause, and for the
public advantage. The infancy of an undertaking like the present would be most effectively
protected by a society, who, whilst they risked
the possible loss, should be entitled to the
undisturbed profit. It was prohibited by the
States-general, on pain of death, and forfeiture
of ship and goods, that any, save the Dutch
India Company, should for twenty-one years
pass eastward of the Cape of Good Hope. And
surely, continued the judge, the Dutch have

ever been our greatest and most dangerous rivals in trade. The King, by his charter, makes the plaintiffs, as it were, his ambassadors to concert a peace with the Indians, and Mr. Sandys has complained that he is not one of them. Because the King may pardon every offender, but will not pardon any highwayman now in Newgate, must those gaol-birds, therefore, think themselves injured in their liberty and property? The most flourishing trades have begun by united stocks and policies. The company have been at the trouble of discovering places, of erecting forts, of keeping forces, of settling factories, and of making leagues and treaties; and it would be against natural equity to wrest the benefits from them which they have thus earned. Let the plaintiff take his judgment.'

On the 3d of June, 1684, the claim of Lady Ivy for some property in Shadwell came to be investigated before a judge as intelligent and keen as ever enlightened the bench at Westminster, or a special jury assembled upon an occa-

---

' The other judges who concurred, were Sir Francis Wythens, Sir Richard Holloway, Sir Thomas Walcot. A paper in the Mss. Lansd. 1219. folio, contains the introduction of Sir George Jeffreys's speech, which is not in the State Trials, but is otherwise imperfect.

sion so important. She was in possession; the
action, therefore, was brought against her, and
it seems that the plaintiff had been once before
unsuccessful. The judge plainly showed his
disposition in the outset to sift the cause *in pe-
netralibus*, and, accordingly, showed the counsel
on either side very little mercy. They began
with an old book found among the evidences of
the dean and chapter of St. Paul's, in which
some alteration had been made, the object of
which did not appear. " It is plain," said the
chief justice, " that in this slippery age we live
in, it is very easy to make a book look as old as
you would have it." Now the attorney-general,
who conducted Lady Ivy's case, was shrewd
enough to take advantage of this hint, and
knowing that his was the side on which forgery
was suspected, he declared, seemingly with
much innocence, " They threaten us with for-
geries, and I know not what; I believe it will
be found on Mr. Neale's side." However, the
tide was soon to turn against his client. Jeffreys
fastened himself upon Lady Ivy's first witness;
and unless a man were the very image of truth,
he had but little chance under such an ordeal.
But here was a man who undertook to tell the
contents of a deed he had never looked into,
and who swore that he knew its owner on first

finding it, from a superscription, which was
proved to have been written long afterwards.
" I am sure," quoth the judge, "thou swearest
wildly." And the next witness made so little
account of time, that he veered so lamentably
from one day to another as to draw upon him
a most formidable lecture from the judge. And
the solicitor-general was pleased to make this
very polite address to the Lady Ivy, his client,
then in court,—"Your witness is drunk, madam!"
Every step in this cause was against the defendant; and not only did the jury find a verdict
disallowing her claim, but she had the misfortune to encounter two informations for forging
and publishing indentures, which were very
soon afterwards filed against her. The most
ingenious device in this singular cause was a
plan which suggested itself to a Mr. Bradbury for the developement of these fraudulent
practices. The indenture relied upon by Lady
Ivy was stated as of such a day in such years
" of the reigns of our Sovereign Lord and
Lady Philip and Mary, by the Grace of God,
King and Queen of England, Spain, France,
both Sicilies, Jerusalem, and Ireland, Defenders,
&c., Archdukes of Austria, Dukes of Burgundy,
Milan, and Brabant, &c." Bradbury urged,
and he brought records in proof of his allega-

tion, that Philip and Mary were never then called King and Queen of Spain and both the Sicilies, but King and Queen of Naples, and that Burgundy never stood before Milan. The judge was extremely pleased with the demonstration of this theory, while the attorney-general, who felt the shoe pinch, was vainly striving to silence an interloper so dangerous. However, the contriver of this detection was so much elated by the encouragement he met with, that he could not help interfering again on one or two occasions, which brought the wit of Jeffreys upon him, seasoned with that admirable knowledge of the world and of human nature, for which the judge has never had sufficient credit with posterity. Probably Mr. Bradbury had been diving into all the old rat-eaten records for days and nights before the trial; " for," cried he, " I dare affirm that there are none of the rolls of that year so till after Easter Term ;" and then he was stopped with " Lord, sir, you must be cackling too; we told you your objection was very ingenious, but that must not make you troublesome; you cannot lay an egg but you must be cackling over it."

Nor did the chief of the court use his brother judges with much greater respect, if he thought they deserved a lesson. We shall give an instance of this kind here in the treatment of Mr. Baron Gregory,[1] who was subpœnaed as a witness upon this occasion. When the learned baron came into court, the counsel were pleased to behave very civilly to him, and proposed that he should be examined forthwith; whereupon Sir William, whose delicacy exceeded his foresight, declared himself very unwilling to interrupt the course of the evidence. " Nay, we will take you at your word," said the chief, whose notions of such scruples were very contracted; " but if it be long, pray remember we would have eased you, but you complimented yourself out of it; now you are likely to abide by it a while, I assure you, brother." The baron waited some considerable time, and his evidence at length was not wanted; upon which he retired, with another friendly hint from the bench: " Well, brother, we cannot help your staying now; but remember you had an offer made you at first, and you are punished for refusing it."

[1] William Gregory was chosen speaker of the House of Commons in 1679, by the recommendation of Lord William Russel, the King absolutely refusing to confirm the nomination of Mr. Edward Seymour. In 1679, he was made a baron of the Exchequer, but made way for Jenner, the recorder of London, early in the reign of James II. Being a man of integrity, he was immediately placed judge of the King's Bench at the Revolution, and died in 1696.

Here was a sure and sound principle in human life recognised by the chief justice, and false delicacy justly lashed.

Yet, whatever respect he might have shown to the common law, he had no prejudice in favour of settled forms; and, indeed, it is an observation common to those times, that when a judge desired a precedent, he would have it. Jeffreys, the last of these worthies, was heard to say, that if there were no precedent for what he did, he did not see why he had not as good a right to make one as any of his predecessors. And, so little respect did he pay to the great oracle, Sir Edward Coke, that he used to stop the counsel who were wont to quote him, and gruffly tell them, that if Lord Coke really had said what they were urging, his opinion was not law.

Had he, however, always persisted in establishing precedents as honourable as his conduct to the mayor and corporation of Bristol, his name had been immortalized for philanthropy. A very roguish practice had obtained in that money-getting city. The mayor, aldermen, and justices, had been in the habit of selling their transported criminals for slaves into the American plantations; and finding the barter very lucrative, they only regretted that crime

was not more on the increase within their good
territory. So they hit upon this expedient.
When any little pilferers got into a scrape, all
the horrors of hanging were held out to them;
and through the officers, who were creatures of
the corporation, they were induced to pray for
transportation; and then each alderman had his
turn to sell one, about which, by the way, they
sometimes quarrelled. Jeffreys knew how to
protect the rights of men as well as any; and
having received a hint of this custom, which had
passed unnoticed for years, he instituted an inquiry, whence it appeared that the mayor was
equally criminal with the rest of his brethren.
He gave out publicly to the citizens, that he
had " brought a broom to sweep them." This
was a crisis which exactly suited a man of our
judge's temperament. There was no state policy to interfere with him, and even-handed
Justice was therefore to be exalted in all her
magnificence. Slowly, in all his scarlet and fur
robes, did the chief magistrate descend from
the bench of justice, by order of Jeffreys, and
having reached the common bar, he stood there
like a criminal to answer for his misdeeds. At
first, indeed, he hesitated, and slackened his
pace, but he was quickly overawed by the resolute
chief, who, stamping, called for his guards, for

M

he was " general by commission." And surely
justice might have overtaken him and his friends,
had not the Revolution introduced a general
amnesty, by which the informations against
these persons were cancelled. They had been
compelled, however, to give large security that
they would answer the charges, and doubtless
thought themselves amply fortunate to come off
so easily, with all their unrighteous gains secure
in their pockets. The mayor, Sir Robert Cann,
was so much terrified, that he employed some
friends in London to appease the great man,
who at length yielded, saying, " Go thy way,
sin no more, lest a worse thing come unto
thee."

Before we speak of the great western tragedy,
the conduct of this hot-headed judge to Richard
Baxter, the celebrated nonconformist, who refused the see of Lichfield and Coventry at the
Restoration, shall be just adverted to. His real
offence was expounding some passages of the
New Testament in his paraphrase rather too
strongly against the Roman religion, for which
a prosecution was instituted against him as a
seditious libeller of the Church of England
bishops. The passages selected for the charge
were picked out by Sir Roger L'Estrange and his
companions. Baxter asked for time.—Jeffreys.

" I will not give him a minute's more time to save his life. Yonder stands Oates in the pillory, and says he suffers for the truth; and so says Baxter; but if Baxter did but stand on the other side of the pillory with him, I would say, two of the greatest rogues and rascals in the kingdom stood there." On the 30th May, 1684, he came to trial. Wallop, Williams, Rotheram,[1] Atwood, and Phipps,[2] were his counsel. The clerk was reading the title of a cause.—" You blockhead you," cries the judge, " the next cause is between Richard Baxter and the King." Wallop said, that those who had drawn the information were the libellers, in attributing the defendant's words to the English bishops, which he evidently meant for the Roman hierarchy. " Mr. Wallop," quoth my lord, " I observe you are in all these dirty causes; and were it not for you gentlemen of the long robe, who should have more wit and honesty than to support and hold up these factious knaves by the chin, we should not be at the pass we are at."—Wallop. " My lord, I humbly conceive that the passages accused are natural deductions from the text."—Jeffreys. " You

---

[1] Afterwards a baron of the Exchequer. Evelyn mentions him as a trustee for Boyle's Lectures.

[2] Afterwards Sir Constantine, and chancellor of Ireland.

humbly conceive, and I humbly conceive! swear
him! swear him!" Wallop went on again. Jeffreys. "Sometimes you humbly conceive, and
sometimes you are very positive: you talk of
your skill in church history, and of your understanding Latin and English; I think I understand something of them as well as you; but in
short must tell you, that if you do not understand your duty better, I shall teach it you."
And this silenced Wallop, for he sat down.
Then Rotheram began; and Baxter added, that
he had incurred the censure of many dissenters
on account of his moderation. "Baxter for
bishops!" saith Jeffreys; "that's a merry conceit indeed! turn to it, turn to it." On which
Rotheram pointed out a place where Baxter
had declared that great respect was due to those
who were called to be bishops. But he was
interrupted with, "Aye! this your presbyterian
cant! truly called to be bishops! that is himself
and such rascals called to be bishops of Kidder-
minster, according to the saying of a late author,
'and every parish shall maintain a tithe pig
metropolitan.'" Baxter was beginning again,
but—"Richard! Richard!" ejaculated the judge,
"dost thou think we'll hear thee poison the
court? Richard, thou art an old fellow, an old
knave; thou hast written books enough to load

a cart. Hadst thou been whipt out of thy writing trade forty years ago, it had been happy;" and with many other such observations he closed his harangue, which had the effect of putting down Rotheram. But it was now Mr. Atwood's turn: and he was going to read some of the text.—— " You shan't draw me into a conventicle with your annotations, nor your snivelling parson neither," exclaimed Sir George. However, Jeffreys met with his match, for the counsel would go on; and so the one inveighed, and the other urged his client's defence, till he had made an end. And then the chief justice finished with— " Well, you have had your say." Williams and Phipps were quite confounded, and so were silent; and Baxter soon had his quietus also: on which Jeffreys turned to the jury:—" 'Tis notoriously known," said he, " that there has been a design to ruin the King and nation: the old game has been renewed, and this has been the main incendiary: he is as modest now as can be; but time was, when no man was so ready at, ' Bind your Kings in chains, and your nobles in fetters of iron;' and, 'To your tents, O Israel!' Gentlemen, for God's sake, don't let us be gulled twice in an age." Of course the jury found him guilty, and he was fined £500, and bound to his good behaviour for seven years.

But through the mediation of Lord Powis,
a Roman Catholic nobleman, he had great kindness shown him: his fine was remitted, and he
soon afterwards was left at liberty to preach,
which he did to a separate congregation unto
the day of his death in December, 1691.

Here, however, is an opportunity of telling
something much to the credit of Jeffreys, and the
more so, because a dissenter is our theme.

Philip Henry, a man of unblemished character, a nonconformist, had refused to pay a fine
which some Shropshire justices had imposed
upon him for attending a conventicle; upon
which his goods were distrained,' and carts were
even pressed upon the road for the purpose of
carrying them away. This minister was the
only nonconformist in Flintshire, which was
Jeffreys's county; but he always remained unmolested, although this great foe to dissenters was
chief justice of Chester, and came that circuit.
And upon the occasion we have above mentioned, Sir George withheld his approbation of
the measure, and even inquired jocularly, by
what new law the gentry pressed carts to remove goods distrained for the offence of going to

---

' The conviction was certified from Shropshire into Flintshire.

meeting. He spoke with respect of Mr. Henry, declared that he knew him and his character well, and that the preacher was his mother's great friend. Mrs. Jeffreys was a very pious good woman; and, as her son openly acknowledged, had sometimes requested Henry to examine him when a school-boy, who, moreover, was in the habit of commending his proficiency. There is something of filial regard and a respect for old acquaintance in this.

There is a stronger instance still of the judge's forbearance towards the same man. Mr. Henry was in the habit of attending a meeting for prayer every Monday morning; and this assembling, having created some notice, was mentioned very innocently to some person in London by means of a letter. This communication fell into the hands of a busy-body, or malignant of some kind, who laid an information against the writer and receiver of the letter, which greatly pleased Jeffreys, who imagined that it might be a branch of the presbyterian plot. He, accordingly, " rallied the parties very severely ;" and then it came out, that the project had its rise with Mr. Henry, which occasioned the most serious fears for his safety. But the whole matter was suddenly dropped, and no inquiry made, which astonished the

vulgar : whereas it only proves the consistency
of Jeffreys when he knew that a man of high
character was in the right, and remembered him
in happy youthful days, of which the impressions
are so kind and so lasting.

When Jeffreys had left Mold (the assize
town), after the distraining we have talked of, the
enemies of Mr. Henry began again, and presented him for keeping conventicles ; but all the
parchments against this favoured minister had
been cast into the dead sea with as good success,
for the chief justice frowned upon them, and
they were never more heard of. It is proper
that we should give Mr. Henry's opinion of this
mercy. His son, Matthew, who wrote his life,
says, that he " acknowledged the hand of God,
who turneth the hearts of the children of men,
as the rivulets of water."

CHAP. VI.

EVERY one is familiarized with the history of Monmouth's invasion in the early part of the second James's reign, with his fallen fortunes, his luckless capture, and his much-lamented fate. To punish his adherents, a special commission was issued by the crown, at the head of which was placed Lord Jeffreys, and, in addition to his rank as prime judge, he had, by a second commission, the authority of general.

The conduct, moreover, of this powerful minister in the execution of his dangerous trust, is, as it were, naturalized in our minds, and, perhaps, it cannot be very much palliated; although we do not profess to be governed by the raving invectives of historians, or the teeming abuse of copying scribes. For the foregoing reason, therefore, the reader shall be but scantily troubled with stories which he can trace the mention of from his childhood, and, consequently, the severity of executions, the dying speeches and confessions, the clamours of distressed relatives, and, above all, the lugubrious dirges of contemporary writers, will be rarely introduced.

We have no concern with the fury of the famous little ale-house woman in the west, whose rage kindled instantly at the name of Jeffreys; a passion, be it said, *en passant*, which she caught from a mother, who was an eyewitness of that dreadful personage: nor with that tenacious feeling of the rabble which urged

them to insult the Countess of Pomfret, grand-
daughter to their hated judge, when passing on
the western road.[1]

Possibly, Sir Bartholomew Shower's mode of
treating the subject might be, after all, the best:
it is excellent for it's brevity. "In Trinity term
Monmouth's rebellion in the west prevented
much business; in the vacation following, by
reason of that rebellion, there was no assize held
for the western circuit; but afterwards five
judges went as commissioners of oyer and ter-
miner and gaol-delivery, *and* 351 *of the rebels
were executed, &c.*"

Something, however, for the sake of justice
or humanity, must be said concerning these
three hundred and fifty-one[2] persons; and something for the judge's sake, whether he were the
avenger of sedition, or the brutal navigator in
a sea of blood.

In the autumn of 1685, Jeffreys went forth,
guarded by a party of Colonel Kirk's soldiers,
taking with him as his assistants, the lord chief

[1] We might add, nor with poets; especially when they
write thus :—

"This demy-fiend, this hurricane of man,
Was sent to butcher all i' th' west he can."

[2] Some books speak of 251, but the number is differently
stated from 330 to 350.

baron[1] and three puisne judges;[2] although it may
be said, that these last were mere cyphers, for
all the fierce deeds are imputed to the chief,
and all the odium rests singly upon him.   He
acted up to his commission, gave daily the word
and orders for going the rounds, and ordered
what party of troops he pleased to attend him.

Winchester was the first place where the
ministers of justice halted; for here was the
Lady Alicia Lisle awaiting her trial,—a very obnoxious lady, for her husband had been no other
than the great John L'Isle,[3] one of King Charles

---

[1] William Montague, Esq. He was one of the judges
whom James turned out afterwards for resisting his attempted
power of dispensation. He lived in retirement to a great
age; and from his known uprightness of character, it is to
be presumed that he had little share in these scenes of blood.

[2] One of whom was Sir Robert Wright, a baron of the
Exchequer, and afterwards chief justice of the King's Bench
at the trial of the seven bishops. He was one of the true
butcher-birds, and was the man who promised to hang the
poor soldier for deserting his colours upon Hounslow-heath,
if he were promoted, which was done by moving Sir Edward
Herbert, and the promise was performed. Judge Jenner
was another.

[3] He was son of Sir William Lisle, Knt., of Wootton,
Isle of Wight: went to Magdalen Hall, and thence to the
Temple, and soon distinguished himself at the bar. He was
returned for Winchester in 1640, and became master of the
hospital of St. Cross near that city, which he gave up to

the First's judges, a zealous republican, some time lord president of the high court of justice, and joint commissioner of the great seal. Her offence was the harbouring one John Hicks, an alleged traitor, who was hung afterwards at Glastonbury, and who·fled for shelter after the defeat of the duke. One of the most singular incidents, however, which accompanied this trial, was the appearance of Henry Pollexfen'

Mr. Solicitor Cook in 1649. Jeffreys told his wife pretty clearly how well his presence at the condemnation of King Charles was remembered. He was one of the council of state, sometime president of the high court of justice, and was very instrumental in making Oliver the lord protector. He was excepted out of the act of oblivion at the Restoration, and fled into Switzerland, where, at Lausanne, he had great respect paid him, and was treated as chancellor of England, being clothed with the robe of that high officer. In 1664, some Irishmen, angry at his kind reception on the continent, thought proper to shoot him with a musquetoon, whereupon he was honourably buried.

' Henry Pollexfen, or Polixphen, was a native of Devonshire, the family being settled at Kitley, near Plympton. His business at the bar was very steady and considerable; and it is observable, that he was in all the principal cases in the latter part of Charles the Second's, and in the succeeding reign. In 1688 he was returned for Exeter, and at the Revolution made attorney-general, whence he was presently removed to be chief justice of the Common Pleas. He died in 1692. Roger North calls him " the veriest butcher of a judge;" but Burnet vouches for his honesty. He was the author of some Reports.

as counsel for the crown. This lawyer had
been deep in the confidence of the country
party, or, according to North, " in all the desperate designs against the crown," and yet was
selected for the King's advocate upon this emergency; and, which is yet more strange, consented to the employment. Fanatic as he is called,
he had contrived hitherto to preserve a great
character for consistency; and in spite of his new
retainer, was made chief justice of the Common
Pleas on the accession of King William.'

But to return: Hicks and one Nelthorp, both
of Rye-house Plot notoriety, were found in the
house of the prisoner under these circumstances: they had escaped from Weston Moor,
and entreated an asylum at the hands of Lady
Alice. When the application was made to her,
she entertained it with great civility, being entirely ignorant of the route which her guests had
taken. Hicks either had the candour or the temerity to acquaint her with the truth, on which she
instantly dispatched her principal servant to a
justice of the peace with information concerning
them, but gave especial orders that they might

ı The conciliation of Pollexfen upon this occasion was no
indifferent stroke of policy, since the writers who have under-
taken to defend the conduct of King James, rely upon that
lawyer's appointment to be the crown counsel, as a proof that
the monarch wished to adopt a course of moderation.

be suffered to escape. At this crisis a party entered, and made the fatal discovery. Jeffreys, bitter foe as he ever showed himself to the dissenters, was transported with rage beyond himself at this trial; for in addition to a prisoner who had been harbouring dissenters, he had a very reluctant presbyterian witness to deal with. It would seem, in fact, that this judge had worked himself up to a lunatic pitch of frenzy against nonconformists, and that he could scarcely be said to command his senses when one of such a persuasion was brought before him. And yet he displayed his usual knowledge of men's characters by the use of many religious admonitions, and even imprecations of the divine wrath against liars, which greatly tended to alarm the presbyterian witness, who in reality did shuffle in his testimony for the purpose of screening the culprit, but was entirely mastered by the chief justice. The expressions used towards him were such as he would be most likely to have heard in the places of worship which his creed taught him to attend, and the repetition of them in so awful a place as a court of justice would render them the more formidable to his mind.

One part of Jeffreys's conduct at the trial has been strongly reprobated. He told the jury

that Nelthorp had privately informed him of the
whole conversation which took place between
the prisoner, Hicks, and himself, when they
were together at supper. And although it might
have been a very flat and just contradiction of
the witness, who was then swearing most out-
rageously for his mistress, the judge had clearly
no right to mention it from the bench. " I would
not mention any such thing as any piece of evidence to influence this case," said he; but the
jury must have been shamefully biassed by such
a statement, because the Lady Lisle was clearly
made out to have been cognizant of the rebellious
designs of those she sheltered, by evidence of
that conversation.

The Lady Lisle said, that had she been tried
in London, several persons of quality would
have testified how strongly she had condemned
the rising of Monmouth; that she had shed more
tears for King Charles than any woman; that she
apprehended the object of Hicks's visit to be no
more than an anxiety to escape the general warrant against nonconformists; and that her son
was actually in arms against the rebels through
her advice.

The good woman, seventy years of age, is said
to have slept during great part of the charge to
the jury; and, beyond doubt, she was well pre-

pared for the scene which was to follow, and
well apprised of her judge's outrageous prejudice. But the jury betrayed a feeling which
did them some credit. They asked, whether
the prisoner could be found guilty of concealing
a person who had not been convicted of any
offence, for Hicks was not as yet tried; and a
very sensible question it was. Jeffreys said, it
made no difference, and this opinion of his was
one ground for reversing the judgment after the
Revolution. However, the jury were still dis-
satisfied; they thought that there had been no
proof of Lady Lisle's knowledge that Hicks had
been in the army. Nothing more palpable,
according to the judge's opinion; and at length
the death-sealing verdict was obtained.'

" If I had been among you, and she had been
my own mother, I should have found her
guilty," said the satiated Jeffreys, who now had
his victim bound to the horns of the altar; and
then he passed judgment on her, in common

' Oldmixon, in his History of the House of Stuart, tells
us that the jury brought her in twice " Not guilty;" and
Rapin says that this happened three times; and further,
that Jeffreys threatened an attaint of jury: the report, however, in the State Trials, is widely at variance with this aggravated statement, and Hume adopts the more moderate
story.

with the other criminals who had been capitally convicted at the assizes. Moreover, the sheriff was ordered to prepare for her execution on that afternoon; but Jeffreys threw out this hint, " We that are the judges shall stay in town an hour or two. You," addressing himself to the prisoner, " shall have pen, ink, and paper brought you; and if, in the mean time, you employ that pen, ink, and paper, and this hour or two well (you understand what I mean), it may be you may hear further from us, in a deferring the execution." This intimation might have been applied to a discovery of more state-prisoners, or, it is possible that the great man looked keenly for a bribe. For, although writers may have been incorrect in attributing venality to our chief justice upon all occasions, it must be confessed that he began a system of corruption on this circuit, to say the least; and being himself originally without an estate, now spared no means of acquiring one.

At the intercession of some Winchester clergymen, the lady was respited for a few days; and it was revenge, probably, at his pecuniary disappointment, that induced the inexorability of Jeffreys against petitions for a final reprieve. There was, however, one more turnpike-gate, before the aged prisoner had fully arrived at the

close of her sufferings. Access to the throne was
ostensibly open; and very considerable interest
was made at court to preserve so blameless a
life. One thousand pounds were offered to
Lord Feversham, the King's general, if he should
succeed in saving her; and the noble lord went
to His Majesty, and begged her life, but heard
from the mouth of royalty, that the King *had
promised Jeffreys not to pardon her.*

Although this latter story comes from Burnet,
who, in spite of his vivid phraseology and occasional want of correctness, has been more and
more confirmed of late in his principal state-
ments, James's want of clemency has been
established by other accounts. When he was
petitioned for a reprieve by two tory peeresses,[1]
he declared that he would not respite her for
one day; and these news we have from one who
was bent upon excusing the whole transaction;[2]
and we are assured again, that Jeffreys had
acquainted His Majesty that Lady Lisle's pretensions to loyalty were feigned. She was
accordingly beheaded[3] as soon as her brief re-

[1] Lady St. John and Lady Abergavenny.
[2] The author of the " Caveat."
[3] Mr. James Macpherson would have us believe that no
application was ever made to the King for a pardon; and he

spite expired, declaring, with her dying breath,
that the judge omitted to recount her defence to
the jury, which, indeed, was but too true. Her
guests, Nelthorp and Hicks, soon followed.
When Hicks's brother, then dean of Worcester,
was importuned on behalf of his relation, it is
said he coldly answered, that " he could not
speak for a fanatic." Some intemperate expression might have fallen from that very learned
and religious man,[1] but a total want of feeling is

attributes the changing of her sentence [*] to Jeffreys. This,
however, is a prerogative which the King has always exercised in person, and there are many authorities which prove
that a request for mercy reached the highest quarter, and that
it failed, though the causes of that failure be variously represented.

   [1] George Hicks, dean of Worcester, the author of " Jo-
vian," was a very learned, but intolerant man. He indi-
rectly reflected upon Tillotson, whose pupil, Edmund Pri-
deaux, was supposed to have been implicated in the rebellion

   [*] From burning to beheading, not hanging, according to Mr. Macpherson. This gentleman has another incorrect passage in a page or two after
the above statement; for he says that the unhappy Mrs. Gaunt was tried
before Sir Edward Herbert, who was, in fact, a mild, clement man; whereas chief justice Jones presided at the trial, and treated the prisoner with a
severity as fully deserving of censure as any violences of the Lord Jeffreys;
and, which was worse, he mixed insidiousness with his behaviour. But
this Jones had established a character for honesty, and thus escaped the
lash of the whig writers, and the traditional anger of historians.

highly improbable, since his brother acknow-
ledges, in a letter written just before his death,
that the dean was gone up to London to see
what could be done for him.

The only disquisition, (and that as short as
need be,) to which we feel disposed to ask the
reader's patient attention, is, whether the chief
justice did actually incur an undivided responsibility respecting the career which he pursued
against the western malefactors; or, whether
he was the instrument, willing enough it may
be, of his Royal Master. This very serious inquiry shall be postponed a little, while we proceed in the history, or, as lawyers would say,
go the circuit.

Having dispatched their business at Winton,
the judges advanced to Salisbury, where their
proceedings were so light, in comparison of the
memorable punishments then in immediate
prospect, that they might almost have demanded

of 1685, as though the divine were answerable for his pupil's
future prejudices; not reflecting, at the same time, that his
own brother had suffered for the same fault. He could not
take the oaths at the Revolution, and therefore was ejected
from his deanery. William Talbot, kinsman to the Earl
of Shrewsbury, was his successor. Hicks was, moreover, a
very considerable author.

the pair of white gloves, the pure and innocent emblem of a maiden assize.[1] Some few of
the rebel whigs were whipped and imprisoned,
but there was no political execution.[2]

The good people of Salisbury have not to this
day forgotten the remarkable loyalty which was
manifested by their townsmen in this struggle,
as they reason from the sparing of blood within
their city ; and truly, it is no small confirmation of their professed love for the then sceptred
monarch, that King James was no way backward to trust himself within their walls at the
commencement of his troubles. The only set-off
against their claim is, that Jeffreys had made
Dorchester his head-quarters, and that he had
been gleaning prisoners from the time he first
entered Hampshire, whom he carried along with
him like oxen to a general slaughter-house, as
the enemies of our judge would say.

And now the fearful cavalcade moved on to
Dorchester, where the first great thunderbolt

[1] A maiden assize is said to be, when there is not a single
prisoner for trial at a circuit town.

[2] According to one account, there was a single execution
at Salisbury ; but by another, no prisoner was there indicted
for high treason. Possibly the execution might have taken
place for some other offence.

was destined to fall on the ill-fated sons of rebellion. These might indeed say:

Omnes eòdem cogimur, omnium
Versatur urna, seriùs, ocyùs
Sors exitura, et nos in æternum
Exilium impositura cymbæ.[a]

which may be thus paraphrased:

" We are all in a trap at the mercy of the
same man; for each of us he shakes his raffle;
and sooner or later will the lot leap forth, the
signal of our journey on the sledge to an eternal
exile."

It is customary for the judges to attend divine
service before they proceed to the business of an
assize town, and Jeffreys was not the man to
neglect a ceremonial so customary, as well as so
imposing; for he would, if possible, do all things
with due form.

It was on Friday, the 4th of September, that
he proceeded to St. Mary Dorchester, having
opened his commission on the preceding day.
Here the clergyman spoke of mercy; but it was

[a] Thus all must tread the path of fate;
Thus ever shakes the mortal urn,
Whose lot embarks us, soon or late,
On Charon's boat, ah! never to return.
FRANCIS.

observed that the Lord Jeffreys laughed both
during prayers and sermon;¹ a pretty plain
sign that he was (according to the singular conceit of an old writer,) about to " breathe death
like a destroying angel, and to sanguine his very
ermins in blood."

The minister finished, and the chief went

¹ One is irresistibly reminded of the fine pictures which
the " Great Unknown " has given us of the famous Claverhouse and General Dalzell, just before the battle of Both-
well Brig. Henry Morton had gone out to propose terms
on behalf of the covenanters to the gentle Duke of Monmouth ; Colonel Claverhouse (afterwards Viscount Dundee),
and General Dalzell (a guest, by the way, of James Duke
of York), stood beside the Duke. The Duke received the
terms with courtesy. " Here Morton observed Dalzell
shake his head indignantly, and whisper something into Claverhouse's ear, who smiled in return, and elevated his eyebrows, but in a degree so slight as scarce to be perceptible."
The Duke dismisses the plenipotentiary with these words:
" I earnestly entreat," speaking of the answer, " it may be
such as to save the effusion of blood." " At this moment
another smile of deep meaning passed between Dalzell and
Claverhouse. ' Yes, gentlemen,' repeated the Duke, ' I
said I trusted the answer might be such as would save the
effusion of blood. I hope the sentiment neither needs your
scorn, nor incurs your displeasure !' Dalzell frowned, but
made no answer. ' It is not for me to judge the propriety of
your Grace's sentiments,' said Claverhouse, his lip just curled
with an ironical smile. The subsequent carnage was immense."—*Tales of My Landlord.*

forth, inoculated (as we shall prove hereafter) with the royal unction, and attended by his judicial brethren. The court was hung with red cloth, "a colour suitable to such a succeeding bloody tragedy," as our writer says; and in due time their lordships entered with the flower of the west, the gentry of Dorset, Somerset, and Devon. Then came the charge to the grand jury, a vehement and ear-piercing harangue, which astonished and alarmed all who heard it, cognizant as they must have been of the man's character who was addressing them. Not only after " principals" was their most strict inquiry to be bent, but after " aiders and abettors." And who might not have been an " aider or abettor?" for the jury had sheltered many of their relations, which made them accessaries to high treason after the fact. The court then adjourned until eight the next morning.

The panic-struck jury, moulded, as it were, to the will of the court by the well-timed threats which had been held out, soon found bills of indictment against thirty persons; and in the course of the assizes they implicated more than three hundred in the great transaction. But does the reader imagine that it had ever been the intention of Jeffreys to give all his prisoners the benefit of a long and patient hearing?

Well did that sagacious lawyer calculate that
he might have sat in judgment until the spring
assizes if he had been vexed with the " say" of
all these unhappy men. Now, therefore, came
the *ruse de guerre*. He held out the white flag,
and proclaimed that, " if any one of them there
indicted would relent from their conspiracies,
and plead guilty to the same, they should find
him to be a merciful judge." It is very important just to mention here that which we
shall show rather more at large presently, that
the kind of people who were to be dealt with
were such as by no means inclined to " relent
from their conspiracies ;" they were men of conspicuous hardihood and resolute daring, even
while the cloud of death was overshadowing
them.

But, moreover, that there might be menace
as well as encouragement, the prisoners were
informed, at the same time, that those who put
themselves on their trials should, if found guilty,
have very little time to live ; indeed, Jeffreys
did not scruple to say, at once, that their confessions would save him trouble. And the matter was afterwards managed in this way : two
officers took a list of the accused, and went to
them with the sister promises of pardon or execution ; and as many were induced to accept

the proffered mercy, these officers were in a
condition to appear as witnesses of their confession, (as the law was then administered,) in the
case of their retracting. This artifice was not
forgotten when the judge was lampooned some
years after as a fallen chancellor, to the tune of
" Hey brave popery !"

> The prisoners to plead to his lordship did cry,
> But still he made answer, and thus did reply,
> We 'll hang you up first, and then after we 'll try.
>   Sing hey brave Chancellor ! O fine Chancellor !
>   Delicate Chancellor ! O !

However, the first thirty, not so easily caught
by the sham bleating of the wolf, were
minded to venture upon the defensive, and so
they pleaded not guilty. The result of this
boldness is soon told. It was on Saturday that
these prisoners came to the bar, and the same
evening Jeffreys signed a warrant to hang thir-
teen on the Monday following, which was punctually performed. The rest followed very soon
afterwards, save one Saunders, who had been
acquitted for want of evidence. But it is not
to be supposed that all these died without a
word of supplication to save their lives, nor that
they were convicted without an effort to procure a different verdict. There was a constable

of Chardstock who, having some money in his
hands for the use of the militia, was deprived
of it by the Duke's friends, and this was his
offence. The evidences against him were a
woman of bad fame, and a catholic, whose house
had been searched for arms by Monmouth's
party. The prisoner objected to the testimony.
" Villain! rebel!" exclaimed the judge, "methinks I see thee already with a halter about
thy neck;" and he was ordered specially to be
hung the first. Very considerable interest was
made to preserve Matthew Bragg, an attorney,
whose crime was walking home without his
horse, of which the rebels had deprived him,
and thus became an aider and abettor according to the then prevailing construction. People
of the best quality sought a reprieve, and even
a respite of ten days for him; but he was put
to death on the Monday, in company with the
twelve others who have been mentioned. Jeffreys, indeed, was disposed to be facetious, for
he jestingly declared, "that if any lawyer or
parson came in his way, they should not escape
him." This might be a jocose saying, but it
was no joke, for the judge kept his word.

The business now proceeded, but the great
point which Jeffreys aimed at was gained. He
had intimidated the culprits, who pleaded guilty

by dozens; but the ire of their judge was kindled, so that their time-saving plea stood them in little stead.

Two hundred and ninety-two received judgment to die, besides the sacred band of thirty; and of the second batch seventy-four[1] were consigned to the hangmen of Dorchester, Bridport, Lyme, Sherborne, &c. The remainder were transported, severely whipped, or imprisoned. Indeed, the most extraordinary whippings which Jeffreys ordered were little thought of at the instant amidst the more heavy inflictions of justice. Many of the transports were sold for slaves. The whole county was adorned with the gibbeted quarters of the factious, which were distributed up and down as was thought expedient.

Yet the principal terrorist was indulging himself in luxuries during these alarms, solaced by the company of his favourites, who were keen in discovering the sources from whence they might, jackal-like, bring plunder to their lion. The fountain of mercy fell in muddy drops. There was one John Lawrence, who managed an estate near Dorchester; the Duke of Monmouth's party came and took three horses from

---

[1] Some accounts say, eighty-seven.

his care, on which he remonstrated with that
nobleman, and at last recovered one. The giving
up of the two others was deemed an abetting,
and so he was drawn into the plot. Jeffreys
would have had his master in the scrape; but
that being impracticable, this poor fellow, who
had the temerity to stand his trial, was ordered
to be hung at Wareham; and surely so it
would have happened but for one of the judge's
courtiers, who found that money was to be had,
and who got a reprieve upon the payment of
200*l*. down, and a security by bond for 200*l*.
more.

After all, the greatest hardship which befel
any man at these assizes was the sad end of a
Major Holmes, who suffered at Lyme. He had
lost one of his sons in the battle, and an arm
besides,[1] when he was captured, and brought
up to London. King James, as Father Orleans
acquaints us, desired to see him; and the prisoner boldly said upon the interview, that it
would be more advantageous for the King's reputation to grant him his life, than beneficial to

[1] Which he himself is said to have struck off in a kitchen
immediately after the battle. He is called Colonel Holmes
in the accounts of the condemned persons, and is probably
the same with Major Holmes, who was engaged with Argyle
in Scotland in the same cause.

himself to receive it. " No one was more frequently in the King's antichamber," till he was
sent down into the west as a kind of king's evidence, (at least Father Orleans would have it
so,) for the purpose of pointing out the fittest
objects for mercy or for punishment, that he
might " doe some service ere he receiv'd his
pardon." Other accounts state that Jeffreys
caused him to be privately seized; but certain it
is, that he was hanged; and the King, according
to the biographer just mentioned, called Jeffreys
into judgment for this harsh act, but was soon
satisfied perforce on the ground of necessary
justice, which " the King having made him judg
of, knew not how to contradict."

We have seen that Jeffreys was once captivated by a woman's generosity; but he had
learned a most cruel disregard of the fair as he
advanced in life, of which the second Lady Jeffreys might, to be sure, have been partly the occasion, as we shall see by and by. Mr. Battiscomb, a man of very tolerable estate and engaging
manner, was so ill-fated as to become an inmate
of Dorchester gaol, and so ill-advised as to defend the equity of his cause, which had like to
have choked Jeffreys, who furiously ordered him
to a place of execution, there "to be hung by the
neck till he should be dead." All the ladies

in Dorchester were interested in the fate of the young man, who, by the way, when the judge's fit was over, had offers of life made him on the condition of his betraying some friends, which he resolutely repelled; and thus, having shut out the last hope of mercy, had become doubly an object of admiration: several girls, one especially, went to Jeffreys, and asked his life, but he is said to have repulsed them quite *en brute*.[1]

There are some lines written upon this unhappy damsel, and some of them sufficiently curious.[2] The prisoner suffered at Lyme, and

[1] Ralph, in his review of James the Second's reign, gives a story which is too gross to repeat here. It is a most brutal reply of Jeffreys to this young lady. Page 892 of Ralph.

[2] A poem on a lady that came to my lord chief justice to beg Mr. Battiscomb's life, sister to one of the sheriffs in the west, which he denied.

> Harder than thine own native rocks,
>> To let the charming Silvia kneel,
>> And not one spark of pity feel:
> Harder than senseless stones and stocks!
> Ye gods! what showers of pearls she gave!
> What precious tears! enough to save
> A bleeding monarch from the grave.
>
> By every hapless virgin curst:
>> Winter blasts not more unkind,
>> Deaf as the rugged northern wind;
> By some Welsh wolf in murders nurst.

his character is thus given us: "All that knew or saw him, must own Mr. Battiscomb was very much a gentleman. Not that thin sort of animal that flutters from tavern to playhouse, and back again, all his life made of wig and cravat, without one dram of thought in his composition; but one who had solid worth, &c. His body made a very handsome and creditable tenement for his mind; and 't had been pity it shou'd have liv'd in any other;" and so on.

Here is another instance of the judge's brutality to females. Two persons named Hewling were

---

Hast thou eyes? or hast thou none?
Or are they worse than marble grown?
Since marbles weep at Silvia's moan.

Rebels stiff, and supple slaves,
   All the frantic world divide;
   One must stoop, and t'other ride;
Cringing fools and factious knaves:
Tho' falling on the loser's part,
Gently Death arrests my heart,
And has in honey dipt his dart.

Life, farewell! thou gaudy dream,
   Painted o'er with grief and joys,
   Which the next short hour destroys;
And drowns them all in Lethe's stream.
What blest mortal would not die,
Might he with me enbalmed lye,
In precious tears from Silvia's eye!

among the condemned at Taunton, who had two
sisters, and they hung upon the state coach im-
ploring mercy at his hands; whereupon the
incensed magistrate bade his coachman lash
their fingers with his whip. And he moreover
refused one of these sisters a respite of two days
only for her brothers, though she offered him
one hundred pounds for that little favour.[1]

The miseries which were inflicted upon the
inhabitants of this county shall be concluded
with an account of a most horrible sentence of
whipping which was pronounced upon one Tutchin, a young man of Hampshire. This fellow
(who, after all, was but a saucy rogue,[2]) appeared

[1] Sir John Dalrymple has confounded those Hewlings with
one Simon Hamling, of whom we shall presently speak.—
See his Memoirs, p. 78.

[2] This person was a great promoter of sedition by his
writings. He was tried in the reign of Queen Anne for a
libel published in 1703, in his " Observator," but escaped,
through some legal difficulties which were started after the
verdict. He died in 1707, through some violence which his
scurrility had brought upon him.—See *Toulmin's Taunton by
Savage*, p. 510, in the note.

> Careless, on high, stood unabash'd De Foe,
> And Tutchin, flagrant from the scourge, below.
>   *Dunciad*.

This man had the assurance to visit Jeffreys in the Tower,
after his disgrace.

to a charge of rebellion under the assumed
name of Thomas Pitts,' and was acquitted for
want of evidence. This happened at Taunton;
but as Tutchin was a man of Dorset, and was to
be punished in that county, we mention him
here. Jeffreys soon found out his true name,
and asserted, that "he was never so far outwitted by a young or old rogue in his life." He
then tried to fish out of Mr. Tutchin the names
of some of his confederates, but failed; upon
which he grew furious, and not being able to
hang him, issued forth the following sentence:
"Imprisonment for seven years, and once a
year to be whipped through all the market-
towns in Dorsetshire: to be fined one hundred
marks, and find security for his good behaviour
during life." This was a blow indeed; and the
ladies in court immediately burst into tears;
but Jeffreys called out, " Ladies, if you did but
know what a villain this is, as well as I do, you
would say that this sentence is not half bad
enough for him." And the clerk of the arraigns
was so much astonished, that he could not help
observing upon the number of market-towns in
Dorset: he said, that "the sentence reached to
whipping about once a fortnight, and that Mr.

' Thomas Pitts, gent., was the author of the " Western
Martyrology."

Tutchin was a very young man."—" Aye, he is
a very young man, but an old rogue," retorted
the invincible judge; " and all the interest in
England shan't reverse the sentence I have
passed on him." Tutchin himself had that keen
regard for his bones, and was so fully sensible
of the discipline intended him, that he actually
petitioned the King to be hanged with his fel-
low-prisoners. It seems that the court felt the
enormity of the chastisement proposed; but all
that transpired was, " Mr. Tutchin must wait
with patience." Then the young man tried to
buy a pardon, but in vain; and then came the
small-pox, a day or two before his first lashes
were to have taken place, and reduced him so
low, as to occasion a reversal of the sentence by
Jeffreys himself. Most probably, as in Rosewell's case, the King had peremptorily commanded the change.'

The doom of the Dorsetshire men being fixed,
the judges went forward to Exeter. Jeffreys
was beset on all sides by petitions from the inhabitants of the places through which he passed,
that he would compassionate their relations.
But a little incident occurred, which had like to

' We are told also, that a boy of Weymouth, about ten or
twelve years old, was most cruelly whipped for being in
possession of some popular pamphlet.

have driven away the veriest shade of mercy.
The cavalcade had stopped to sleep at the house
of some honourable gentleman, when in the
midst of a disorder, occasioned, it is said, by the
servants, some pistols were fired in the night.
The great man took the alarm instantly, for he
had a suspicion that a design was on foot against
him; and, at parting, he declared, that " not a
man of all those parishes that were of that vici-
nitude, if found guilty, should escape."

However, the severity exercised in Devonshire fell short of that which had occurred
in Dorset, as did the dreadful punishments,
which awaited the next county: yet the same
method of economising time was resorted to,
and with much success. There was one John
Foweracres who had sufficient nerve to stand a
trial, but by no means the fortune of gaining his
acquittal; and the precedent of going before a
jury was considered so obnoxious, that the prisoner was ordered for instant execution. This
had the desired effect, for the rest of the culprits
immediately pleaded guilty, which saved " further trouble." Nevertheless, thirty-seven were
hanged in different parts of the county, and
several transported, whipped, and imprisoned.
The number of accused amounted to two hundred and forty-three.

We cannot forbear to insert here a description, which was given at that time, of the beautiful western country.

" He" (Jeffreys) " made all the west an Aceldama; some places quite depopulated, and nothing to be seen in 'em but forsaken walls, unlucky gibbets, and ghostly carcases. The trees were loaden almost as thick with quarters as leaves : the houses and steeples covered as close with heads, as at other times frequently in that country with crows or ravens. Nothing could be liker hell than all those parts; nothing so like the devil as he. Caldrons hizzing, carkases boyling, pitch and tar sparkling and glowing,' blood and limbs boyling, and tearing, and mangling, and he the great director of all; and in a word, discharging his place who sent him, the best deserving to be the King's late chief justice there, and chancellor after, of any man that breath'd since Cain or Judas." If this be an exaggerated picture, it must be confessed that there is imagination in it. The prisoners, however, received great kindness from the city of Exeter. " Most sorts of provisions, as hot broth, boyled meat, roast meat, divers sorts of

' It was Kirk who is said to have ordered the boiling the rebellious carcases in pitch.

pies, were daily sent into the prison; the persons that sent them unknown to them."

Five hundred unfortunates still lingered in the county of Somerset, and thither Jeffreys was now come, determined upon expedition, and in no wise abated from his zeal. He began at Taunton, so lately the scene of boughs, herbs, and flowers, in honour of Monmouth, where twenty-six virgins had presented the invader with colours made by their townsmen; the captain of the young women going forth to meet the duke with a naked sword in one hand, and a Bible in the other. Some of these were children, ten or twelve years old; and yet their little frolic cost their parents dear; for when all was hushed, and the circuit over, the girls were excepted out of the act of amnesty for presenting the rebel chief with the standards. But then the knavery peeped out; for on payment of certain small *douceurs* according to ability, their pardons came out piecemeal, and they were delivered from a public trial which was threatened. Some gave £50, some £100; and the money went, not to Jeffreys, but to the Queen's maids of honour as a Christmas-box. They sent an agent into the country to discriminate, as it should seem, and complained at first of the small sums which were extorted, for they expected seven thousand pounds; but they were compelled to be satisfied, and the matter dropped.*

On the first night of the chief's arrival at Taunton, he not only opened the commission, but gave his charge, which was furious enough; and Ralph tells us, that he declared " it would not be his fault if he did not depopulate the place." A sad omen for the men in Taunton

---

* The affair did not pass away without a struggle, for the Duke of Somerset interfered on the behalf of the court ladies. He wrote to Sir Francis Ware,* urging him to secure some of the rebellious girls, and, above all, the schoolmistress. Another letter from his grace to the baronet, recommended the giving a power of attorney to some one, which the maids of honour were to sign; but Sir Francis represented that the teacher was a woman of low birth, and that the scholars worked the banner by her orders, without knowing any offence, upon which the greater severities were abandoned. One Miss Mary Blake, who worked the colours, died in Dorchester gaol, as some say, of the small-pox, whilst her sister received a pardon. Another girl surrendered herself in court, when the judge looked so furiously upon her, telling the gaoler, at the same time, to take her, that she pulled her hood over her face, and fell to weeping, and not many hours afterwards died through fear.—See *Toulmin's History of Taunton*, p. 162; and the same book, edited and enlarged by J. B. Savage, where the original letters may be seen. Taunton, 1822, p. 529.

* Baronet of Hestercombe.

Castle. But the old game was, notwithstanding, very available for confessions. This is celebrated in a poem called " Jeffreys's Elegy :"—

> He bid 'um to confess, if ere they hope
> To be reprieved from the fatal rope:
> This seem'd a favour, but he'd none forgive;
> The favour was, a day or two to live;
> Which those had not that troubled him with tryal,
> His business blood, and would have no denyal.
> Two hundred he could sentence in an hour, &c.

One Simon Hamling, a dissenter, had gone to Taunton to advise his son to remain neuter; but as the Duke of Monmouth was at that time in the town, the father was taken before a justice on suspicion. Now, it seems, that the magistrates loved a bribe as well as the chief justice; and as the rage of the day waxed very hot against sectaries and conventicle preachers, Hamling, who would not, or did not know how to attack the justice's weak side, stood no chance of escaping a committal. William Gatchett, or Gatchell, a constable, had been compelled to execute a warrant for bringing provisions to Monmouth's army, on pain of having his house burnt, &c., and was accordingly sent to gaol as an accomplice. Now these two men had most excellent defences, but unhappily, perhaps, had the courage to make use of them;

they therefore gave in their pleas, Not guilty.
Of course the jury convicted them, and thus
secured them the advantage of being hung first:
so they were sent to the gallows the morning
after their trial. The constable was a very decided character; for as he went to execution, he
looked upon the Taunton men very calmly, and
said, "A populous town, God bless it!" But
Hamling's case was the most hard. The evidences against him were profligate fellows, who
would do any thing for the committing justice;
and the prisoner proved that fact, but in vain.
And what was still more remarkable, the justice
himself was there, and could not help telling the
judge that there certainly was a mistake concerning that man. And now, unless we had
positively told the history of his execution, the
reader would have looked for an instant acquittal. Jeffreys was made of sterner stuff.—"You
have brought him on; if he be innocent, his
blood be upon you!"[1] exclaimed the judge.
What a scene does all this bandying reveal to
us! The magistrates were corrupt, and cared
little or nothing for justice, and Jeffreys despised
the magistracy. As far as appearances went,

[1] That was a dry speech of Nero, who, when he was told
that the wrong man had been executed, coolly replied,
"Doubtless he deserved to die as well as the other!"

he did not respect any one on the earth who differed from his gigantic opinions. There was a tory nobleman in those parts, Lord Stawell, who was so much displeased with the severity which had been exercised, that he refused to see the chief justice. The peer resided at Cotheleston at that time; and very soon afterwards came forth an order that one Colonel Bovet, of Taunton, should be executed close by my Lord Stawell's residence. Indeed, there was but little scruple or delicacy as to the place of death; for it was not by any means impossible in those days to find a man hanging by a rope out of a chamber window; and in fact, such an event is said to have happened at Taunton, and the hanging to have been accomplished by an executioner of Exeter.

It is not practicable to be correct to a man; but we have authority for saying, that one hundred and forty-five were adjudged to die at the assizes held for Taunton, and that one hundred and forty-three of these actually suffered. The following warrant was sent by the sheriff of Somerset to the mayor of Bath:—

" Edward Hobbes, esq. sherreiffe of ye countie aforesaid, to the con^{bles} and other his Maties officers of the cittie and burrough of Bath, greeting: Whereas I have rec^d a warr^t under the hand and seale of the right hon^{bl} the Lord Jeffreys for the executing of several rebells within yor said cittie, These are therefore to will and require yo^w immediately on sight hereof to erect a gallows in the most publike place of yor said cittie to hang the said trayto^{rs} on, and that yo^w provide halters to hang them with, a sufficient number of faggotts to burne the bowells of fower traytors, and a furnace or cauldron to boyle their heads and quarters, and salt to boyle therewith, halfe a bushell to each trayt^r, and tarr to tarr y^m with, and a sufficient number of speares and poles to fix and place their heads and quarters: and that yo^w warne the owners of fower oxen to be ready with a dray and wayne, and the said fower oxen at the time hereafter mentioned for execusion; and yo^w yor selves, togeather with a guard of fortie able men att the least, to be present on Wednesday morning next by eight of the clock, to be aiding and assisting to me, or my deputie, to see the said rebells executed. Given under my seal of office this 16th day of November, A° 1° Jacobi Secundi, 1685.

"Edward Hobbes, Vic.

"Yo^w are also to provide an axe and a cleaver for the quartering the said rebells."

If mercy had been suffered to enjoy even the triumph of a moment, Jeffreys's great boast had been idle; for he vauntingly puffed forth, on his return, that " he had hanged more men than all the judges of England since William the Conqueror." Colonel Kirk was left far behind by this seasonable brag. Jeffreys once asked a major how many the soldiers had killed; the officer said one thousand. " I believe I have condemned as many as that myself," returned the peer.

Two hundred and eighty-four were ordered for transportation at this town, and forty-three were recommended for a pardon. There was another little list of fifteen very lucky beings who were intended for execution, but were accidentally omitted in the warrant. The whippings went on as usual. " I will pay my excise to King Monmouth," said one Mrs. Brown, an unfortunate gossip of Lyme, to an officer of excise, but quite jestingly. This tattling occasioned her some smart floggings through the market-towns of her county. There was a Captain Madders, who bore the character of being a good Christian and an honest man, and was, moreover, positively instrumental in giving due and loyal notice of the duke's rising. All this was told Jeffreys; but whether the captain had refused to *pouch* the chief, as we say at Eton, or otherwise howsoever, as the special pleaders say, is not quite capable of solution. "Oh! then," cries my lord, when he had heard the recommendation, " I'll hold a wager with you he is a presbyterian: I can smell them forty miles." He was hung. There is a great triumphing with some writers about the death of John Hucker.[1] Sir John Dalrymple says that this execution escaped censure. Hucker,[2] who gave the alarm to Feversham's army, pleaded his treachery in mitigation. " He deserves a double death," said the impartial judge; " one for rebelling against his sovereign, and the other for betraying his friends." However, Hucker had no mind to die under so gross an imputation; for in a letter which he wrote a few hours before his execution, he thus complains:—" I also lye under a reproach of being unfaithful to an interest that I owned, which I utterly deny and disown." Men sometimes go to the gallows under false colours, if they think that their reputation will be saved by the disguise.

The carts with prisoners were now put in motion again, for there was to be another visi-

[1] Dalrymple calls him Robert, which was the name of his son, who had no concern in the matter.

[2] It has been asserted, that he did this because the duke refused to make him governor of Taunton.

tation for Somerset at Wells; and to be short,
after the accustomed manœuvring to gain confessions, and menaces to enforce verdicts, one
hundred capital convicts were obtained, of whom
ninety-seven died by the executioner. There
was a general settlement of accounts here;
three hundred and eighty-five were delivered
over to different people for transportation, a
few were pardoned, and about five escaped, who
were fully destined for the other world, but left
out of the warrant. Upwards of one hundred
more were bound, each for the other, to appear
at the next assizes, in the penalty of 100*l.* And
then the chief justice proposed to jog towards
home, taking Bristol in his way.

We must stop for an instant to speak of the
excellent Bishop Ken, of Bath and Wells.
This prelate had checked the severities of
Feversham, (who was anticipating Jeffreys very
ably,) by hinting that persons were entitled to a
trial by jury after the first heat of victory had
subsided. And, afterwards, he spared neither
expense nor pains in soothing the truly wretched
state of the accumulating prisoners in Wells,
who were gnawed by despair, fear, and disappointment.

This divine was a remarkable man in other

respects: he was one of the seven bishops who
came under the lash of the privy-council for
opposing the King's declaration, and yet lost
his see at the Revolution, because he could not
subscribe the new tests.

We left Jeffreys on his road to Bristol, where
it was really intended to make some examples,
for that city had shown some readiness to open
the gates to Monmouth, though such lengths
were not gone. It will be recollected, that a
severe usage of the mayor and aldermen has
been already told, and a magnificent harangue
against slavery with all the consequences detailed to the reader in a former page. It is to
be feared, that the merit of arresting the evils
of kidnapping must be considerably lessened,
when we find that the whole affair was a political attack upon the place for its inclination to
rebellion, and not a pure emanation of justice:
not but that a more heavy penalty would have
been inflicted than the mere bullying and fining
of the corporation, had it been practicable; but
as Ralph says, " Jeffreys, to his great mortification, found no traitors to fatten upon here
(Bristol)." So that he was obliged to content himself with pulling their strong holds to pieces,—
the pride and ostentation of their magistracy,

which he certainly found means to mortify in a
very painful degree; and as he never could endure
that any one should be greater than himself, he
was delighted beyond measure at the opportunity. He began by putting himself at the
head of the commission before the mayor, which
had not been usual, and this must have displeased
the Bristol men not a little ; but they were too
much terrified by the fame of his exploits to
show their teeth. They received him, therefore,
with great state and splendour, and this was
meant to soften him; but, " Lord !" said he,
"we have been used to these things;" and very
coolly proceeded to business. His charge is so
precious a *morceau,* that it cannot be entirely
omitted, because it so plainly bespeaks the man;
nor can we give it quite at its length, for fear of
wearying those who read. Here are some
extracts:

" Gentlemen, I am, by the mercy of God,
come to this great and populous city; a city that
boasts both of its riches and trade, and may
justly indeed claim the next place to the great
and populous metropolis. Gentlemen, I find
here are a great many auditors who are very
intent, as if they expected some formal or prepared speech; but assure yourselves, we come
not to make neither set speeches nor formal de-

P

clamations, nor to follow a couple of puffing
trumpeters; for, Lord! we have seen these
things twenty times before: no, we come to do
the King's business."—"But I find a special
commission is an unusual thing here, and relishes
very ill; nay, the very women storm at it, for
fear we should take the upper hand of them
too: for, by the by, gentlemen, I hear it is much
in fashion in this city for the women to govern
and bear sway." Then he told them that he
should give them no trouble about points or
matters of law, but only mind them of events
which had happened, "for I have the calendar
of this city in my pocket," said he; and he then
complained of the stone, and the unevenness of
their roads, which was a bad omen for them.
After this came a long sermon about the blessed
martyr, King Charles, and rebellion the sin of
witchcraft, a panegyric on King James, and an
ample acknowledgment of his absolute power
as God's vicegerent on earth: and then he
opened on the Duke of Monmouth, by way of
antithesis:—"On the other hand, upstarts a
puppet prince who seduces the mobile into rebellion, into which they are easily bewitched;
for, I say, rebellion is like the sin of witchcraft.
This man, who had as little title to the crown as
the least of you (for I hope you are all legi-

timate), being overtaken by justice, and by the
goodness of his prince brought to the scaffold,
he has the confidence (good God! that men
should be so impudent!) to say, that God Almighty did know with what joyfulness he did die
(a traitor!)."—"Great God of heaven and earth!
what reason have men to rebel? But as I told
you, rebellion is like the sin of witchcraft: fear
God and honour the King is rejected by people,
for no other reason, as I can find, but that it is
written in St. Peter. Gentlemen, I must tell
you, I am afraid that this city hath too many of
these people in it; and it is your duty to search
them out."—[Here the grand jury were in as
many words directed to the mayor and aldermen.]—"For this city added much to that
ship's loading; there was your Tylys, your
Roes, and your Wades, men started up like
mushrooms, scoundrel fellows, mere sons of
dunghills: these men must forsooth set up for
liberty and property! A fellow that carries the
sword before Mr. Mayor must be very careful
of his property, and turn politician, as if he had
as much property as the person before whom
he bears the sword, though perchance not worth
a groat. Gentlemen, I must tell you, you have
still here the Tylys, the Roes, and the Wades:
I have brought a brush in my pocket, and I

shall be sure to rub the dirt wherever it is, or
on whomsoever it sticks. Gentlemen, I shall
not stand complimenting with you: I shall talk
with some of you before you and I part, I tell
you; I tell you, I have brought a besom, and I
will sweep every man's door, whether great or
small. Must I mention particulars? I hope
you will save me that trouble."—" I do believe it
would have went very hard with you if the
enemy had entered the city, notwithstanding
the endeavours which were used to accomplish
it. Certainly they had, and must have great
encouragement from a party within, or else why
should their design be on this city? Nay, when
the enemy was within a mile of you, that a ship
should be set on fire in the midst of you, as a
signal to the rebels, and to amuse those within!
when, if God Almighty had not been more gracious unto you than you was to yourselves, (so
that wind and tide was for you,) for what I
know, the greatest part of this city had perished; and yet you are willing to believe it
was an accident. Certainly here is a great
many of those men whom they call trimmers:
a whig is but a mere fool to these; for a
whig is some sort of a subject in comparison
of these; for a trimmer is but a cowardly and
base-spirited whig; for the whig is but the

journeyman-prentice that is hired, and set over
the rebellion, whilst the trimmer is afraid to
appear in the cause."—" Gentlemen, I tell you,
I have the calendar of this city here in my
hand. I have heard of those that have searched
into the very sink of a conventicle, to find out
some sneaking rascal to hide their money by
night. Come, come, gentlemen, to be plain
with you, I find the dirt of the ditch is in your
nostrils."—[Now he opens upon the chief offence, alluded to by his having the calendar in
his pocket,—the selling convicted criminals for
slaves.]—"Good God! where am I—in Bristol?
This city, it seems, claims the privilege of hanging and drawing amongst themselves! I find you
have more need of a commission once a month
at least. The very magistrates which should be
the ministers of justice, fall out one with another
to that degree, they will scarce dine with each
other; whilst it is the business of some cunning
men that lie behind the curtain, to raise divi-
sions amongst them, and set them together by
the ears, and knock their loggerheads together:
yet I find they can agree for their interest, or if
there be but a kid in the case; for I hear the
trade of kidnapping is much in request in this
city: they can discharge a felon or a traitor,
provided they will go to Mr. Alderman's plan-

tation at the West Indies. Come, come, I find
you stink for want of rubbing. Gentlemen,
what need I mind you of these things? I hope
you will search into them, and inform me. It
seems the dissenters and fanatics fare well
amongst you, by reason of the favour of the
magistrates: for example, if a dissenter, who is
a notorious and obstinate offender, comes before
them to be fined, one alderman or other stands
up, and says, He is a good man (though three
parts a rebel)! Well then, for the sake of Mr.
Alderman, he shall be fined but five shillings.
Then comes another, and up stands another
good man alderman, and says, I know him to
be an honest man (though rather worse than the
former). Well, for Mr. Alderman's sake, he
shall be fined but half-a-crown; so, *manus ma-
num fricat:*[1] you play the knave for me now,
and I will play the knave for you by and by. I
am ashamed of these things: and I must not
forget to tell you, that I hear of some differences
among the clergy,—those that ought to preach
peace and unity to others: gentlemen, these
things must be looked into."

The scope of this tirade, peculiar and without
precedent, was to alarm the jury, to extort

---

[1] They tickle each other's palms.

mutual criminations and confessions, and thus build up a calendar of malefactors. The mayor and aldermen of Bristol would have filled Jeffreys's purse most marvellously, if their necks could have been drawn within the hempen circle; but the experiment was idle, and all that remained was to make a due inquisition into the slave trade. Much of the result of this charge has been related: to be very brief, therefore, the corporation were presented as kidnappers; and as they descended from the bench to the bar, Jeffreys bawled out, "See how the kidnapping rogues look!"

This was not, however, the first time that our judge had mortified a sleek citizen. Sir James Smith, lord mayor of London in 1685, bitterly complained to Sir John Reresby of the superciliousness which he met with from the great man: he declared, that he was but the mere *ombre* of a lord mayor, the authority being entirely usurped by another chief magistrate; and he added, in a tone of pity, that haughtiness would be the ruin of my Lord Jeffreys. Good easy man! he thought of acquainting the King with it, and Reresby even advised him to do so; but Monmouth and Argyle, then in arms, gave way, and other matters supervened. Sir Robert Geffery, some distant relation to the then

new chancellor, sat in the civic chair the next
year.

But both Smith and Reresby agreed together
that this judge had a method of ejecting as many
as five aldermen at a time (which was done at
York), without hearing their defence. Such was
the virtue of the " ring,"—such its giant-rearing
qualities.

However, six men were convicted of treason
at Bristol; and three of these were executed,
although they have been considered ever since
as " martyrs to political revenge."[1]

The work was now fully done, and the
horses' heads were turned towards the metropolis. Most writers have declared, that Jeffreys
hastened home to pounce upon the great seal,
which had become vacant by the death of Lord
Guilford. And there seems to be very good
reason for believing that the King wrote a letter
with his own hand to the chief justice on the
circuit, urging him to return home and receive
the seal, for that he was obliged to be chancellor himself in the meanwhile. But it is quite

[1] See Bristol, by Corry and Evans, vol. ii. p. 8. The
names of the persons executed in the west may be found in
" The Life and Death of George Lord Jeffreys." London,
1693, 8vo. p. 54. and in " Proceedings against the Rebels
in 1685, &c." Lond. 1716.

clear that the vacancy happened at a most favourable juncture, for the commission had been
opened at the last place, and three or four hundred men hung, and what more could be done
for the King's service? The men of Cornwall had
not involved themselves in the disaster, being
quite satisfied, perhaps, with the resistance which
their ancestors had made to King Henry the
Seventh, and with the unlucky fate which attended them in that rebellion. As it therefore
suited the convenience of our judge to go home,
the purse and insignia of the chancery were
very agreeable things in prospect for him after
his sanguinary labours. Indeed, according to
Evelyn, it was the common talk of the time,
that the seal was to be bestowed in this manner as a reward for the rigorous prosecution of
the rebels. A great blunder, which has been
frequently imitated, is that of ascribing Jef-
reys's peerage to his services in the west, whereas he had been created baron of Wem in the
May preceding, of course before the landing
of Monmouth.

A cry for mercy harassed the returning magistrate, as might be expected; for those who
pleaded guilty were not sacrificed quite so soon
as the people who dared to say that they were
innocent. When the cavalcade was passing

from Somerset into Wilts (Jeffreys still in the quality of lieutenant-general, with a body of dragoons as his life guard), a major in the regiment took the liberty of saying to him, that there were two Spekes, and that one of these, being left for execution, was not the man intended; and that, perhaps, favour might be shown him. " No, his family owe a life," replied the general-judge; " he shall die for his namesake." The mayor of Taunton also interceded for this person, but Jeffreys silenced him with the same reply, and a violent motion of his arm. These Spekes were brothers, and he who had been intended for the rope had escaped. There is an old fable, which warns us never to adventure ourselves within reach of the lion's mouth, if we can by possibility escape; and there was a man of those days called Tory Tom, who knew the moral of this very correctly. The major, above-mentioned, had sent this fellow to the guard-house at Wells for sauciness, and, after some time, Tom begged for his liberty; but while he sent a letter with this view, he took care to procure some people to intercede with the major that his name should not be mentioned to Jeffreys, for that, right or wrong, Tory Tom would be hanged if any one gave him an ill word in that quarter. Upon submission he got his discharge, and was not left " to the mercy of his own tory judge." How great men are sometimes outwitted by their confidants and underlings ! What would the embryo chancellor have said, or rather what would he not have sworn, had he known that one of Monmouth's professed and dear friends was travelling very safely to London, nearly about the same time with himself? And yet nothing is more certain; for Dr. Oliver, a physician to Greenwich Hospital, (the man who advised the duke after the battle to seize a passage-boat and make for Wales, where he might have been concealed,) was safely stowed with the judge's clerk, to whom he had been recommended by a tory, and both were moving on towards the east in company.

But if it should be imagined that all the rigors and penalties were now over, we must bring again to remembrance the mulcting of the poor Taunton children, who were long vexed with threats of punishment, and demands of heavy fines : and the most remarkable instance of exaction still remains behind. Edmund Pridaux, Esq.,' of

' Son of Mr. Attorney-General Pridaux. Mr. Attorney was of the Inner Temple, and sat in parliament for Lyme; he was a busy man " in examining the King's cabinet of letters,

Ford Abbey, Devon, was brought to London in
June by Lord Sunderland's[1] warrant, and committed to the custody of a messenger: this was
two days after the Duke of Monmouth's landing. He was kept in imprisonment for a month
without examination, and was then discharged
upon his habeas corpus, giving security to the
amount of 10,000l. for his future appearance.
On the 14th of September, he was again sent
prisoner to the Tower, charged with high treason. The agents on the circuit had by this
time satisfied themselves of his capacity to ransom his life, and all hands were at work to
hatch an accusation; while Jeffreys boldly declared his resolution to hang; and this he
would have done with the greater pleasure,

taken at Naseby, and in the bustles of those times made a
very conspicuous figure. He was sometime a commissioner
of the great seal, and was made a baronet by Oliver, who
made him post-master for all the inland letters. He was also
recorder of Exeter, and practised within the bar. At the
Restoration he managed to make his peace, and died, very
rich, August 19, 1669. The great Archbishop Tillotson was
employed to instruct his son; and he so far ingratiated himself with the attorney-general, as to obtain 1000l. out of the
Exchequer for the improvement of his college (Clare Hall).
This money, however, was seized by the parliament forces,
and applied towards the fortifying Cambridge Castle.

[1] Then secretary of state.

because Edmund Pridaux, the commonwealth attorney-general, was the father of this hardly-beset gentleman.

Pridaux applied to the King, but received this damning answer,—" That the King had *given* him to Jeffreys." Mrs. Pridaux, who was refused access to her husband, until she had consented to remain with him in confinement, found the case very desperate, for the alternative of instant execution or pardon was holden out to many of the western prisoners, if they persisted in a refusal to accuse him on the one hand, or would come forward and impeach him on the other. So being informed that His Majesty's gift had been conferred for the eminent services which had been rendered to the crown, she ventured to ask the terms on which the agents would guarantee her husband's temporal salvation. 10,000*l.* she received for answer. There was a demur to this extravagant demand. It has happened not once nor twice to men who have been extremely anxious to purchase estates, that on their hesitating to give the sum required, a considerable advance has been forthwith propounded in place of the expected abatement; and thus it happened here. The price was raised to 15,000*l.* and actually paid, a

set-off of 240*l.* being allowed for the prompt payment of a part. The prisoner had been in duresse
for seven months, and without knowing the particulars which had occasioned his misfortune.
Another person of respectability in that country
laid down fifteen or sixteen hundred guineas
which came into the same coffers.[1] With part of
this money the chancellor bought the manor of
Broughton, or Nether Broughton, in Leicestershire, in 1687. He gave 34,000*l.* for the property,
which he mortgaged in the course of a year afterwards.[2] Some disposition was manifested, on the
accession of William III. to compensate Mr. Pridaux for his losses; and a bill was accordingly
brought into the Commons "for charging the
manors of Dalby on the Woulds, and Nether
Broughton in Leicestershire, with the repay-
ment of 15,000*l.* and interest, extorted by him
from Mr. Pridaux." It was unsuccessful, and
one of its most strenuous opponents was my Lord
Chief Justice Pollexfen, the same man who
conducted the crown cases in the west, and who

[1] Jeffreys certainly received 1416*l.* 10*s.* for the job in the
West from Graham and Burton, the crown solicitors, as
appears from the parliamentary inquiry which was instituted.
[2] He bought two estates of the Duke of Albemarle with
this money.

became a trustee, with others, for the children and creditors of the deceased peer.

These lands were sold, however, about the year 1709, by virtue of an act which was passed for that purpose, it being found impossible otherwise to satisfy certain settlements made by the first lord in 1688.[1] Thus the rude untutored boy, who came up from Wales in 1658, without an acre of ground, is found in possession of capital messuages, woods, pastures, manorial rights, and royalties. But an old writer applies the saying of Juvenal to him:—

> Criminibus debent hortos, prætoria, mensas,
> Argentum vetus, et stantem extra pocula caprum.

> Great men to great crimes owe their plate embost,
> Fair palaces, and furniture of cost.—*Dryden*.

[1] It was an act for " vesting the barony of Wem, and manors of Wem and Loppington, and several lands and tenements in the county of Salop; and the manors of Dalby and Broughton, and lands thereunto belonging, in the county of Leicester; and the manor of Fulmer, and several lands and tenements in the county of Bucks (amongst which was Bulstrode), late the estate of George, late Lord Jeffreys, deceased, in trustees, to be sold."—" George Jeffreys died seised of the manor of Broughton, with its rights, members, and appurtenances; and also of all that capital messuage, mansion-house, park, and all those messuages, woods, lands, meadow,

No sooner had Jeffreys regained the court, than he was strictly questioned upon his conduct, according to Father Orleans, the great apologist for James; but he palliated and excused himself so ably by reason of the King's welfare, that no further notice was taken; and so the manes of the innocent sufferers, if any such there were, remained unpropitiated.

Now is the fittest time, were we so disposed, to recount all the bitter imprecations which men have poured forth against the subject of this memoir, and then, in the true strain of panegyric, to palliate his faults, till they first slide gently into failings, and presently ascend into the scale of virtues. There must, however, be some extenuating circumstances in the conduct of every one, be it never so reprehensible in the general; for nature can hardly be so depraved, as not to let in good at some time or another. But there will be no elaborate attempt to excuse or explain away in these pages, and the very sting of the transaction will be suffered to remain as

and pasture, parcel or reputed parcel of the manor of Dalby, in possession of Timothy Hemsby, at the yearly rent of 157*l.* 10*s.* and also of Brandriffe's tenement, parcel of the said manor, in possession of Christopher Hawley, at the rent of 14*l.* &c."—See *Nickolls's Leicestersh.* vol. ii. part 1. p. 119.

acute as the judge's severest censurers can wish. But it must just be told what sort of people the special commissioners had to deal with, and in doing this, no disrespect is intended to any class or sect in religion. They were not a broken-down, repentant, spiritless race, who had pluck-ed up their muskets in a moment of excitement, and then laid them quietly down again in pa-tient expectation of punishment, like wayward schoolboys who await the lash. Archdeacon Echard, who speaks very strongly against the effusion of blood, admits that the behaviour of the prisoners was such as rather tended to exas-perate the judges, than to encourage a feeling of compassion for them ; and this was a highly dan-gerous exploit, if it be considered that a patient under a raving fit of the stone was to try them.

Kirk[1] had determined to know their temper

[1] Colonel Kirk was a soldier of fortune, and had acquired, by a long command at Tangier among the Moors, a consi-derable appetite for military execution. Amongst other cruelties which he practised at Taunton after the battle, was a massacre of thirty persons, whom he caused to be hung whilst he was feasting. Ten went off in a health to the king, ten to the queen, ten to Jeffreys. Some say that he caused the drums to beat, when the criminals were struggling in death, that " they might have music to their dancing." Others doubt the cruelties altogether, and contend that such a man could never have been employed at the Revolution as

Q

after the battle which had marred all their
hopes, and so hanged a man on the White

major-general, if he had been guilty of such enormities. But
William, only three days after his landing, would hardly
have troubled himself with the character of a man, who was
a brave and active soldier, and ready to serve him, for Kirk
disliked and deserted the fortunes of James. Indeed, according to the colonel's opinion, the monarch knew so little
how to profit by his victory at Sedgmoor, that when he took
leave of a Mr. Harvey at Bridgewater, who had been very
civil to him, he said, " I believe it will not be long before I
see you again :" and there was something about his manner
which intimated that it would not be on the same side.
Kirk, as well as Jeffreys, always said, that he did nothing
but by express orders from the King and his general, and that
he put a restraint upon the power and instructions given him.
When James wanted him to turn papist, he very drily said,
that he was " really very sorry, but that he was pre-enga-
ged." The King smiled, and asked him what he meant. " Why,
truly, when I was abroad," answered Kirk, " I promised
the Emperor of Morocco, that if ever I changed my religion,
I would turn Mahometan ; and I never did break my word
in my life, and must beg leave to say I never will." As to
the famous story of Kirk's ill-usage of a young lady, there
being many doubts and much argument upon the subject, we
cannot do better than to refer the reader to the History of
Taunton, by Dr. Toulmin, the new edition by J. B. Savage,
pp. 540—549. A story tending to exculpate Kirk is given
there. When he was standing at a balcony with his officers
to view the execution of twenty rebels, a Mrs. Rowe begged
the life of one; Kirk turned to Bush, a stupid lieutenant,
and said, " Go bid the executioner cut him down." Bush

Hart sign-post, at Taunton, three times, to see if he would own his fault. The man affirmed, that if it was to do again, he would engage in the same cause. And another refused his life, which was offered him on condition of his crying " God bless King James!" Some of them asserted the righteousness of their enterprise in open court; and such as these, with all our mercy and clemency, would be hung now if they should be esteemed of sufficient consequence. A great number of the disaffected were dissenters; and this was a race that Jeffreys would call

never asked the man's name who was to be cut down, * so that when he came to do his bidding,—" Cut him down?" quoth Ketch, " which him? for there are twenty." The culprit to be saved was praying most devoutly, and heard none of all this; but another, who was thinking of something else besides his prayers, told Mr. Bush that he was the man. Bush took his word; he was cut down, and away he went. Why should not this be a different story, and so both be held authentic, since there has always been an unsuspecting tradition of the other? See also Holt's Characters of the Kings of England, p. 263.

* How strikingly this fact resembles a passage in " Coriolanus!" Coriolanus is begging the freedom of his host, with whom he had sojourned in Corioli. Cominius, the general, agrees instantly to the request. Then Lartius speaks—

Marcius, his name?

Coriolanus.—By Jupiter, forgot:

I am weary; yea, my memory is tired.

" stiff-necked," and hated as sincerely as he
loved power: and truly there had been some
very furious fanatics among them, the fifth mo-
narchites, for example. The judge was not to
be blamed, if he kept a very jealous eye over
people who were not backward to introduce in-
novation under an appearance of the most godly
sanctity, or unbridled enthusiasm. There were
some good well-meaning Christians among them;
but we say that Jeffreys had met with a great
deal of detestable and snivelling hypocrisy, and
that he was led away by his passions to condemn the general body. God forbid, that there
should be any persecution for conscience sake;
but let those beware who would remove the ancient land-mark, and thus endanger the security
of a well-compacted and firm constitution. They
may gratify the visionary ideas of liberty which
are splendid and effulgent enough for regions of
fanciful romance, but by far too intoxicating for
the heads of sober citizens. Slow, and tardily
moving with the opening intellect of the times,
should be the pace of improvement, neither excited by passion, nor overawed by menace. The
clinging crusts which clothe the rock, mark truly
its years and strength : the naked offspring of vol-
canic fire is spouted wildly from the ocean, soon
to sink back into its bosom. The judge was in-

volved with sons of violence, and it was not more
than his duty, pledged by oaths, to crush them.
At the justice of the execution the more moderate
writers have not cavilled; the source of regret is,
that the divine attribute of mercy was not imitated. " I have indeed sometimes thought,"
says the author of a Caveat against the Whigs,
" that in Jeffreys's western circuit, justice went
too far before mercy was remembered, though
there was not above a fourth part executed of
what were convicted. But when I consider, in
what manner several of these lives then spared
were afterwards spent, I can but think a little
more hemp might have been usefully employed
upon that occasion." For this he is most un-
mercifully censured by Ralph, which is not surprising; but it shows the resolution of the insur-
gents, and explains the zeal of the high tory
judges. Even Tutchin, who had been excused
his manifold scourgings, went off to the Tower
to see the old persecuting judge in his dark
hour; and as it no where appears that his visit
was charitable, it would not have been amiss, if
he had been whipped out of that garrison for
his intrusion. And if we should find, moreover,
that orders had been issued from the seat of
royalty to spare none, the case of Jeffreys will

assume a very different complexion, especially
if it should appear that he was " snubbed at" on
his return for not doing more. A wise and good
man would have resigned his place rather than
have obeyed such orders, but an ambitious courtier would probably retain it; and so did Jeffreys, who was behind no man in pushing his
own advancement.

But although thus much has been said to ex-
tenuate, or (if that be too kind an expression) to
explain this conduct on the part of Jeffreys, it
is impossible to say otherwise than that he
either was an infuriated maniac, or had a very
inhuman thirst for blood   The rigours of tardy
justice could never have fallen at once for the
same crime upon three hundred and fifty persons, unless the minister of their fate had been
most painfully averse to mercy.

One more consideration remains—it is that
which we have promised; but, courteous reader!
be not alarmed, we have vouched for its brevity.
Was the monarch guiltless of this blood, or did
he remain plausible but reckless in his eastern
metropolis? Was James the unrelenting tyrant,
or did he pity as a father the sad punishment
of his subjects? If he were cognizant of the un-

' His own expression.

sparing rope, and calmly parried back the
written plea for mercy, the controversy is no
more—

The King, the King's to blame!

If, as at the Boyne, he had said, " Oh! spare
my British subjects!" then has the royal head
been stamped with most unsightly blemishes,
and the angry page of both priest' and layman
must be tarnished with one common blot.

There are several *evidences in favour of the
Monarch;* first,

Sheffield, Duke of Bucks.—Speaking of the
King's sudden and silent retreat to the continent,
he tells us, that " the mysterious carriage of this
absconding, cost the Lord Chancellor Jefferies his
life, (a thing indeed of little value to any body
besides himself,) &c."—" This proceeding of his
was imputed to neither ill-nature nor carelessness, two faults His Majesty was not guilty of,
but rather to his generosity; which made him
compassionate his very enemies so much, as
never to forgive that lord's cruelty in executing
such multitudes of them in the west against
his express orders."

' Bishop Burnet, and many others.

The Hon. Roger North.—"Upon the news re-turned of his (Jeffrey's) violent proceedings, his Lordship saw the King would be a great sufferer thereby, and went directly to the King, and moved him to put a stop to the fury, which was in no respect for his service, but in many respects for the contrary. For though the executions were, by law, just, yet never were the deluded people all capitally punished; it would be ac-counted a carnage, and not law or justice: and, therefore, orders went to mitigate the pro-ceeding; but what effect followed, I know not. I am sure of his Lordship's intercession to the King on this occasion, being told it, at the very time, by himself."

From the Stuart Mss. edited by the Rev. J. S. Clarke.—"His imprudent zeal, (speaking of Jeffreys), or, as some say'd averice, carrying him beyond the terms of moderation and mercy, which was always most agreable to the King's temper; so he drew undeservedly a great oblo-quy upon His Majesty's clemency, not only in the number, but the manner too of several exe-cutions, and in showing mercy to so few, parti-cularly an old gentlewoman, one Mrs. Alice Lisle, who was condemned and executed (Sept. 2,) only for harbouring one Hicks and Nelthorp, both ill men enough indeed; and the latter in a proclamation; but as pretended, was ignorant of it, and therefore perhaps might suffer for a common act of hospitality." The case of Major Holmes is then mentioned, and the palliating circumstance of Pollexfen's appointment to be the leading counsel. Speaking of the chancellor, it is said,—" Certainly His Majesty had acted more prudently, had he refrain'd from heaping such distinguishing favours upon a person, who had by an imprudent zeal (at best) drawn such an odium both upon his master and himself."

Again : " Though this was made one of the popular topicks to decry His Majesty's government, 'tis certain, the King was hugely injur'd in it : his inclinations were no ways bloody, but ever bent to mercy; and after all, he pardon'd thousands on this occasion, who had forfeited both life and estate." The escape of the peers who were involved in the rebellion is then adverted to; and great stress laid upon the few executions which took place in London, by comparison with those in the west.

Père d'Orléans.—" Beaucoup d'autres furent punis, et en plus grand nombre même que le Roi n'avoit prétendu. On en accuse la sévérité du

Chevalier Jeffreys leur juge, depuis chancelier
d'Angleterre, la cruauté du Colonel Kirke, et en
général l'avarice des commissaires préposez
pour exercer envers les rebelles ou la sévérité
des lois, ou la miséricorde du prince : car on dit
que le plus ou le moins de part dans le crime
commis, ne fut pas en cette occasion le motif de
la peine ou de l'indulgence, que les moins en
état de racheter leur révolte furent ceux qui la
payèrent plus cher, et que si beaucoup de gens
perdirent la vie, ce fut parce qu'il s'en trouva
peu qui eussent assez d'argent pour la con-
server. Le Roi fut trop tard averti de ce dés-
ordre, mais on ne l'en eût pas plutôt informé,
qu'il en témoigna de l'indignation ; et si des services importans, qu'il avoit reçu de ceux qui en
étoient accusez, l'obligea de les épargner, il ré-
para autant qu'il put leur injustice, par le pardon général qu'il accorda à ceux des révoltez,
qui étoient encore en état d'éprouver les effets
de sa clémence."

"Notwithstanding the rigour generally ascribed to the government of James," says Macpherson, "there is great reason to believe that
the chief justice followed more the bent of his
own mind, than the commands of his sovereign,
in his behaviour in the west. The terrors of

others for Jeffreys's power prevented any impartial account to come to the ears of the King." Then comes Major Holmes's story.

Very different accounts are given by writers on the opposite side of the question. The first we give more for its curiosity, than for any use we desire to make of it.

" How can we choose but see, unless we have winkt ourselves blind, that the hand of the same Joab has been in all this? that 'twas the famous D. of Y. who was at first as deep in Godfrey's murther, as in the fire of London; the same who was at helm all along after, and as good as managed the executioners axes and halters for so many years ?"

" He who shew'd so much mercy to the poor west country men, women, and children, destroying so many hundreds in cold blood, and hardly sparing one man that cou'd write and read, by his chief hangman, Jeffreys."

Gilbert Burnet, bishop of Sarum.—" That which brought all his (Jeffreys's) excesses to be imputed to the King himself, and to the orders given by him, was, that the King had a particular account of his proceedings writ to him every day : and he took pleasure to relate them

in the drawing-room to foreign ministers, and
at his table, calling it Jefferies's campaign:
speaking of all he had done in a style that
neither became the majesty nor the merciful-
ness of a great prince. Dykfield was at that
time in England, one of the ambassadors whom
the States had sent over to congratulate the
King's coming to the crown. He told me, that
the King talked so often of these things in his
hearing, that he wondered to see him break out
into those indecencies."

*Jeffreys's declaration when Tutchin visited him
in the Tower.*—He said, that " his instructions
were much more severe than the execution of
them; and that, at his return, he was SNUBBED
AT COURT, for being too merciful."

*Jeffreys's declaration to Dr. Scot on his death-
bed.*—Scot told it to Lord Somers, Lord Somers
to Sir Joseph Jekyll, and the last to Onslow.
The divine was drawing the attention of the
dying man to the famous expedition, on which
Jeffreys thanked him, and said with some emo-
tion,—"Whatever I did then, I did by express
orders; and I have this further to say for myself, that I was not half bloody enough for him
who sent me thither."

What! desire a man who had been embruing

his hands in blood against the will and in violation of the honour of his sovereign, to come back
and take the seals of England, to become keeper
of his prince's conscience! yet so did James.
What is the meaning of giving one subject up
to another? And yet such an event happened—
for the King had GIVEN Pridaux to Jeffreys.
What shall we say, if we find the very fountain-
head of mercy dried up at the suit of a subject?
And yet we hear, that the King had promised
Jeffreys not to pardon the unhappy Lady Lisle.
Who went shares in the extorted bribes of which
those who could ransom were despoiled? The
Queen,—the maids of honour. There was an
act of amnesty which the royal apologists most
loudly applaud. Who were excepted out of
the indemnities? The poor Taunton children of
twelve years old, that their parents might enrich the coffers of the court favourites.

" We must rely upon great facts," said Parr,
whilst he was asserting that all history was obscure
in the detail. We are content to follow the advice
of that considerable scholar, and we have great
facts to adduce. The Duke of Monmouth came
before his uncle, and begged for mercy: the King
extorted a signed declaration from him of his
illegitimacy, and then left him to the insults of

the Queen, and to his fate. The duke rose from
his knees with the scorn which became a brave
man, and died under the axe. Here was no
chief justice, it was the pure act of the monarch,
who had decided upon death as his nephew's
portion. If it be said, in allusion to the sentiment in Euripides, that in defence of empire a
King may shed blood at his liking, let it be remembered, that the principal object intended,
is to remove from the memory of Jeffreys those
contaminations which have marked him as the
contriver of those dreadful scenes. Again, Mrs.
Gaunt, the good anabaptist, (or baptist,) a
woman of known beneficence, was burnt for concealing one Burton; and this happened in October, when the King had been of necessity acquainted with the past transactions, and had
been dealing out his threats and reproaches,
if we pay any credit to the Mss. Her judge
was Sir Thomas Jones, a person of a reputation
the very opposite to Jeffreys, yet she found no
mercy. Cornish followed, whose fate is said
to have been afterwards commiserated by the
monarch, his accusers being condemned to perpetual imprisonment; but these signs of kindness and repentance were hardly visible till the
kingdom was passing away, and the last hope

of safety was fast flitting with the tide of popular feeling.

The mercy shown the great peers is relied on as a proof of James's clemency. These noblemen were the Lords Grey, Stamford, and Brandon Gerrard.* The first played the part of treachery at Bridport, and at Sedgemoor fight; so that, when the Duke of Monmouth asked Colonel Matthews, after the former action, what he should do with the Lord Grey, the answer was: " That there was not a general in Europe that wou'd have asked such a question but himself." No wonder that a man was pardoned who had done such essential service to the King's forces under the disguise of a malecontent.

Stamford was imprisoned so long without a trial, that he petitioned the House for an inquiry into his conduct, and it was finally fixed for the first of the following December; but instead of sustaining the prosecution, his adversaries were content to have his name inserted in the general pardon, certainly because they had no evidence against him; and he was glad to avail himself of their vaunted clemency, being sensible how much a day might bring forth.

Lord Brandon, according to Echard, con-

* Lord Delamere was actually brought into jeopardy for his life, but acquitted.

trived to obtain a pardon by some means; and, considering that the archdeacon was not over favourable to rebels, it is little short of a clear proof that he came off, not from the compassionate bowels of the King, but by much the same manœuvre which saved Hampden,— that is, by a good round bribe. Jeffreys had 6000*l.* from the patriot as the price of his ransom; and yet, in the Stuart Papers, we find Hampden mentioned as a remarkable object of clemency; but North says, that his brother told the King of the game which was going on, and that it was instantly checked. Whether the wary old courtier had waited until the last minute, that is, until the country could not be burdened with more gibbets, we cannot pretend to say; but the facts are rather in opposition to any very successful opposition on the side of my lord keeper. Upwards of eighty were hung at Dorchester, one hundred and thirty-nine at Taunton, and one hundred at Wells. If the soft distilling dew of mercy had fallen so early, we should have had a converse ratio of the condemned and executed; less than eighty would have died in Somerset, in place of the numbers who suffered.

And with respect to Bristol, it was found impossible to " rear the bloody hand," in that

place, for the duke had left the city rich in all
her loyalty. If, therefore, my Lord Guilford
had represented the matter when very young,
it militates still more against His Majesty that
Jeffreys did not return in custody for such an
outrageous disobedience, the executions being
at once suspended: if it was mentioned late to
the ears of royalty, Roger North is hardly borne
out, in saying that "orders went to mitigate the
proceeding;" and his brother scarcely escapes a
suspicion of having connived at the great punishment. He says indeed, " What effect follow'd,
I know not. I am sure of his lordship's intercession to the King on this occasion, being
told it at the very time by himself." The most
that can be made of the whole proceeding is,
that the lord keeper, though at the point of
death, had discovered the sanguinary measures
which were going forward, and had advertised the
King, who knew better than himself what was
in hand; and that the monarch made a show of
wonderful mercy when some hundreds of his
most obnoxious subjects had been consigned to
the halter, and when Jeffreys had nothing left
but to say, as Monsieur Le Sage did afterwards, when Charles XII was killed at the
siege of Frederickshall,—" The game is up; let
us be going." And when we are told, that

R

James declared when his throne was in danger,
that "Jeffreys was an ill man," making a compensation at the same time to some person at Sarum; let it not be forgotten, that this King would
have sacrificed his favourite chancellor at that
time; first, because, being unpopular, he had no
further use for him; and next because he refused
to go all lengths in establishing popery. And
he actually did sacrifice the judge, for he stole
off privily at night without acquainting the unlucky chancellor, who fully counted upon going
with him, whereby he left the keeper of his conscience behind, soon to become a captive, and
at the mercy of an infuriated multitude. If he
could have exterminated the name of Protestant
from his dominions, and erected the triumphant
host in all his cathedrals, James had attained
his wish: the prince made but a mere tool of
his chief justice, who, hating dissenters, cut
them off joyfully with the august permission
which accompanied him; but seceded most in-
opportunely, when he found that the Catholic
religion was to reign "lord of the ascendant."
No sooner was it the policy of the court to conciliate the dissenters, dictated by that subtle
courtier William Penn,¹ than Sir Edward Her-

¹ King James was heard to say to some one, "William
Penn is no more a quaker than you are."

bert went down into the west, a meek, kind
judge, who healed all the wounds of the preceding year, issued forth the most ample promises
of pardon, and strove to unite the dissenters
against the church establishment. But long
disquisitions are odious; we have therefore determined to stop, merely chaining together the
few facts following,—

Which nobody can deny.

King James put Monmouth to death, and then
sent out his chief justice to punish some western
rebels. He refused to respite Lady Lisle for a
day, because he had promised the said judge that
he would not do so. Either he sent out an order
to save the prisoners after three hundred and fifty-
one had been hung,—or he made a judge, who
had disobeyed his orders, lord high chancellor of
England, tarnished as that person must have
been with a very massacre, if he had no orders
for his conduct. The King, moreover, made a
present of a rich man to the said judge, and
permitted the members of his court to enrich
themselves at the expense of some poor western
widows.

After the strong collateral confirmation which
has been supplied; the testimony of Burnet,
and the dying words of Jeffreys will bear a

stamp of authenticity which no kingly apologist can explain away.

From the London Gazette, Oct. 1, 1685.

Windsor, Sept. 28.

" His Majesty, taking into his royal considera- tion the many eminent and faithful services which the Right Honourable George, Lord Jef- freys, of Wem, lord chief justice of England, had rendered the crown, as well in the reign of the late King, of ever-blessed memory, as since His Majesty's accession to the throne, was pleased this day to commit to him the custody of the great seal of England, with the title of Lord Chancellor."

In December, John Hampden came to his trial, not before Jeffreys, according to the report in the State Trials, but Sir Edward Herbert, who had succeeded. The prisoner's petition for mercy was so abject, and his fee of 6000*l.* to the chancellor so softening, that he obtained his pardon; but, it is said, that shame haunted him ever afterwards, and in about ten years he cut his throat. About this time, also, Danger- field came to his end. He had been tried be- fore Jeffreys shortly after Oates's sentence, and had judgment to receive such terrible whippings,

that he chose a text for his funeral sermon.
But that which concerns Jeffreys in the affair
of his death, is the resolution which that nobleman persevered in to punish the author of it.
The truth seems to be, that Mr. Frances, a barrister of Gray's Inn, incontinently, and certainly
indecorously, accosted him after his flogging
with these words:—"How now, friend! have you
had your heat this morning?" Dangerfield spat
in his face : Frances then thrust a bamboo cane
into his eye, which, according to the evidence
of a surgeon, occasioned his death. There are
different representations of the whole business,
which became at length a popular affair : it is
said, in one place, that the wounded man died
directly; but Bevil Higgons tells us, that he
lived so long afterwards in Newgate, as to occasion a doubt among the surgeons who attended
the coroner's inquest, whether he did not die by
reason of his punishment. Attempts were made
to influence the widow of Dangerfield to consent that the prisoner should be pardoned; but
she refused, although the application was backed
by a bribe, and she even had an appeal ready.
She would have had occasion too to press her
appeal, had it not been for Jeffreys, there being
a strong disposition at court to overlook the

matter; but he posted to Whitehall as soon as
he learnt the chance of mercy, and declared
firmly that Frances "must die, for the rabble
was throughly heated." And so the poor "state
martyr was hanged." Yet with all this anxiety
on the part of Jeffreys to avenge Dangerfield
(the better opinion is, that Frances was a political martyr), the ghost of the whipped sufferer
arose, and poured forth a lamentation in print,
in which the judge, who sentenced the body to
be scourged, is not spared. It begins with

> Revenge ! revenge ! my injur'd shade begins
> To haunt thy guilty soul, and scourge thy sins.

A little further on, are these lines :—

> The trembling jury's verdict ought to be,—
> Murder'd at once by Frances and by thee.

There was also a long wild elegy published
upon Thomas Dangerfield, where Jeffreys is
dyed still blacker than the deepest plungings
mentioned in the Dunciad would make him. A
most unmerciful sentiment is contained in it :—

> But since nor friend nor poet can invent
> Deeper damnation for his punishment,
> May he be Jeffreys still, and *ne're repent.*

The Jews are held to be mild in comparison of the judge.

> Tho' milder Jews far more good nature have ;
> They forty stripes, Jeffreys four hundred gave.

Poisoning is then imputed to the chief justice :

> Two strings to 's bow, for fear one should not do ;
> Stellettos sometimes fail ; take poison too.

This reproach is ridiculous, for the body of Dangerfield might have appeared bloated after his punishment from the severity of the stripes.

The whip, so unfeelingly dealt, while it reflected great discredit upon the person who promoted its use, no less disgraced the monarch who could have arrested its terrors. There might soon have been a mandate a little more controlling than the poor solace which was sent to Tutchin, " that he must wait with patience ; " when, but for an acute disease, he had been whipped a morning or two afterwards.

The elegy concludes with such a mountain of curses as might weigh down the loftiest head ; but as they came probably from a near relation who must have written so fierce a declamation, there is some slight palliation of the matter.

Posterity will now admit, probably, that truth could hardly have shone forth amidst such a vapouring; and we hope, therefore, to gain a better evidence for any good qualities we may find in the vilified chancellor, whom we are about to introduce, fraught with purse and mace, in the next chapter.

CHAP. VII.

The great seal—Conduct of the lord chancellor in parliament—
Lord Delamere arraigned before the Lords Triers at West-
minster—Ecclesiastical high commission court—Dr. Sharp—
Compton, bishop of London—The chancellor's cause-room—
Anecdotes of the lord chancellor—Account of Sir John Trevor—
Doctrine of passive obedience—Trial of the seven bishops—
James throws off the mask with regard to his religion—Dr.
Peachell—University refractoriness—Determined conduct of
the mayor of Arundel—Duke of Ormond—The royal dispen-
sing power—Domestic life of the lord chancellor—Scandalous
stories of his second lady — Evelyn—Lord Clarendon—Mr.
Jeffreys's father—Sir John Trevor, speaker of the House of
Commons—Anecdote of Tillotson—Lord Castlemaine's mission
to Rome—Father Petre—Earl of Tyrconnel—Acquittal of the
bishops—Birth of the Pretender—Privy-counsellors present—
Legal character of the lord chancellor discussed—Sir Basil
Firebrass—Gathering of the political storm—Religious contest
—The city charter—How far Lord Chancellor Jeffreys is personally involved in the national and civic dissensions—Landing
of William III.—The court of James in confusion.

"HERE, my lord, take it, you will find it
heavy," said the prophetic King Charles to his
lord keeper North, when he delivered the seal
to that statesman. And Roger North relates a
confession made by his brother when dying,
which was, that "he had not enjoy'd one easy

and contented minute since he had had the seal."
Jeffreys was enjoying himself over his bottle with
some friends soon after his new preferment,
when one of them told him that he would find
the business heavy. " No," said he, " I'll
make it light." What would my lord of Eldon
give if he could as unconcernedly throw into
the balance his huge tribunal of bankruptcy,
his cabinet and parliamentary toils, with the
superincumbent weight of equity jurisdiction,
dragging its slow length along?

So strongly was the charge of corruption entertained against the new chancellor, Lord Jeffreys, that his unwillingness to take office has
been absolutely asserted; and, farther, that a
bribe was necessary to induce the relinquish-
ment of his scruples. Perhaps this is saying
too much; but, whether chief justice, or chief
judge in the Chancery, his promotion was so
much feared and disliked by the community
at large, that no difficulty was made of propa-
gating any insidious stories to his disadvantage.
And now we find him fairly seated in the great
chair, quite resolved to be " top fiddler of the
town." It was by no means the scope of his
ambition merely to vindicate his court from Lord
Coke's imputation, who called it, *Officina jus-*
titiæ, a workshop to frame writs in; Jeffreys

had been a discontented man, if, in his own
estimation, he could not have controlled the
common, statute, and equity law by a single
effort. *Boni judicis est ampliare jurisdictionem,*[1]
was an old maxim, which was destined to come
into fresh remembrance upon this event: so
that, even in matters within their own province,
the judges of the common law courts ceased to
receive the courtesy and decorum which were
due to their stations. Sir Thomas Jones, then
chief justice of the Common Pleas, soon felt the
power which was above him.[2] Sometimes a
chancellor will direct an issue to be tried in a
court of law that he may have the verdict of
twelve men as to some particular fact, and this
is called a feigned issue. A case of this kind
came to be heard at the bar of the Common
Pleas, on which the plaintiff obtained a verdict
with the approbation of Sir Thomas, the chief
justice, and of the whole court. The defendant
asked for a new trial, saying, that some of the
jury had been tampered with; but his suggestion
failed to meet with the countenance which he
desired, and his motion was therefore unani-

[1] It is the part of a skilful judge to enlarge his jurisdiction.
[2] Jones had obtained this place in defiance of Jeffreys who
coveted it, as one of more profit than the chief place in the
King's Bench.

mously refused, as being made merely for the
purpose of delay. It was a matter of some consequence, and the defendant was not so easily
persuaded to remain quiet. He accordingly
ventured into Chancery to ask for the same
thing, and on the same grounds, where he gained
a very different reception, for he had his motion
granted presently, and a new trial was " roundly
ordered." Yet this proceeding, which, if suffered
on the sudden, was at best a little disrespectful
to the other court, was intolerably seasoned
with sallies of wit against the learned persons
who had delivered the judgment, so that there
was a plain design to mortify them. With a
due degree of deference to the high authorities
from whom he might dissent, a chancellor of this
day might arrive at a similar conclusion, and in
so doing, he would not transgress the practice of
his court; but the keeper of King James's seals,
steering quite clear of all common civility, was
pleased to indulge in the most free personalities,
and never hesitated to accuse his brethren of
carelessness in the distribution of justice. But
the admirable part of the affair was its issue;
for when the defendant came to his second
hearing, the plaintiff got a great accession of
damages from the new jury.

The conduct of this magistrate of equity shall

now be laid aside for a time, whilst we give some
account of him upon other occasions. And first
with regard to his carriage in the House of Lords.
No doubt he imagined that the august assembly
would bow down before him, and that he might
soon overawe his co-peers by his bluff figure and
well-appointed swagger. He had an opportunity of making the experiment before he had
held the seals two months. The King had addressed his parliament in very courteous terms;
but in the course of the speech two very awkward propositions were developed: one was,
that the militia were not sufficient, and thence
came the dilemma of a standing army. The
next was, an admission that some of his
officers had not conformed themselves to the
tests, and that he would not deprive himself of
their services on that account, after the efforts
they had made on his behalf: whence the dispensing power might easily be detected in its
most odious forms. Both Houses were alarmed
at this avowal; but they rendered back their
thanks to His Majesty: the Lords *in totidem ver-
bis*, the Commons with a proposition to indem-
nify the popish recusants, (most unsavoury words
for the ear of royalty,) and a modified grant.
James was warm in his answer; upon which
both Lords and Commons proposed to take the

King's speech into consideration. The latter,
however, were terrified into an adjournment:
for Coke (of Derby) was sent to the Tower for
saying, "I hope we are all Englishmen, and
not to be frighted out of our duty by a few high
words." He was the seconder of the motion.
But the thing took a very different turn in the
Lords. Compton, bishop of London, introduced
the subject there; and the courtiers forthwith
took the alarm, saying, that as the House had
thanked the King for his speech, the sentiments
contained therein had been adopted as of
course. This ingenious snare was soon laid open
and rejected; and the test was manfully com-
mented upon as the bulwark of liberty. And
then came on my Lord Jeffreys. He answered
the popular speakers as though he had been addressing an obstinate jury, or menacing a ter-
magant prisoner; a carriage so entirely out of
place, that all his frowns and arrogance were
unable to beat down the uncompromising argument which the other side had made use of: and
so, out-voted and " out-argued," as Ralph has
it, the minister gave way, and a day was fixed
for investigating the subject. But it was to the
infinite mortification of Jeffreys that such a crisis
happened; and Burnet delights in recounting
the defeat which he endured. Soon afterwards,

the parliament was prorogued; and as the great
seal was thrown into the Thames before the
meeting of another, the chancellor had no room
for improving himself in the tact and method of
senatorial eloquence.* But this smart rebuff seems
to have had some slight effect upon him; for being
appointed to preside at the trial of a peer for
treason, he managed, though still very tenacious
of authority, and intoxicated with his power, to
deport himself before the assembled lords with
a decency quite remarkable: yet, it was evident,
that after this the peers regarded him with
jealousy, and mainly suspected that he took "his
law from the King," according to his motto, as
serjeant.ª

   Although the western circuit had been pretty
thoroughly travelled, there remained some men
of noble blood in the Tower charged with the
late transactions, reserved, as it were, to grace
the greater triumph, by ransom, or by death.
The escape of these lords has been already explained; but as Lord Delamere stood his trial,
the manner and method of it must have some

* His civility may be compared to that of a bailiff towards
a man of rank under his arrest, such bailiff having been
lately kicked for insolence upon a similar event.

   ª John Jeffreys, probably his son, was member for Brecon
Town, in this parliament.

mention here, as they involve some strange
actions of Lord Jeffreys, white staff upon the
occasion.

It had very early suggested itself to the
favourite, that if he could cause the noble prisoner to be conveyed into Cheshire, he would
have him most conveniently within the sphere
of his local influence. The main accusation
rested on a proposal for a rising in that county;
so that by the course intended, a conviction
might be quietly obtained in the very territory
of the accused, to the sore mortification of his
high blood. Besides this, the people would be
awed, the trial by peers averted, and the influence of Jeffreys in the neighbourhood would
have done the rest. Indeed, some disrespect
which had been shown him when chief justice
of Chester, might now be amply avenged—a gratifying crisis not to be sacrificed without an
effort: therefore it was boldly declared, that
the treason having happened within a County
Palatine, the prosecution must be there. This
was said by Jeffreys under the King's command
to the assembled peers, who were indignant that
the Lord Delamere should be absent, and had
addressed the King upon the subject. The bill
of indictment was then presented and found in
Cheshire, and so far the plan had succeeded;

for had the prisoner been tried in the King's
Bench, which it is but fair to say would have
amounted to a breach of privilege, Sir Edward
Herbert, a more mild judge,[1] would probably
have marred the prosecution, by conceding every
indulgence, and ratifying every excuse consistent with the law. But it was soon determined
to remove all the proceedings by *certiorari* before a select body of lords at Westminster,
called Lords Triers.[2] Jeffreys, the lord high
steward, was somewhat out of his element; for
he now no longer addressed " mean men," but
spoke in the presence of the first men in his
country, who very little regarded his newly-
fledged nobility, and would utterly scorn any
menace if he dared employ any. The King and
Queen, moreover, graced the solemn occasion,
an unusual degree of polish and courtesy was
therefore observable in the judge's deportment
towards the whole court : yet, in the course of his
first speech to the accused, he could not help
thinking how comfortably he would be spared

[1] Yet this Herbert was the man who first proposed to dispense with the tests. He had urged the matter to King
Charles, who was too shrewd to give any encouragement to
such a dethroning fantasy.

[2] This selection is abolished by 7 Will. III., so that
a nobleman must now be tried by all his peers.

any further pains, if a plea of guilty could be obtained; and to this end, with a very crafty insinuation of mercy, he begged of my lord at the bar, that if he were guilty, "he would give glory to God, and make amends to his vicegerent, the King, by a plain and full discovery." But Lord Delamere was engaged upon any other subject rather than a confession, and indeed, what seemed to trouble him the most just then, was whether a peer was bound to hold up his hand at the bar like a commoner, but this was resolved to his satisfaction: and then he asked another question, which he doubtless considered mainly important:—"I beg your Grace would be pleased to satisfy me, whether your Grace be one of my judges in concurrence with the rest of the lords?"

Lord High Steward.—No, my lord, I am judge of the court; but I am none of your triers.

The song of the siren could not have enchanted the ears of her captives more deliciously. Some delay then arose before the prisoner would plead, and at length he put in a special plea which contained two objections to the course then pursued: first, he said, that being summoned to parliament, he ought to be tried by all the peers of parliament; and, secondly, he claimed this privilege still more strongly, because the parliament was still con-

tinuing, and not dissolved. Sir Robert Sawyer, the attorney-general, answered the difficulties which were started, on which Lord Delamere prayed the aid of counsel; but not having
any ready, the plea was rejected: although, in
the case of Edward Fitzharris, four days were
allowed that prisoner to procure and instruct
advocates. Jeffreys's temper was rising once.

Lord Delamere. "I hope your Grace will be
pleased to advise with my lords the peers here
present."—Lord High Steward. "Good my
lord, I hope you that are a prisoner at the bar
are not to give me direction who I should advise
with, or how I should demean myself here." On
which an apology was made him. He was ne
vertheless somewhat confounded in his new
state, and had a little committed himself, for he
let slip that he thought the plea frivolous.

Lord Delamere saw the blunder at once. "I
hope, my lord, that the privilege of the peers
of England is not frivolous."—"Pray, good my
lord," returned the disconcerted judge, "do not
think I should say any such thing, that the privilege of the peers is frivolous." He then gave
his charge to the peers in a very fulsome harangue; in the course of which the expressions
" fierce, froward, and fanatical zeal of the late
House of Commons," "Arch-traitor Monmouth,"

" hellish and damnable plots," could not fail to
have pleased the royal auditors. The chief
evidence for the crown was a man who swore
that he was introduced to Lord Delamere and
two others, with a recommendation from Lord
Brandon, and that he received money from
them. This reward was for carrying a message
to the Duke of Monmouth, respecting a sum of
40,000*l.* which was wanted to maintain ten
thousand men, to be levied in Cheshire against
King James. But however this may have been,
he made a decided blunder in the date, which
gave Lord Delamere an opportunity of calling
witnesses to prove an alibi.

This was done most satisfactorily, and the
peers gave an unanimous verdict of acquittal.
They evinced, however, a strong dislike to the
control of the lord high steward, who, on his
part, was equally obstinate in insisting upon his
own supposed rights. The accused desired an
adjournment, that he might have time to prepare his defence: the matter was referred to
the judges, but some lords were determined that
the court should withdraw to debate the question amongst themselves, alleging that their
privileges were concerned, though Jeffreys denied that privilege was in any way at issue:
and they withdrew accordingly. The judges

were against the adjournment, and the lord
high steward then chose to discourse of his own
power :—

"My lords, I confess I would always be very
tender of the privilege of the peers wherever I
find them concerned; but truly I apprehend,
according to the best of my understanding, that
this court is held before me: it is my warrant
that convenes the prisoner to this bar: it is
my summons that brings the peers together to
try him; and so I take myself to be judge of the
court. My lords, 'tis true, may withdraw, and
they may call the judges to them to assist them,
which shows they have an extraordinary privilege in some cases more before the high steward,
than juries have in inferior courts in cases of
common persons." He then went on to say,
that he could not withdraw with the lords if
they desired to consult him, but that all questions must be asked of him in open court. "This,
I confess, my lords," added my lord high steward, " has a great weight with me ; and I know
your lordships will be very tender of proceeding
in such a case, any way but according to law:
for though you are judges of your own privileges, yet, with submission, you are not judges
of the law of this court; for that I take to be my
province." He ended with a wonderfully clement speech.

"Certainly, my lords, your lordships and I, and all mankind, ought to be tender of committing any errors in cases of life or death; and I would be loth, I would assure you, to be recorded for giving an erroneous judgment in a case of blood; and as the first man that should bring in an illegal precedent, the consequence of which may extend I know not how far." However, with all this fair language, the old heresy was broached again, that the testimony of one witness to an overt act of treason, corroborated by other substantial circumstances, was sufficient proof of a treason. And this opinion was mentioned in the House of Commons some years afterwards, upon the bill for attainting Sir John Fenwick. "It was told him [Jeffreys] then," said a member, "that if ever they met him in the House of Lords, he should answer it with his head."

James was exceedingly exasperated against the poor witness: the day after the trial he declared that Saxon should be first convicted of perjury, and then hanged for high-treason. This last threat was not put into execution; but the man was twice pilloried, twice whipped, and fined besides for his mistake.[1]

[1] According to the Stuart Papers, it seems that the court really believed Saxon's story, and that his discomfiture arose from a mere slip in the date.

This was the despotic treatment which the
new monarch loved : his minister was one whom
"he delighted to honour," because he was content to take his cue so obediently from the court;
and all things were now arranged so as to promise the English a speedy change from freedom
and liberty of conscience to the papal and any
other obnoxious yoke which it might please the
Sovereign to impose.

The pulpits were now teeming with discourses against popery, for the nation had become seriously alarmed at the King's determined
inclinations; and the clergy already fancied
that other hands would soon shear the fleeces
of their flocks, while they themselves would be
compelled to own a divided allegiance. The King
was not backward to perceive, on his part, the
rising temper of the times : he had not forgotten
the flaming preachments of the forty-one, nor the
stern hum of the Cromwellians, nor the sacred
hurricanoes of the covenanters. So there went
forth letters mandatory to the bishops, forbid-
ding their clergy to attempt controversial dis-
cussions in public; and having promulged the
order, James decided also on prescribing the
punishment of disobedience.

The ecclesiastical high commission court, a
name lost to the British annals since the reign of

Charles the First, was erected, and seven commissioners [1] were appointed to superintend and
enforce its powers. The crown expected that
some severe animadversion would be passed
upon this new creation, and an answer was
therefore at hand. It was said, that in the new
commission no power was given to fine or im-
prison or tender the oath *ex-officio,* [2] and that
its judges were enjoined to keep within the
bounds of ecclesiastical censures; that the ordinary power of the archbishops and bishops had
been revived at the Restoration, although the
high commission court of Charles, which permitted fine and imprisonment, and the tender-
ing the oath *ex-officio,* was indeed abolished;
that this was therefore a legal constitution, even
more so than Doctors' Commons and the bishops'
courts, where the proceedings would run in

---

[1] George, Lord Jeffreys, lord chancellor; Sancroft, archbishop of Canterbury; Crew, bishop of Durham; Sprat,
bishop of Rochester; Chief Justice Herbert; Lawrence
Hyde, Earl of Rochester, lord treasurer; Robert, Earl of
Sunderland, lord president. The following were afterwards
added: the Earl of Mulgrave; Cartwright, bishop of Chester,
in the room of Sancroft, who declined to act; Chief Justice
Wright; Sir Thomas Jenner.

[2] A perfect inquisition, by which they compelled a man to
swear that he would answer all questions put to him. In
default of obedience, he might have been tortured.

the names of the episcopal judges, whereas this mandate ran in the King's name. Most people were obstinate enough, however, to think, that the law had been invaded upon this occasion ; but in a country where four judges had been turned out at once (a circumstance just then of recent occurrence) for questioning the royal competency of dispensing with the laws; and where again, a great verdict had just been obtained by a defendant,[1] whose defence was that the monarch could waive a penal enactment, as supreme lawgiver; it was not to be expected that public opinion would be regarded with any very particular respect. Amongst other capabilities with which these great commissioners were invested, they were enabled to summon such as " seemed to be suspected of offences ;—to correct, amend, and alter the statutes of the universities, churches, and schools; or, where the statutes were lost, to devise new ones," &c. It was no small aggravation of the horrors which the clergy had already attached to this junto, that it could not assemble without the lord chancellor. Jeffreys, consequently, with all his grandeur and majesty, was the awful genius of the place. Nor

[1] Sir Edward Hales, prosecuted in an action of debt by a coachman, for not taking the test.

did he long remain unemployed; and very plea-
sant it seemed to him, that he was again so
highly elevated as to mortify great dignitaries
at his capricious pleasure. Sharp, the rector
of St. Giles's, who is called the " railing parson,"[1] had expressed his contempt of such as
could be converted by Romish arguments. He
was constantly inveighing against popish errors;
and Compton, bishop of London, who had so
obnoxiously moved the consideration of the
royal speech, was his diocesan. These were
fit subjects to begin upon. The King sent
forth a mandate to the bishop to suspend
Dr. Sharp; the bishop very civilly declined,
on the ground of his inability to condemn
any man who had not been cited, and heard in
his defence. This happened in August, 1686;
and the high court had been formed in April.
It was deemed proper that the new terrors and
penalties should be inflicted upon these two
holy offenders, though Sharp had been the
bearer of the bishop's letter, and had made an
effort to save himself by very tame submissions.
Accordingly, on the 4th of August, the lord
chancellor was at his place in the Commission
Court, and the bishop made his appearance.

---

[1] Father Orleans.

There was but one question, " Why did you not obey the King?" But Compton was disposed to procrastinate, and so he asked for time till November, as counsel were absent on the circuit. " Hah! that's unreasonable," quoth Jeffreys; " His Majesty's business cannot admit of such delays; methinks a week should be enough: What say your lordships, is not a week enough?" And their lordships said that a week was enough. The bishop complained that he could not get a sight of the commission; but the answer was, that " all the coffee-houses had it for a penny a piece." On the ninth day, the business was resumed, when the bishop declared, that a whole week's search had, with difficulty, put him in possession of the authority which had been mentioned as so common in every coffee-house. " My lord, when I told you our commission was to be seen in every coffee-house," says my lord chancellor, " I did not speak with any design to reflect on your lordship, as if you were a haunter of coffee-houses: I abhorred the thoughts of it; and intended no more by it, but that it was common in the town."

This vaunt of the chancellor's got the bishop a fortnight's further indulgence. But, at length, the day must arrive for an answer to " Why did you not obey the King?" And at the ap-

pointed time the spiritual peer came, attended
by four doctors of the law as his counsel. But
the civilians made a very left-handed defence
for their client : indeed, the first, Dr. Oldish, ventured beyond the precincts of his scarlet tribe,
and was rash enough to affirm, that "if an attorney takes a man's word for his appearance, there
would lie no action against the attorney."—
"*Cujus contrarium,*" (which means, only just the
contrary,) exclaimed Jeffreys, who was pleased
to advertise the doctor of the existence of actions for escapes. Some of the commissioners
were disposed to accept the bishop's submission,
but the King plainly told Rochester, that unless
he gave way, his treasurer's white staff was
gone. Most of the others would have agreed
upon the question being put, that the bishop
had done treason, if the King pleased ; and he
was forthwith suspended by a formal and solemn
sentence, together with his subject rector, Dr.
Sharp, both during the royal pleasure. They
dared not meddle with his revenues, notwithstanding ; for that being a measure affecting tem-
poralities, the matter would have been translated into the King's Bench, where Herbert
presided ; and as he was not satisfied with the
sentence of suspension, he might probably have
rendered the bishop justice, which at that time

would have been a precedent highly inconvenient.

The parson of St. Giles's was soon relieved, but the prelate remained under the ban till the fright about the Prince of Orange became very considerable, and then all the great rough riders were unhorsed: Jeffreys was sent to the corporation of London with their long-lost charter, and the people of London saw their bishop very civilly restored to his episcopal functions.

The chancellor showed himself quite equal to Serjeant Bradshaw, who presided at King Charles's trial. Both the accused desired to speak, the bishop before, the monarch after sentence; both were repulsed most unceremoniously:—

Lord Bishop.—My lord, may I have leave to speak before sentence is read?

Lord Chancellor.—My lord, we have heard you and your counsel already.

King Charles to Bradshaw.—Will you hear me a word, sir?

Bradshaw.—Sir, you are not to be heard after the sentence.

King.—No, sir?

Bradshaw.—No, sir. By your favour, sir. Guard, withdraw your prisoner.

King.—I may speak after sentence, by your

favour, sir! I may speak after sentence, ever.
By your favour!—Hold! the sentence, sir: I say,
sir, I do—I am not suffered to speak.—Expect
what justice other people will have.—And then
he was carried away by the guard.

And now, not as suitors, but as admiring
reporters of the greatness and dominion of our
Jeffreys, we must return to the court of Chancery, from whence so many think themselves too
happy to be emancipated.

He held his court at Dr. Shepherd's Chapel
in Duke-street, Westminster, and made the adjoining houses towards the park his residence.
But just before we relate the judicial extrava-
gancies of this legal despot, it will not be thought
out of place, as we are upon the subject of
houses, if a specimen of his dealings respecting
them, and of the treatment with which he would
annoy persons who had an equitable claim upon
him, be briefly told. Moses Pitt, a bookseller,
brother of the Western Martyrologist, complains
very strongly against his tenant, the chancellor.
This gentleman had been captivated by the
boundless promises of building; and amongst
other dwellings which he established in the vi-
cinity of the Park, was one at the south end of
Duke-street of a superior order, which he let,
with coach-houses and stables, to the judge at
300l. per annum. Jeffreys came with the rich

Alderman Duncomb to see the house; and observing a vacant piece of ground adjoining, he
said, he would have a cause-room (by which he
meant a chancery tribunal) built upon it.[1] Pitt
said, that the ground was the King's property;
but it was agreed that James should be importuned for the gift of it, and that it should be
made over to the builder by grant for 99 years
at a peppercorn rent, in consideration of which
the builder would erect the desired cause-room.
It seems, that in addition to the court which was
required, Mr. Pitt raised two large wings on
either side of the chancellor's house, which cost
him altogether about 4000*l.* and that his tenant
never paid a farthing for the fitting-up of the
new erections, and the necessary offices which
appertained to the cause-room.[2]

[1] " It is easily known," says Pennant, " by a large flight
of stone steps, which his royal master permitted to be made
into the park adjacent, for the accommodation of his lordship.
These steps terminate above in a small court, on three sides
of which stands the house. The cause-room was afterwards
converted into a place of worship, called Duke-street Chapel,
and is on the left. When Jeffreys found it inconvenient to
go to Westminster or Lincolns'-inn, he made use of this court."

[2] " In three or four months' time I built the two wings of
that great house which is opposite to the bird-cages, with the
stairs and tarrass, &c. which said building cost me about
4000*l.* with all the inside work," &c.—Pitt's *Cry of the
Oppressed,* p. 22.

However, when the whole was finished, the
promised grant was looked for very anxiously,
and very respectfully demanded ; but Jeffreys
found means of evading the fulfilment of his
pledge from time to time till the architect's patience was exhausted, and King William had
approached too near to render the chancellor's
downfall by any means equivocal. Finding his
ruin at hand, and a speedy flight necessary, he
sent for several tradesmen ; and Mr. Pitt, the
landlord, who had ever found him quite inac-
cessible, although a near neighbour, contrived
to get into the great man's parlour, and there
renewed personally his long neglected claim.
" I shall leave your house," quoth Jeffreys,
" and I shall not take away the ground and
building with me." This was the utmost indulgence of the answer. Half a year's rent was
then nearly due, but Pitt expressed himself
much more anxiously respecting the grant, than
the payment of the arrears. The next day the
chancellor departed to the Jesuit Petre's lodging at Whitehall.' It turned out, that Sir Edward Hales, a vast favourite at court, the same
who gained so great a triumph in behalf of

' 1688, Nov. 29. " In the morning, I went to see my
lord chancellor : he now lodgeth at the duke's old little
chamber at Whitehall."—*Clarendon's Diary.*

the dispensing power, had begged away this ground from Jeffreys; so that the judge, perceiving how impossible it was to complete his contract, shuffled out of it in the best manner he was able.[1] The learned counsel who attend the high court of Chancery at the present day,

[1] The history of the case was this: Pitt, when he received this promise from Jeffreys, discovered that John Webb, the King's fowl-keeper, had a grant of the land from Charles II. during life; and thereupon gave him a consideration for a great part of it. Then Sir Edward Hales got it from the King, which overturned the chancellor's pledge; and though Sir Edward seems to have paid half a year's rent to Mr. Pitt for a parcel of this land, which was used as garden-ground, he, in common with some others who had recognised Pitt as the landlord, refused all subsequent payments. This unfortunate architect and bookseller, after having spent 12,000*l.* in the improvement of buildings at Westminster, was thrown into prison, where he remained long enough to be sensible of the dreadful enormities which were perpetrated on the persons of poor debtors at that period,—See his *Cry of the Oppressed,* in two parts. He was a man of considerable enterprise, as may be collected from the statement already given; and moreover, he took the theatre at Oxford for the purpose of printing his Atlas, in twelve volumes, folio: an undertaking which was fraught with ruin. Jeffreys's large house was let to the three Dutch ambassadors, who came from Holland to congratulate King William upon his accession in 1689. It was afterwards used for the admiralty-office, until the middle of King William's reign.

T

who rather give than take the law from the considerable individuals who preside there, can scarcely form an idea of the disrespect with which their quondam brethren were treated in the reign of James. We have seen how Jeffreys, when chief of the King's Bench, disregarded their just pretensions to a courteous reception; how he set at naught their high blood and birth, and held as valueless the honourable stock from whence the larger number sprang. And truly no greater share of civility was reserved for the advocates in equity: the furious lecture of a quarter or half an hour, proportioned to the offence of the patient, was of daily occurrence. There was no room for boasting on the part of those whom he occasionally spared.—" This is yours," they would drily say; " my turn will be to-morrow." [1] His angry opposition, however, to one custom would probably be lauded by the public press of this day. Six, eight, or ten of the best counsel would be retained on a side, and of course each would indulge the court with a view of the case. This, doubtless, was a tire-

---

[1] Sir John Trevor, the master of the rolls, treated the counsel with equal freedom. He said something to his nephew, a very promising young lawyer, which cut him so severely, that he died in consequence.

some practice, and called for the most trying patience; but the new chancellor soon decided against it. " It was troublesome—it was impertinent—he could not bear it—it was all repetition; and, therefore, he would not hear it."[1] Yet in the progress of these sallies, he sometimes broke loose so wildly as to be obliged to beg pardon, which he would do to the great satisfaction and amusement of the audience. But if the ornaments of the court met with this unsightly violation, what might not the unfortunate attornies expect? What might be the situation of the still less respected suitor? Here Jeffreys was indeed himself; and often verified his own observation, that he would " give a lick with the rough side of his tongue."

A city attorney had a petition filed against him; and whether or not he had done wrong, it appears that some one had threatened him with my lord chancellor; an admirable bugbear beyond question at that time of day. " My

---

[1] In the new act of parliament which has been propounded for the amendment of the Chancery practice, a proposition has been introduced to limit the number of counsel on either side. The evil alluded to rarely occurs in the King's Bench; and in the court of Common Pleas only two serjeants are accustomed to address the bench.

lord chancellor!" returned the citizen; "I *made*
him." This very natural vaunt was put carefully into an affidavit, and read over to the judge.
"Well," says that nobleman, "then I will lay
my maker by the heels." And the patron of
the young Hicks's-hall pennyless advocate was
sent to gaol. Another very sharp decision
against a solicitor is recorded. The lawyer was
ordered to give up certain papers in a cause,
some of which had got into the hands of his
client, and, in fact, were quite out of his reach;
but, finding that the master in Chancery had reported him for disobedience, he made an application to the court, stating the hardship, and
his readiness to do any thing that could be rea-
sonably required of him. This was, nevertheless, a trifling with the high order, and the
unlucky solicitor found his way to the Fleet.
But half an hour afterwards the chancellor
called the registrar, and bade him inform the
master that some arrangement must be made
for the performance of the order, and that the
master should exercise his discretion. On this
the counsel for the prisoner took courage; and
after several wily insinuations for his client,
such as that the end of the motion for papers
had been obtained, and that the solicitor had

acted as well as he could under the circumstances, he begged that the rule for the commitment might be rescinded. Jeffreys. " Sir, I make no new order: I only add to what I have already pronounced." And the man remained in custody. Instances have been remembered of his placing even counsel themselves in the safe guardianship of the Fleet prison, and this, for errors in judgment; whilst he sent men, women, and children promiscuously to the warden, in a proportion of ten to one as compared with the commitments of his predecessors.

His bare threats, however, were no small punishments; at least in this nervous age we should be apt to think so: and although the great judge made a common practice of uttering them, it is agreed that his countenance betokened most fearfully the likelihood of their execution. A poor scrivener felt this awful influence, when he opposed a petition for relief against a bail bond. The plaintiff's bill was about to be dismissed, and the scrivener would have gone off triumphant; but one of the counsel against him very waggishly said, that this man was a strange fellow, sometimes going to church, sometimes to conventicles; in fact, " it was thought he was a trimmer." Jeffreys's old re-

collections revived in a moment. "A trimmer?"
said he; "I have heard much of that monster,
but never saw one.   Come forth, Mr. Trimmer;
turn you round, and let us see your shape."
The defendant was frightened out of his senses;
and lucky it was for him when the bill against
him was dismissed with costs, so that he could go
his way from the court.   " How did you come
off?" said a friend of his, as he came into the
hall. " Come off! I am escaped from the terrors
of that man's face, which I would scarce undergo
again to save my life; and I shall certainly have
the frightful impression of it as long as I live."
The sequel of the history will show how true
this saying was, and how fatal this tirade had
been to the chancellor's welfare.   It cost him
his life.

Sir John Trevor had now succeeded Sir John
Churchill as master of the rolls: he had been
fostered by Jeffreys, and owed his elevation to
that powerful favourite; but far from bending to
the will of his patron with the abject submission
which was expected, he was bold enough to turn
again when trampled upon, and had even the
hardihood to look with an ambitious eye towards
the great seal. Strange to say, he had some
chance of supplanting his master; but as he is

connected, in some measure, with the chancellor's private life at this time, a more full account of him, and of the disputes which he maintained in defence of his jurisdiction, shall be deferred, till we come presently to detail the little that can now be ascertained of the judge's domestic history.

In 1687, Jeffreys had another opportunity of indulging his master's spleen against the church, and of upholding the dispensing power which was the darling aim of his sovereign. To attain this end he had laboured extremely in the previous year; indeed, the monarch himself has informed us of the zeal with which his chancellor acted, how he summoned the judges, and enforced the doctrine of passive obedience as part of the English law, till all the twelve, saving one,[1] declared themselves converts to his argu-

[1] Sir Thomas Street, judge of the Common Pleas. He was first made a baron of the Exchequer, and thence advanced to the Common bench. Lord Clarendon attempted to patronize this judge at the Revolution, and intended to have presented him to the prince; but meeting with Lord Coote, he was dissuaded from doing so. "While I was in the outward room," says the noble journalist, "my Lord Coote came to me, and told me he was sorry to see me patronize Street. I told his lordship I had long known the judge, and that I took him to be a very honest man. My lord answered to this effect:—I know he did not join in the

ments, or, which was more probable, bowed
before an influence which could presently strip
off their ermine.'

Devoted to the Catholic tenets, James now

judgment for the dispensing power: he has married my relation; but he is a very ill man. I have given the prince a
true character of him," &c. When Street came the next
day to Lord Clarendon, he was told that the prince had ill
impressions of him, and was advised to wait a little; which
he did long enough, as far as related to the restoration of his
place, for he was never made a judge again.

' It should be kept in mind, that in delineating the extraordinary character of Jeffreys, we say decidedly that he would
go *nearly* all lengths for the sake of his place; but that he would
never desert his religion, though, under the apprehension of
disgrace, he certainly persecuted its functionaries upon occasion. In the course of an inquiry which took place before the
House of Commons in 1689, this power of stripping off the
ermine was most strictly proved in the cases of Baron Nevil
and Judge Powell. The speaker asked the reasons of their
discharge. Nevil said, he was sent for to Chiffins's
chambers, when the King came in with a paper in his hand,
and asked his opinion upon the dispensation. The baron
said, he thought the King could not dispense with the
penal laws, but that he would consider of it. Jeffreys then
took up the affair, and sent for the judge several times; but
received a positive declaration from him against the King's
wishes. Street and Holloway were with Nevil at different
times upon the subject; and notwithstanding the chancellor's
long harangues, and disapproval of the reasons, they maintained the same resolution. When Judge Holloway con-

resolved to bear the mask no longer; the pre-
cepts of his mother church swayed him with an

curred, it was in the presence of the King, Jeffreys, Sunderland, Rochester, and Godolphin. The chancellor at length
sent for Baron Nevil to his house, and said, that if he persisted, he must expect to be discharged; and seven or eight
days after he had his quietus. To a subsequent question,
the baron replied, that the chancellor managed the whole
thing. Sir John Powell thought he was turned out for his
opposition to the dispensing power, and an opinion against
the crown in the case of a *quo warranto.* He said, that
Jeffreys was present at the consideration of these decisions
in private, and took an active part in bringing the judges
over to the royal will. But Powell was inexorable; and he
had the honour of being acquainted with his discharge in the
first instance by the chancellor, who told him, at his house,
that he was sorry for it, but would not send the patent of
revocation till the end of the term.—" And I sat out the
whole term," added Powell.

Sir Edward Nevil seems to have been a very honest judge :
he contrived to escape in those days with very little observation, and was rewarded with his old place in the Exchequer
when King William returned. He was afterwards promoted to the bench in the Common Pleas, and died in 1705,
at Hammersmith, August 8.

We have had three judges named Powell, and they were
contemporaries. The first was the gentleman alluded to
above; a man of considerable abilities and integrity. He
once laid a blame on a brother judge (Holloway), which
the latter denied, and retorted the charge upon Powell. It was
upon the much worn subject of the dispensing power. Powell
said he was at some distance from his brother, and thought

absolute dominion, and these prompted him to
bring back his backsliding subjects to the pure

that he assented to the King's demand; Holloway, on the
contrary, asserted that he had never agreed to such an opinion, and he is certainly acquitted of this by the testimony
of others.

Powell was in disgrace for the resolution he displayed at
the trial of the seven bishops, where he zealously and successfully strove in their favour. The following curious interference is related to have taken place on the bench on
that occasion. The Solicitor-general Williams was advert-
ing to the dispensation, upon which Powell spoke aside to the
chief justice,—" My lord, this is wide, Mr. Solicitor would
impose upon us : let him make it out, if he can, that the King
has such a power; and answer the objections made by the
defendant's counsel."

Wright, chief justice—" Brother, impose upon us ? He
shall not impose upon me ; I know not what he may upon
you : for my part, I do not believe one word he says."

Sir John Powell was the only judge of the twelve in
Westminster-hall when this famous libel case was contested,
who was restored to the bench. But he was called to account for the sentence passed upon the Earl of Devonshire ;
and severely questioned by the House of Lords. The noble
earl struck Colonel Culpeper in the King's palace with a
stick, for some affront which had been given him : upon which
he was compelled to give bail in the King's Bench to the
amount of 30,000*l.* personally, with four sureties bound in
penalties of 5000*l.* each. He pleaded guilty to the information exhibited against him, and was fined 30,000*l.* ; and
Powell was implicated in this exorbitant mulct. The judge
declared he was very sorry ; that he had been misguided by

faith of the Virgin. It had been discovered that

books; that he conceived 3000*l*. fine enough, and begged Lord Devonshire's pardon.

Sir Robert Wright followed in the same mercy-begging strain, saying, that the large fine came, according to the course of the court, from the puisne judge first. Holloway tried to show that all four judges were equally guilty. Allibone was dead. But the lords had possessed themselves of certain information, which induced them to ask whether this enormous fine had not been privately cogitated and agreed upon before they came into court. Wright denied it flat. Holloway prevaricated, and said, they had no orders from the King or the chancellor about it.—" But," said Mr. Justice Powell, " Sir Richard Holloway may remember, there was a discourse of the fine, five or six days before, at the lord chancellor's, where Sir Robert Wright, Sir Richard Holloway, Sir Richard Allibone, and himself, were." Then Holloway declared he did not remember that ; and Wright said, they did not meet about the fine. However, upon this, Sir John Powell told the discourse ; and it was, that Jeffreys first proposed 20,000*l*., but afterwards said, it had better be 30,000*l*., and then the King might abate 10,000*l*. Sir John added, that he expressed his dislike to this before the other judges, but not before the chancellor. The lords voted the sentence a breach of privilege; but Powell was allowed to retain his place in the Common Pleas, which he held till the summer circuit in 1696, when he died, at Exeter.

Thomas Powel came up from the Exchequer, to succeed his namesake in 1688 ; but continued a few months only, and was entirely laid aside.

John Powell, junior, called, by way of distinction there, of

Dr. Lightfoot[1] had not taken the oaths when he
was admitted to his master's degree at Cambridge; and this afforded a very convenient precedent for sending a candidate to that university for the degree of M.A., who should be sheltered against the usual ceremonies by the King's
dispensation. Accordingly, Alban Francis, a
Benedictine monk, armed with a letter under
the sign-manual, presented himself at Cambridge, for the purpose of having the degree
conferred upon him. But the vice-chancellor,
Dr. Peachell, or Rachel, as some call him, finding that the mandate required not only the dignity which was sought, and to which no objection
would have been offered, but that it was to be given

Gloucester, (there being two John Powells in the Common
Pleas at the same time,) was a judge very eminent for his
learning. He came up successively from the Exchequer and
Common Pleas into the King's Bench, where he sat a great
many years, and proved a most able assistant to the lord chief
justice Holt. He died at the latter end of Queen Anne's
reign. These are but mere samples of the promotions of
puisne judges, so much objected against of late. It is not
for the author to presume or suggest any thing here; but such
as will take the trouble to examine the elevations of judges,
will find the custom of advancing them entirely identified with
the constitution.

[1] Most probably the great rabbinical scholar and learned
writer. He was a prebendary of Ely, and rector of Much
Munden, in Hertfordshire.

without the administration of an oath, quickly
determined upon a respectful opposition to a
measure so novel and insidious. So, after various
expressions of their dislike to the proceeding, the
members of the university, after admitting some
one to the degree of doctor of physic, who took
the oaths, sent to Mr. Francis, and declared
their readiness to admit him also, on condition
of his submitting to the same ordeal. But Father
Francis of course declined to do this, insisting
as he did upon the King's dispensation; and,
therefore, he was refused, upon which he went
to Whitehall to make his complaint in form. A
second letter came down some time afterwards,
upon which Dr. Peachell wrote to the Duke of
Albemarle, then chancellor, begging him to
represent the illegality of the proposed admission
to the King. His Majesty highly resented this
obduracy as he considered it; and the consequence was a summons from the awful ecclesiastical commission to the vice-chancellor and
senate, commanding the former to appear in person, the latter by themselves, or their deputies.

The sting of this body was the all-powerful
chancellor: he was so admirably calculated to
intimidate offenders, that, as we have elsewhere
mentioned, the court could not be convened
without him. The vice-chancellor, according

to Burnet, was an honest, but a weak man; indeed his imbecillity is evident by his starving
himself at the Revolution after a rebuke which
Archbishop Sancroft gave him for drunkenness;[1]
so that a more unfit man could scarcely have
been found at this juncture, when the rights
and privileges of so venerable an assembly
were to be called critically into question.—
Nevertheless, every thing was to take place
with due ceremony, and a show of as much
respect as the commissioners could make use of;
and the Head was in decency compelled once
again to throw the lambskin over the wolf's
shoulders.

On the 21st of April, the judges and the
parties summoned made their appearance, and
the burden of the questions on that day was
simply, " Why did you not obey the King's
command?" However, the vice-chancellor obtained with some pains the delay of a week.
At the next meeting the university delivered in
an answer to the charge, and in about ten days
from that time all met again for the purpose of
deciding the subject. Jeffreys, terrible even in
smiles, scared all the wits of Dr. Peachell with
the first question,—" Pray what was the oath?"

[1] He tried to resume his eating functions, after three days
of abstinence ; but nature refused, and so he died.

The Doctor had forgotten the oath which he took when he was made vice-chancellor. At last he stammered out:—"I cannot call to mind the very words of the oath, but the substance of it is this;— that I should well and faithfully *præstare,* or *administrare munus,* or *officium Pro-cancellarii."*

Lord Ch. — " Ay, *munus,* or *officium;* well what then ?"

Then the vice-chancellor said that the office was declared by the laws of the land. Jeffreys was desirous of establishing the fact, that masters of arts had been made without taking oaths, with the sanction of vice-chancellors who had taken the same oath as Dr. Peachell; and he pressed the doctor with Lightfoot's case.

Lord Ch.—" Don't you remember any master of arts made without oaths?" Dr. Cook (a doctor of the civil law who interposed now and then, and seemed to be the main stay of the vice-chancellor)—" Not under the quality of an university nobleman, my lord."

Lord Ch.—" Nay, good doctor, you never were vice-chancellor yet; when you are, we may consider you."

The civilians had no chance with Jeffreys. Cook was soon at his post again. " My lord,

Dr. Lightfoot did subscribe."—Lord Ch. "What subscription do you mean?"—Dr. Cook. "To the thirty-nine articles, and the first of them is the King's supremacy."—Lord Ch. "Is subscribing swearing, doctor?" And so he was silenced for that time. Then Mr. Stanhope began, but he was stopped in the outset.

Lord Ch.—"Nay, look you now, that young gentleman expects to be vice-chancellor too: when you are, sir, you may speak; but till then, it will become you to forbear." It was impossible for any man to have a fairer object for his raillery than this Dr. Peachell. After a strict examination of the unfortunate Head, the noble lord fell upon Dr. Smoult, the professor of casuistical divinity, who had carried up the opinion of the non-regent house regarding Francis. —Lord Ch. "And pray, sir, who are you that you should be thought fit to represent a whole house? why should they choose you rather than any body else?"—Dr. Smoult. "My lord, I suppose because I was one of the seniors."—Lord Ch. "One of the seniors! if you come to that, why was not the very senior chosen?" Dr. Smoult. "I cannot tell, my lord; they came to me."—Vice-Ch. "My lord, he is one of our professors."—Lord Ch. "Nay, when I ask

you questions, they prompt you, and now you
prompt them; but I must tell you, Mr. Vice-
Chancellor, you ought to take an account of
what is done in the house yourself and not from
others." Soon afterwards Jeffreys became tired
of all argument and explanation; and having
made a blunder which was corrected in open
court by the bishop of Rochester, one of the
commissioners, a circumstance which by no
means improved his temper, he cut short another deputy from the university, who was trying to elucidate some act which took place
there, with—" Ay, sir, we took both what was
done, and what was not done; therefore withdraw." Poor Dr. Peachell was turned out of
his high office, and suspended from the head-
ship of Magdalen College; but, notwithstanding, Dr. Balderson, the new vice-chancellor,
being a very spirited man, Father Francis was
refused.

The chancellor had now established himself
not only as the head, but the bull-dog of his
party: he was ever zealous to worry all who
were not within the sacred fold, and approved
himself a most fitting successor of that worthy
person,—

Who still his clenched argument would end
With this home thrust,—he is not Cæsar's friend.

U

The courtiers soon turned their wrath against the other Magdalen College in the sister university, where the temperate Dr. Hough had been acknowledged as president by a large majority, in opposition to the royal mandate, which directed that one Anthony Farmer should be chosen. This was a man of so ill a reputation, that his patrons were at last ashamed of him, although he professed the utmost affection for the popish cause. To say that the inveteracy of the Fellows in adhering to their choice would be the means of bringing them before the ecclesiastical inquisition, and that Jeffreys would be at his post, prepared to repudiate the new Head, and to punish the disobedient fraternity, is to relate a history most consistent with the arbitrary wishes of the Sovereign. But the angry peer transcended himself upon this occasion; for in place of a weak and watery vice-chancellor, he met with a doctor who bearded him on the throne of his holy office. The name of this college champion was Fairfax, and the manner of his resistance presented a scene which cannot but be classed with the ridiculous; though the countenance of the judge, indeed, changed from an expression of the most fawning benignity to the sternest threatenings of vengeance.

We are told, that the university put in an answer to the charge of disregarding the King's recommendation, but that Dr. Fairfax's signature to this defence was wanting. Jeffreys, imagining no less than that he had found at least one man who had separated himself from the bed of heretics, was in ecstasies; and on the doctor's applying to him for leave to explain his reasons for declining to subscribe the answer, said on the instant, " Ay, this looks like a man of sense and a good subject : let 's hear what he will say."—" I don't object to the answer," said Fairfax, " because it is the vindication of my college : I go further; and as according to the rules of the ecclesiastical courts, a libel' is given to the party that he may know the grounds of his accusation, I demand that libel, for I do not know otherwise wherefore I am called here ; and besides, this affair should be discussed in Westminster-hall."—" You are a doctor of divinity, not of law," exclaimed the disconcerted judge ; that smile, which had bewitched so many hapless defendants into an unavailing though ingenuous confession, being now pursed up. " By

' The same writing as a declaration at common law, intimating the nature of the charge against the defendant, or party libelled against.

what commission or authority do you sit here ?"
rejoined the undaunted Fellow. As long as Jeffreys could enjoy the pleasure of indulging his
pretensions to special pleading by quibbling at
the weaknesses of defendants, he could preserve
a tolerable share of humour, though at the expense of those upon whom he might exercise
it ; but here was a man, not only emancipating
himself from the answer which would be a
favourable subject for the judge's raillery,
but absolutely questioning the very right and
essence of his dominion. So he broke out :—
" Pray what commission have you to be so
impudent in court ? This man ought to be kept
in a dark room. Why do you suffer him without a guardian ? Why did you not bring him to
me to beg him ? Pray let the officers seize him."[1]

---

[1] King James was not more polished in his behaviour than
his chancellor. He very officiously went to Oxford in person, to expostulate with his rebellious college ; and after
remonstrating with the chief men of it, he addressed them
thus, while they were kneeling to him, and begging for
mercy and liberty of conscience : —

" Ye have been a stubborn, turbulent college ; I have
known you to be so this six-and-twenty years: you have
affronted me in this. Is this your Church-of-England loyalty ? One would wonder to find so many Church-of-England
men in such a business ! Go home, and show yourselves
good members of the Church of England : get you gone !

The college continuing contumacious, it was left to the Bishop of Chester, Chief Justice Wright,[1] (a creature and *protégé* of Jeffreys) and Baron Jenner, of punning memory, to subdue them; and the matter ended with the expulsion of seventy-five Fellows, and the installation of papists in their room.

Yet, notwithstanding this turbulence and vapouring on the part of Lord Jeffreys, no man better knew the world, and the particular respect which one member of society, whether public or private, owes to another. The following is as brilliant an example as can be furnished, not only of this strong sense of propriety, but of the command of passion in a man who commonly allowed no bounds to his resentment.

Know, I am your King! I will be obey'd, and I command you to be gone. Go, and admit the Bishop of Oxon Head, principal, what d'ye call it of your college; (one that stood by said, President,) I mean president of the college. Let them that refuse it, look to it; they shall feel the weight of their Sovereign's displeasure."

[1] Like master like man. And so the chief justice followed, *longo sed proximus intervallo*, at the heels of the chancellor. Mr. Fulham, one of the Fellows, received this repartee from Wright: " Pray, who's the best lawyer, you or I? Your Oxford law is no better than your Oxford divinity: if you've a mind to a *posse comitatus*, you may have one soon enough."

There being a contested election for Arundel,
the government showed great anxiety that the
court candidate should be returned, and Jeffreys
went down to further this object. The mayor,
an attorney of good character and fortune, was
the returning officer, and he did not fail to notice
the busy interfering chancellor intriguing at the
hustings for every feasible vote. But he determined on concealing his knowledge of the great
political person present. With inviolable firmness he impartially scrutinized the pretensions
of every man who came up to poll; till, at length,
having rejected one of the court voters, Jeffreys
rose up in a furious passion, and declared that
the vote should be admitted; " I am the lord
chancellor of this realm," said the enraged nobleman. The mayor, surveying him with scorn,
thus replied : " Your ungentlemanlike behaviour
convinces me it is impossible you should be the
person you pretend ; were you the chancellor,
you would know that you have nothing to do
here, where I alone preside. Officer, turn that
fellow out of court." The crier proceeded to
do his duty; and my lord, not over desirous of
proving at that moment that he actually kept
the King's conscience, retired to his inn. The
popular candidate was elected. In the evening
Jeffreys begged the favour of the mayor's com-

pany at his lodging; but the independent magistrate declined this suspicious honour: upon which, nothing daunted, the chancellor proceeded to the house of his antagonist, and introduced himself with this winning speech: " Sir, notwithstanding we are in different interests, I cannot help revering one who so well knows, and dares so nobly execute the law; and though I myself was somewhat degraded thereby, you did but your duty. You, as I have learned, are independent, but you may have some relation who is not so well provided for; if you have, let me have the pleasure of presenting him with a considerable place in my gift, just now vacant." The mayor could not resist this flattering bait; and having a nephew to whom such a place would be very acceptable, he named his relative, and the appointment was immediately signed by Jeffreys.

It must not be supposed that the universities would easily forget the carriage of the high ecclesiastical commission judge towards their great men: the indignation against him was like that which the Roman senators manifested when the Gauls plucked their beards; and occasion was not wanting to gratify the resentment which had been aroused. On the 21st of July, 1688, the Duke of Ormond, chancellor of Oxford, died,

and it was the royal intention that the chancellor of England should succeed to that rank, in
the room of the deceased duke. But the college had shrewdly suspected an interference in
this matter; and, accordingly, on the 23rd of
that month, James, the late duke's grandson,
was elected in convocation without a dissentient
voice. On the next day came a mandate from
court to choose George, Lord Jeffreys; but letters being sent for the purpose of satisfying His
Majesty that the election could not be revoked,
the favourite was obliged to rest contented ;¹ and,

¹ Jeffreys was outwitted more than once, as every man necessarily must be who is striving for all things. In 1684,
Dr. Grenvill was made dean of Durham, and proposed to
resign his prebendal stall. Jeffreys got a promise of this
preferment; but the affair got to the Earl of Bath's ears, and
he contrived to make Crew, bishop of the see, acquainted
with it. So it was agreed, that while the instrument of the
dean's elevation was passing the broad seal, the dean himself
should give up his prebend : upon which Sir George Wheeler,
who had married his niece, was forthwith installed ; and the
chief justice was balked by speed, in the same way as he
lost the university honours.

He was rebuffed on the northern circuit by a coroner
about the same time. Mr. Baddiley was the person, and he
had been fined by my lord for a misdemeanour of some kind.
After dinner he got admittance to the judge.—" How now,"
said Jeffreys, who expected to pocket what he could get, " I
suppose you are come to beg off your fine !"—" No, my lord,

moreover, the King, though displeased at first, delivered to the new Duke of Ormond the George and Garter which had been worn by his late grandfather.

We must now go back to the year 1686, for the purpose of recounting a defeat which the chancellor sustained at the Charter-house, where he acted occasionally as a governor. It seems that the King's first experiment in favour of the dispensing power was tried at this institution, although it was not concluded till after the quarrel with the universities. Andrew Popham, a papist, was recommended for an out-pensioner's situation. The master[1] desired the applicant to wait till the governors had met to consider his case. At this meeting Jeffreys attended; and the business being propounded, he proposed a ballot for the man's admission without discussion. But it was ordered otherwise, and the master was heard upon the impropriety of receiving any person into the hos-

have a care of that," was the reply; " for as you have laid it on, it belongs to me to take it off." Fines and amerciaments were excepted out of the King's commission as belonging to the see; and Jeffreys perceiving the drift, was plaguily disconcerted at it. These two anecdotes are from Crew's Memoirs, in Nichols's Leicestershire.

[1] Dr. Burnet, author of the " Theory of the Earth."

pital, who would not take the oaths of allegiance and supremacy. He cited the clause in
the act of parliament expressly relating to the
Charter-house. " What 's that to the purpose ?"
said a governor. " I think it is very much to
the purpose," answered the Duke of Ormond ;
" for an act of parliament is not so slight a thing,
but that it deserves to be considered." So the
question was put, and Popham was refused.
However, several governors were anxious to
have a letter written in answer to the King's
message ; but, as Oldmixon says, Jeffreys
" flung away ;" and he carried so many with
him, that the rest were not sufficient to consti-
tute an assembly. The letter was eventually
sent, notwithstanding, on which the King gave
it to his chancellor, saying, " Find out a way
that I may have right done me at that hospital."
This produced the grand threats of the *quo
warranto*, and the ecclesiastical commissioners ;
but whether it was that the governors' had too

¹ The signatures of the governors were these :—

W. Cant.*	Danby.
Ormond.	Nottingham.
Hallifax.	H. London.†
Craven.	T. Burnet.‡

* William Sancroft.   † Henry Compton.   ‡ The master.

much influence, and too good a cause, (which
they had spirit enough to defend,) or that the
court discovered their weakness in attacking
Oxford and Cambridge, it is clear that the
Charter-house was left in peace, as it had been
once before in the time of James the First, when
the great chief justice Coke stood forward as
its champion, and pronounced a decisive judgment against the party who had ventured to
claim it.

But it is time to look homewards for a while,
and to see whether any thing more than ordinary
was passing at this time in the chancellor's
family. Nevertheless, it is rarely, indeed, that
we can approach a man's domestic circle; and
proud is that national feeling which tells us we
are so safely sheltered from the crowd ; yet, how
gratifying is the little whispered story of private
life, got even at the twentieth hand with all its
discrepancies and ambiguities! What a trea-
sure for a newspaper's proprietary is the early
offspring of some well-turned scandal! Our
principle is in brilliant proof at the present moment, when all the fond records of antiquated
memories are brushed up for the general pleasure of a peep behind the curtain. And shall
we be silent, if we can by any means gain access
to the family of that remarkable chancellor,

whose private bearing has already been described as so frolicsome and licentious, and whose behaviour in the marriage state (but that we know how contrary the course of human nature will run on occasion,) might be supposed as full of command as his judgment-seat? To be short, such domestic tales as can be gathered, shall be given at once, according to Dr. Johnson's liberal recommendation, " tell all ;" and considering that the parties have been in their graves for a century and a half, the value of the history will suffer no depreciation from its scantiness.

The second Lady Jeffreys was a dame of most slippery courses, if we are to credit rumour: indeed, the words, " I dare be sworn she 's honest," could never have been predicted of her without a fearfully reminiscent blush. To say truth, the common notion at the time of Jeffreys's marriage was, that Sir John Trevor, of whom more account shall be presently given, was the favoured gallant of the lady's widowhood, and that he left,—who knows what? as the satirist speaks. However, there happened to be a great quarrel between Scroggs, the chief justice, and Sir George, the then newly married recorder, while they were at dinner. Scroggs found out that his friend's wife had got into the straw only thirty weeks after marriage,

which, considering that there was already an
odd story afloat about a Hansen-kelder, and
that Trevor's attentions were no secret, afforded
a high treat to the judge. So, while Scroggs,
who had got out his almanack, was proclaiming
this, Jeffreys was raging and denying, which, as
the story goes, " set him hard as Wakeman's
trial." At last, like rival counsellors who have
been all day clamouring at each other, they
went off very quietly together to pass sentence
upon poor Harris, the bookseller. And really,
these pleasantries were not confined to Sir John
Trevor; for, soon afterwards, a man named Montfort, a licensed parasite of the chancellor, (who
dearly loved flattery,) appears upon the stage. He
seems to have been a successful candidate for
the lady's future favours; so that when the bruit
of the young Prince's birth went abroad, and
created so great a sensation,—the Peter Pindar
of that day, singing of the great achievement,
and of the chancellor's belief in it, exclaims,—

> And he believes the prince is real too,
> But not so certain, nor, 'tis fear'd, so true,
> As he wears horns, that were by M—fort made.

Peter is not content till he has entirely ruined
the fair one's good name :—

For he of Heav'n is sure whene'er he dyes:
Thanks to the care of fond indulgent wife,
To make atonement for his wicked life;
D——s her own soul,   •   •   •
    •   •   •   •   •   •

Sir John Reresby affects to have been quite
surprised at the freedoms which the chancellor
indulged in before this Mr. Montfort, who had
been a comedian.   "I dined with the lord
chancellor," says he, "where the lord mayor of
London was a guest, and some other gentlemen.
His lordship having, according to custom,
drank deep at dinner, called for one Mountfort,
a gentleman of his, who had been a comedian,
an excellent mimic; and to divert the company,
as he was pleased to term it, he made him
plead before him in a feigned cause, during
which he aped all the great lawyers of the age,
in their tone of voice, and in their action and
gesture of body, to the very great ridicule, not
only of the lawyers, but of the law itself, which
to me did not seem altogether so prudent in a
man of his lofty station in the law; diverting it
certainly was, but prudent in the lord high
chancellor, I shall never think it."

To resume for a moment my Lady Jeffreys,
whose husband may truly be said to have

Mist of the maid and caught the dragon,—

she seems to have kept quiet possession of her home, though not much encouraged at court. She was not present at the birth of the young chevalier; but she had the curiosity to ask Dr. Hugh Chamberlayne whether he had any commands to attend Her Majesty; to which he briskly answered, he thought he should, unless their brains were in disorder.

The chancellor never abated his vivacious, though intemperate courses. He was always jollity personified. One day, at Alderman Duncomb's, he, the lord treasurer,[1] and some others, worked themselves up to so high a pitch of loyalty, that it was whispered they had stripped to their shirts, and, but for an accident, would have got upon a sign-post to drink the King's health. Nevertheless, this furious debauch cost Jeffreys a fit of the stone, which had nearly ended all his convivialities for ever. He " virtuously" brought it upon himself, says Reresby. Sometimes, however, he kept very good society. Evelyn, the author of Silva, notes in his Diary, that Jeffreys had always been very civil to him, and that he went to dine with the great man on one occasion. On another day he writes, " I return'd home, when I found my lord chief

---

[1] Rochester.

justice [Jeffreys], the Countess of Clarendon,
and Lady Catherine Fitzgerald, who dined
with me."

Another of the chancellor's high acquaintance
was Henry, earl of Clarendon; but that noble
lord had a purpose to serve by ingratiating himself at Bulstrode, having some concerns at issue,
which needed countenance from the King. He
was treated with great civility; and invited to
dinner, a gentleman, named Graham, having
" prepared my lord chancellor." After a disappointment, occasioned by Lord Clarendon's
illness, the parties met accordingly; and Jeffreys promised to take all opportunities of serving his guest, begging that he might sometimes
see him. And he showed a similar partiality on
many subsequent occasions. In fact, the noble
earl had done well to acquire a judicial friend;
for he was at one time involved in litigation.
He had embroiled himself with the queen dowager in the court of Exchequer, and with a Mr.
Dockmanique, about a New River affair; in which
latter case, Jeffreys interested himself highly to
effect a satisfactory settlement. One day they
came to Bulstrode for this purpose; but all
business being delayed by the default of some
absentees, the chancellor was determined to
amuse his friend. This is the note in the Diary:

"I went in his calash with him. He talked very freely to me of all affairs; called the judges a thousand fools and knaves; that chief justice Wright was a beast : he said, the King and Queen were to dine with him on Thursday next; that he had still great hopes the King would be moderate, when the parliament met. When we came to Dr. Hickman's, my lord was inclined to be merry; saying, he had papists and spies among his own servants, and therefore must be cautious at home."

We have a picture of the chancellor's self-love from the author of his "Life and Character," which exhibits a most inordinate vanity. It would seem that he affected this acquaintance with learned men from a pure feeling of conceit, which his flatterers had found it their interest to foster even in its utmost extravagances: so that he would discourse of religion, philosophy, indeed of any subject which he had been complimented on knowing, and would even delight in pointing out errors in the principal works of art which appeared in his time; though it often turned out that his opinions were not classical, and his conclusions inaccurately drawn. It is related, that the grossest adulation, such as would disgust and affront another man, was the sweetest homage which could be paid him;

x

whether it came from the press in "fustian"
dedications, or from the lips of those who would
" fool him to the top of the bent" for their dinner and wine. These worthies, like all base-
born parasites, repaid him with a silent laugh
at his vanity; whilst men of taste and learning,
who heard his solutions of philosophical and
mathematical problems at second-hand (for he
dared not adventure them in the face of science),
were amazed, when they discovered his want
of skill. One would have thought that the following specimen of dedication had been a mere
mockery and sarcasm, but for his reported love
of the most fulsome harangues. It is prefixed
to the " History of Oracles, and the Cheats of
the Pagan Priests," published in 1688.

" Nor can the unthinking and most malicious
of your enemies reproach your lordship with self-
interest in any of your services, since all the world
knows, when they were thought criminal, nay
even punishable, (for such miserable times we
have seen) when it was enough to have forfeited your fortune, and almost your life; then,
I say, there was found in your lordship that
undaunted bravery, that spirit and fire of loyalty,
that true concern for the royal cause, that
you were the first destin'd victim for the
slaughter, the first to be sacrificed to the *associa-*

tion rage, even when you had nothing left you but honour, justice, and innocence, for your guard."

This character for bravery was sadly at variance with the spectacle of Mr. Recorder on his knees before the parliament; and his justice or innocence might have been bitterly contrasted with the western horrors.

Jeffreys was considered a good judge of music; and during the rivalship of those two famous organ-builders, Father Smith and Harris, he was one of the umpires chosen to decide on their respective merits. An organ was placed by each artist in the Temple church; one at the east, the other at the west end: Blow and Purcell played for Smith, and Lully, Queen Catherine's organist, for Harris. Then Harris challenged Smith to make within a given time the additional stop of the vox humana ; the cremona, or viol stop; the double courtel, or bass flute, &c. The challenge was accepted, and each party laboured to the utmost. Jeffreys decided for Smith, and Harris's organ was withdrawn. Smith, or Schmidt, was a native of Germany; Harris came from France.[1]

[1] See Granger's Biographical History of England, by Noble, Vol. ii. p. 363.

Sometime after his elevation to the chancellorship, Jeffreys bethought himself to visit his father; it is to be hoped through a desire of seeing his parent once more, and not for the purpose of displaying his new glories in the neighbourhood of his birth, whence he had been so cavalierly dismissed before by the old gentleman. However this may be, Mr. Jeffreys of Acton, conscious how odious his son's character had become in the nation, was so much ashamed, that he refused to see him. This respectable man survived all his sons: and Mr. Yorke speaks of a picture at Acton which represents the father in mourning for his seventh and youngest, the canon of Canterbury.

But it is time that we should turn for a while to the fortunes of Sir John Trevor, who was so long intimately connected with Jeffreys. He was also allied by blood to his patron, being a consin,[1] and like him arose from the smallest beginnings. A clerk to Arthur Trevor, another kinsman, and a lawyer in the Temple,—he was allowed to learn, as his relation said, " the knavish part of the law," in chambers. After this he courted the society of gamesters; and

[1] Descended from Tudor Trevor, earl of Hereford.

brought his knowledge of law to bear well with them, so that he was their *point d'appui*, when they had involved themselves in any gambling difficulties, solving their doubts, and playing the judge much to their satisfaction. Whether Jeffreys interested himself for this lawyer by reason of his relationship, or because he was resolved that the acquaintance between his wife and Trevor should appear reasonable, by introducing him as his own personal friend, we need not inquire (both grounds would entitle the young man to a favourable consideration): it is certain, that a silk gown, and the mastership of the Rolls, on the decease of Sir John Churchill, were the rewards or the advantages of this friendship: and in July, 1688, he was sworn of the privy-council. Henry, earl of Clarendon, remarks upon it thus:—"July 6, 1688. Sir John Trevor, master of the Rolls, Colonel Tytus, and Mr. Vane, Sir Henry Vane's son, were sworn of the privy-council. Good God bless us! What will the world come to?"

He had certainly supplanted the chancellor, according to Roger North, if King James's dominion had lived longer, for he never held his superior in much awe; and in Cornish's case, he had the fearlessness to say, " That if he [Jeffreys] pursued that unfortunate man to exe-

cution, it would be no better than murder."
Matters, truly, had gone so far in dispute between them, as to produce mutual scoldings and
upbraidings at Whitehall. The effort to unseat
his master, if true, appears to be ingratitude of
a sufficiently black description on the part of
Trevor; but a writer informs us, that Jeffreys,
most probably through jealousy of his newly-
raised favourite, perpetually reversed his decrees, and discharged his most common orders.
Nay more, he set up officers of his own appointment to affront the master by questioning his
authority, and insulting him publicly on his
seat, without learning or credit to sustain their
objections.[1] Sir John boldly maintained his
ground, and baffled the attempts which were
made to humble him; but it is by no means so
clear that he would have succeeded to the seals.
There was more than one anxious aspirant to
this dignity so soon as it was known that Jeffreys's attachment to the Protestant religion had
diminished his influence at court; and but for
the firmness of a British jury, it is probable that
Mr. Solicitor-general Williams would have had

---

[1] Yet on consulting Vernon's Reports, many of Sir John
Trevor's decrees will be found to have been *confirmed* by the
lord chancellor.

them for his zealous service against the seven bishops.¹

However, the good planet of Sir John Trevor did not set at the Revolution; for he was chosen speaker of the House of Commons in 1690, having filled that high situation before in King James's parliament. He was constituted first commissioner of the great seal in the same year, and presided in Chancery till the elevation of Lord Somers. He met, indeed, with some reverses; which must occasionally happen to every " bold and dexterous man," as Burnet calls him.

The mastership of the Rolls, for example, was given to Henry Powle on the accession of William; but Trevor recovered that place in a few years on the demise of the master, and continued to dispense equity to the day of his death. This dignity was restored to him while speaker, and first commissioner in Chan-

¹ Philip Yorke, in his " Royal Tribes of Wales," tells this story, which he heard from Lord Hardwicke :—" When Jeffreys, who was sitting in the court of Chancery, heard the immense shouting for the bishops' acquittal, he was seen to smile, and hide his face in his nosegay. This was as good as— ' Mr. Solicitor, I keep my seal ;' for he knew that Williams had been promised it, if he could get a verdict against the hierarchy."

cery.   But the worst difficulty he ever fell into,
was the discovery of a bribe which he took from
the city of London, for patronising a bill to satisfy the orphanage debts: no master of the
Rolls ever ran nearer a lee-shore for 1000*l.*
After hearing a variety of personal reproaches
for six hours, he was actually necessitated to
put the question against himself; and, conformably with the sense of the House, having made
the comfortable declaration, that " Sir John
Trevor was guilty of corrupt bribery, by receiving, &c." he departed ; and, sending the mace,
did not care to obtrude himself again as speaker.
In a few days he was expelled, but no impeachment followed to deprive him of his legal rank,
so that the wags cried out: " Justice is blind,
but Bribery only squints." He squinted abomi-
nably.   And he was not troubled with any
qualms of political integrity; but the absence of
these, indeed, has shown a strong digestion in
very many of his fraternity since, and in others,
too, as well.   Burnet says, that he began the
practice of buying off men: a circumstance which
would alone demonstrate the *virtue* of a national
debt, and the righteous appropriation of loans;
and, being a tory himself, he was of course
deemed the fittest to manage that party in parliament.

Not to be too hard upon him, he certainly was a man of great acuteness who could so well recommend himself to every government, and enjoy an office which requires a singular purity in its administration, himself under the galling imputation of bribery, and the sad punishment of being turned out from a post of the highest worth.—" He died at his house in Clement's-lane, May 20, 1717; and was buried in the Rolls' chapel.["]¹

¹ Collins's Peerage. Trevor was once the victim of a repartee from Tillotson, who was in general sparing of his wit. Soon after the archbishop's great promotion, and Sir John's unlucky adventure of the 1000*l.*, the latter meeting the churchman near the House of Lords, muttered loud enough to be overheard, " I hate a fanatic in lawn-sleeves."—" And I hate a knave in any sleeves," returned the doctor.

The bribery spoken of was quite in keeping with his character. He was a decided economist. One day he dined alone at the Rolls, and was taking his wine, when his cousin, Roderic Lloyd, was ushered in from a side-door.—" You rascal," said Trevor to his servant, " and you have brought my cousin, Roderic Lloyd, Esq., prothonotary of North Wales, marshal to Baron Price, and so forth, and so forth, up my *back stairs.* Take my cousin, Roderic Lloyd, Esq. prothonotary of North Wales, marshal to Baron Price, and so forth, and so forth; take him instantly back, down my *back stairs,* and bring him up my *front stairs.*" Roderic kicked against this excessive exhibition of respect, probably anticipating the plot; for while he was being conveyed away

Except in Granger, it is difficult to say, where
George, (Jeffreys) Earl of Flint, Viscount Weik-

down one, and up another flight of stairs, his Honour removed
the bottle and glass. This same Roderic was once dreadfully frightened in Chancery-lane. Coming home rather
fresh from his club one night, he ran against the pump there.
Thinking he had received a blow, he whipped out his sword,
made a lunge, and passed it into the spout. The pump being
somewhat crazy, fell down. Roderic concluded the worst,
left his weapon sticking, and made off to Sir John's house in
the Rolls under the dreadful apprehension of having killed
a man. There he was kept close by the servants for the remainder of the night. In the morning, a faithful valet, who
had been sent to learn the condition of the fallen, made his
report; and forth came the judge to deliver his kinsman from
his horrors and confinement in the coal-hole. The above
anecdotes are from " Yorke's Royal Tribes of Wales."

There were two other judges of the same family. All
three owed their immediate descent to Edward ap David,
who died in 1448. John, of whom we have been speaking,
had the eldest son of this Edward for his ancestor; while
Thomas, whom we shall now introduce, was derived from
the third (Richard), whose fifth son he was. Thomas was
born July 6, 1586: he was observed to smile as soon as he
was born (an augury as well applicable to a tailor as a
judge); went to the Inner Temple, and became serjeant-at-
law. Collins informs us, that he was successively judge of
the Common Pleas and lord chief baron; but from the au-
thorised law reports of the period in which he lived, it appears, that he was made a baron of the Exchequer in the
early part of King Charles's reign; and we find from history,
that he continued in that station till the death of his mas-

ham, is mentioned. The reverend biographer
once thought that this title was a "ridiculous

ter, when, in common with five others, he refused to act under
the new commission. He was impeached during the troubles of 1641; and though he escaped the vengeance which
fell upon his contemporary Berkley, who was fairly taken
off the bench, he was obliged to pay 10,000*l*. After this,
he was, at one time, the only judge who sat upon the Exchequer bench, when certain messengers delivered the King's
writ to him and Judge Reve, for an adjournment of the term
from London to Oxford: he caused the person who served
him to be apprehended, and so did his fellow judge. One of
these men was hanged as a spy. He married, first, Prudence,
daughter of Henry Boteler, Esq.; and secondly, Frances,
daughter and heir of Daniel Blennerhasset, of Norfolk.
By his first wife he had Thomas, who was made a baronet,
but died without issue male, in Charles II.'s reign. The judge
himself died December 21, 1656, aged 83; and was buried
in Leamington Hastang, in Warwickshire.

Thomas Trevor, the first Lord Trevor, and ancestor of the
Viscounts Hampden, was nephew of Baron Trevor. His
father was Sir John, of Trevallin, Flintshire; and his eldest
brother was Sir John, principal secretary of state to King
Charles II. This gentleman studied the law with such effect,
that he became solicitor-general in 1692, and attorney soon
afterwards. When Treby died, he was advanced to be chief
justice of the Common Pleas, and in 1711 was made a
peer. He was a tory at this time, and so met with little
mercy at the Hanover succession; for he was compelled to
quit his place in favour of Sir Peter King.

Had the question, whether the judges were removable on
the demise of the Crown been new, Trevor would have

sarcasm," till he was shown a book entitled,
"Dissertatio Lithologica, auctore Joanne Groenevelt, Transisalano, Daventriensi, M. D. E Col.

tried it, on the principle of his being appointed during good
behaviour; but Holt had been alarmed on the accession of
Queen Anne, and had procured a new commission; and Sir
John Trevor, the master of the Rolls, had followed his example. Archer had attempted the same thing, in the reign
of Charles II.; and so had the Chief Baron Walter, in the preceding reign. Yet Sir Joseph Jekyll, chief justice of Chester
at the death of King William, boldly set the court at defiance;
and though he was threatened with a prosecution, and great
interest made for the place by Mr. Conyers, he prevailed.
Lord Trevor had started a whig, and had been attorney some
years before he deserted his party; he then gradually withdrew himself, and signally dissented from them, by voting
against Sir John Fenwick's attainder. However, he came
back to them, and in 1726 was made lord privy seal, one
of the lords justices in 1727, and president of the council in
1730. "He was," says Onslow, "the only man almost
that I ever knew, who changed his party as he had done,
that preserved so general an esteem with all parties as he
did." We learn from the same authority, that he loved being
at court, but was very awkward there, having been a most
"reserved, grave, and austere judge." Yet the speaker
gives him a character for ability and uprightness as chief
justice; and adds, that he had found him sufficiently com-
municative in conversation. Holt was accustomed to "dis-
parage his law." He died, aged 71, June 19, 1730. He
was a fellow of the Royal Society, and a governor of the
Charter-house. He was twice married. Three of his sons
became successively Lords Trevor; and another was made

Med. Lond. Editio secunda. Londini, 1687,
8vo." It had this dedication :—" Honoratissimo
domino, D.Georgio, Comiti Flintensi, Vicecomiti
de Weikham, baroni de Weim, supremo Angliæ cancellario, et serenissimo Jacobo Secundo,
Regi Angliæ, a secretioribus consiliis."[1]

But let him that thinketh he standeth take
heed lest he fall." Just at the moment when our
chancellor's prosperity seemed to have attained

Bishop of St. David's, and translated to Durham. The eldest son by the second wife, who also inherited the barony of
Trevor, was the first Viscount Hampden.

[1] There would be no room for astonishment on finding that
King James had gratified his minister with an earldom ; but
why was the advanced rank abandoned by his son ? The
creation could hardly have been made for life only : possibly
it might have been fully intended, but never executed ; or,
which is most probable, the patent might never have been
sued out (Nichols says it never was), and the young lord was
clearly in a bad condition to ask for aggrandisement. A
correspondent in the Gentleman's Magazine seems to treat
the promotion altogether as a fiction ; and, referring to the picture by Sir Godfrey Kneller, which represents the judge in
his baron's robes, asks, if the painter would have drawn him
twice? But though the portrait by Sir Godfrey was executed
in 1687, why should not the title have been granted later in
that year, and the dedication by Groenevelt made in anticipation of it ? Here is a book which bears the intended
honour upon the face of it, and a print to confirm its authority.

an eminence, which men might look up to with
wonder, there was a danger at hand, of that
fatal description which ever awaits such as
stand too confidently upon their imagined influence. We have come to the month of December, 1687 ; and although it was not mentioned
in due course, it is sufficient for us to allude to
the well-known historical fact of Lord Castlemaine going ambassador to Pope Innocent,
some two or three years before. With the op-
portune fits of coughing which afflicted his
Holiness as soon as business was mentioned,
with the strict requisitions of ceremonials which
troubled the diplomatist, his failure in the main
object of his mission, and the doubts thrown
upon Welwood's narrative, by such as have
said that the pope never coughed at all, we have
no concern; our object being to reveal the com-
bustibles in this mine which was to be sprung.
In the midst of this it is to be observed, that
Castlemaine's journey to Rome was high-treason; and that Jeffreys was alarmed at it beyond
measure, it being his duty, as a cabinet minister,
to entertain an opinion upon the subject, to advise the King, and be ready to answer for the
consequences. His lukewarmness was detected
by the sharp-sighted priests with a facility
very natural to them; and they followed up this

imputation against him throughout the reign. Father Petre, Sunderland's tool and vehicle, had moreover discovered, that in the proceedings against Magdalen College, a moderation, quite obnoxious to the papists, had been recommended by the chancellor to his sovereign. Now the received maxim was, that "all court merit consisted in promoting the Catholic cause," and the King was well-pleased with the application of it. Jeffreys would not promote the cause, therefore Jeffreys must be sacrificed. The matter stood thus: Tyrconnel, deputy of Ireland, was fearful he should be obliged to yield his place to my Lord Castlemaine; Petre was his friend, and at this father's hands he asked for assistance and continuance in his office. Castlemaine was attached to the pope, and had a promise of great interference from him, which went so far, through the nuncio, as to gain over the monarch in his favour. If the Lords Powis, Bellasis, and Dover, then lords of the Treasury, could be made lords commissioners of the great seal,' Castlemaine might be lord treasurer,

' Horace Walpole tells us, in his Catalogue of Royal and Noble Authors, of a report, that Jeffreys was nearly superseded by the Earl of Anglesey, in 1686; but adds, he could hardly suppose that the minister would be so easily unseated. The event was nearer at hand in 1687.

and so Tyrconnel remain in Ireland, both lord-
ing it over the "dirty roads of power." The
Protestant keeper of the seals was thus in a
fair way of returning the purse and mace; for,
on the 17th of December, it was resolved in the
cabinet, that this alteration was feasible, and
should be made. However, just at the time
there broke out a quarrel between the French
King and the Pope : Tyrconnel, Petre, and Jeffreys, were of the French faction; and Castlemaine followed his Holiness. Father Petre, now
able to save Tyrconnel, dared not alter the balance of the court by introducing Lord Castlemaine; and so Jeffreys profited by the turn of
luck, and was thoroughly re-established.[1]

As far as appearances went, the chancellor
showed the most manifest eagerness to deserve
his continued favour, though it may be shrewdly
suspected (and the momentous case of the seven
bishops[2] affords a remarkable example of this,)
that he never persecuted the establishment but

---

[1] Oldmixon says, that his restoration was effected by Sunderland and the Queen.

[2] William Sancroft, archbishop of Canterbury; William
Lloyd, bishop of St. Asaph; Francis Turner, bishop of Ely;
Thomas Kenn, bishop of Bath and Wells; John Lake,
bishop of Chichester; Thomas White, bishop of Peterborough; Sir Jonathan Trelawney, bishop of Bristol.

with an aching and disapproving heart. Indeed,
at that trying crisis, he was actually in great
trouble, and spoke freely of the apprehensions
he entertained that their public trial would be of
ill consequence to the King. " It will be found,"
said he, " that I have done the part of an honest man ; as for the judges, they are most of
them rogues." And at another time he said,
that the King had once resolved to let the business fall, but that some people would hurry
him to his destruction. And after the trial he
declared, that the King himself was vexed at
it; that he was in a milder temper; and, " now,"
said he, " honest men, both lords and others,
(though the King have used them hardly,) should
appear often at court: I am sure it would do good."
All this smoothness, however, was behind the
curtain : we give his public conduct beneath.

The bishops, after having incensed the monarch
by their famous petition, (when he declared,
as he did oftentimes afterwards, that he would
be obeyed,) were summoned before the privy
council, where the great examinant and interro-
gator was present. The point was soon arrived
at. " Do you own the petition ?" said Jeffreys. It is to be noticed, that hitherto no
evidence of libel had been acquired on the part
of the crown; these dignified persons must, there-

Y

fore, be condemned by their own admissions,
drawn warily forth by the wily judge. But not
so easily : they evaded at first; and at length,
out of mere shame at the fear of acknowled-
ging their own, the archbishop said that he wrote
it, the bishops that they had signed and delivered it. But this was only half the campaign.
" Did you publish it ?" continued the chancellor. This they flatly denied ; they had no
knowledge of the publication. Then a lecture
was commenced upon the wickedness of their
disobedience ; the disturbance of the general
peace ; and many menaces were interspersed to
alarm the bishops for their safety. Finding
that he was wasting his breath, Jeffreys demanded their recognizance to appear before the
Court of King's Bench, and answer the high
misdemeanour. Upon this, they insisted on the
privilege of their peerage, which rather terrified
the council, the rights of nobility being serious
stumbling-blocks to all innovators; but the lord
chancellor soon relieved these apprehensions by
threatening to commit the defendants to the
Tower, as public delinquents. They were ready
to go, they answered, whithersoever His Majesty was pleased to send them. They hoped
the King of Kings would be their Protector and
their Judge. They feared nothing from men ;

and having acted according to law and their consciences, no punishment should ever be able to shake their resolutions. This being felt as a struggle for victory on one side or the other, a warrant was drawn and signed by Jeffreys, and handed round to the board, who all subscribed, save Petre, and he was exempted by the royal order.[1] The acquittal of these great men is familiar to every school-boy; but the difficulty of proving the publication of the libel is not so well known. It is one thing to write a libel; another to make it public: it is again one thing to publish a libel, another to obtain evidence of that publication according to the forms of justice.

In the bishops' case it became necessary to show a publication in Middlesex. It was proved that they had owned the writing of the petition; but their open tender of it was by delivering it into the King's hands. And here was the defect. One witness said, that he did not remember what the bishops owned respecting the delivery; another halted upon his opinion; and a third thought that they had confessed the publication to the lord chancellor, of which opinions and conjectures not a tittle was good

[1] Kennet and Echard declare, that some of the judges declined to sign it. The account we have given is according to Burnet and Ralph.

testimony, while great shouts were set up
in the hall. " Here's wonderful rejoicing that
truth cannot prevail !" cries Mr. Solicitor. At
length, after prodigious pauses, came my lord
president of the council,[1] and he declared, that
the bishops had told him on the day in question,
that they were about to deliver a petition to the
King, and that they offered him the paper; and
he added, that they then went into the King's
chamber. Upon this the court said, that after
such proof, it lay upon the bishops to show that
the paper so supposed to be delivered was not
that charged in the information. The whole matter
was subsequently left to the consideration of
the jury ; who, much to the mortification of Sir
William Williams,[2] then hungering for the great
seal, pronounced the defendants not guilty, having sat up all night without fire or candle.

   And now we come to a very royal scene, at
which the chancellor was present in his official
capacity, and in a very advanced post. This was
the birth of the Pretender, otherwise called King
James III. On the day of the bishops' committal, the Queen intimated her intention of removing from Whitehall to St. James's, for the
purpose of lying-in, and the next morning was
the first of the Chevalier's existence.

   The *entrée* was not quite so indiscriminate as

---

[1] Sunderland.   [2] Solicitor-General.

at the French ceremonial,' but there were men in the room sufficient to distress a woman in that situation, whether delicate or robust. At eight o'clock His Majesty was sent for, and on his arrival, he summoned the Queen dowager and all the council.

The satirist describes the grandees thus:

> Then comes great George of England, chancellour,
> Who was with expedition call'd to th' labour:

' Madame Campan gives a lively description of the motley assembly at an *accouchement* of Marie Antoinette. All the royal family, princes of the blood, and great officers of state, passed the night in a neighbouring chamber; but on the instant of the midwife's exclamation, " La Reine va s'accoucher," the etiquette of general admission was so literally observed, that had it not been for some tapestry-screens, corded, by the King's foresight, near Her Majesty's bed, the torrent of persons would have fallen upon her. Two Savoyards mounted the furniture, that they might have a full view of their mistress. In fact, it was like a place of public amusement. At length, the Queen fainted from disappointment, the softer sex of the infant being discovered to her, and the accoucheur bawled out for air and warm water, and for the chief surgeon to bleed her in the foot. The joy on her revival was so great, that the utmost confusion followed; and the valets-de-chambre took the opportunity of removing divers persons from the room by the collar. This was the last of the legitimately indiscriminate etiquettes.

Lord P——dent[1] comes next, that's now cashier'd;
Then A——del[2] of W—dour, privy seal ;
Then comes my lord[3] All pride with modesty;

with a great many more, some of whom were
not of the council, besides many ladies of
quality.

"The feet curtains of the bed, and the two
sides were open." The Queen was in great
pain, and the King called for Jeffreys, who
" came up to the bedside to show he was there,"
upon which the rest of the privy counsellors did
the same.

Her Majesty was exceedingly annoyed at
this, for all the nobles were close to the bed,
and the chancellor upon the step. She begged
her consort to hide her face with his head and
periwig, for she declared " she could not be
brought to bed and have so many men look on
her."[4] However, the affair then took place,
the child was taken into an adjoining chamber,
followed by the council, who having been advised in dumb show by the midwife's sign, that
it was a son, retreated.

A writer of the last century, no doubt a vio-

[1] Sunderland.
[2] Lord Arundel of Wardour.
[3] Earl of Mulgrave. State Poems, vol. 3. p. 263.
[4] See Appendix to Sir John Dalrymple, part 1. p. 308.

lent whig, who thought no reproach too bitter, and no imputation too severe, declares, that however ill qualified he might have been for his high office, Jeffreys well understood the value of it. Very anxious to attain riches and an estate, he is charged with selling places at a rate the most extravagant, so that art and dexterity were called very considerably in aid to gain purchasers. To promote the traffic, which his demands had rendered difficult, he enlarged the perquisites; and while he was disposing of a situation at five times the usual price, his courtesy and kindness were dispensed with unusual liberality. Although there is such a belabouring in the pamphlet, as must inevitably remind us of the ass who kicked the dead lion, it must be owned, that the acquisition of fortune was a very main object with this nobleman; though, where the author attributes his exactions to avarice, we should lay them to the pressing necessities which must have so closely waited on his careless habits and lavish expenditure.

A circumstance occurred while he filled the equity bench, which amply proves the calumny of satirists, and the prejudices of a multitude] There was a cause before him, which involved a large sum of money to be paid, as his lordship's judgment might be given, to Lord Pembroke's

creditors, or to his heiress. The opinion of the
court was against the creditors, and John Jeffreys, the chancellor's son, was married to the
lady very speedily after the decree. "Loud
and deep reflections were made upon the judge's
honesty and honour," says the martyrologist,
and the greedy ear of slander could have been
scarce ever satiated with such a goodly tale :

> Old Tyburn must groan ;
> For Jeffreys is known,
> To have perjur'd his conscience to marry his son :

says the Pindar of the day ; but the outcry was
quite unfair, the decree being founded on the
most equitable and approved principles, sanc-
tioned by cases, and by several judges in open
court.¹ Nay, which is more, an appeal was

¹ Lord Pembroke, on his marriage, demised lands to
trustees for ninety-nine years, who redemised them to him for
ninety-eight years and eleven months, he agreeing that a
peppercorn should be paid during his life ; after his death, a
jointure for his wife's life ; and at her death, a peppercorn for
the rest of the term. This term, being raised for a particular
purpose, was holden not liable to any debts which would not
affect the inheritance, as bond debts, &c. and, therefore, not
capable of being charged with simple contract debts. And
this was determined by the lord chancellor, Sir John Trevor,
M. R. Mr. Justice Luitwich, and Mr. Baron Powell, and

brought after the Revolution, and heard before
the lords commissioners;' when " every thing,"
says the author of the " Life and Character,"
" was heard greedily that tended to impeach
the chancellor's integrity," and all the influence
of the Pembroke family was used against the
judgment; but it stood its ground, being sustained by the force of just principle, and the
authority of precedents. The appeal was carried still farther, even unto the last tribunal, the
House of Lords, but shared the same fate, for
that high assembly did not think fit to reverse
it. Nevertheless, no acuteness was wanting to
make the bargain sure, for the lady being a
Roman catholic, the marriage was solemnized
two ways; first by a priest, and next by a divine of the establishment.

Mr. Justice Thomas Powel was known to be of the same
opinion. After the second hearing, the decree was, to pay
all the bond creditors of Lord Pembroke with the proceeds
of the sale of these terms, and to apply the *goods*, &c. to the
liquidation of simple contract debts, not barred by the statute
of limitations. The bond debts were 9000*l.* the book debts
and debts by simple contract 18,200*l.* The independent
personal estate was 6000*l.* but the terms in question were
granted, to secure 1800*l.* a year.—See Vernon's Reports, in
8vo. Vol. 2. part 1. pp. 52 and 213.

¹ Sir John Trevor, Mr. Keck, Serjeant Rawlinson.

It may be stated, without fear of contradiction, that this was not the only appeal against a judgment of Jeffreys, which failed of success upon consideration, nor was it a solitary case upon which he might have arrived at a just conclusion, through the interest which he possessed in its result : for though many of his decisions, after the Revolution more particularly, came a second time to be canvassed, they had so strongly the virtue of good law to uphold them, that few, if any, were overturned; and if we consult the able annotator of Vernon,' it seems, that most of those determinations would be admitted as authorities at this day, except the state of equity practice were inconsistent with them.

The perception of the chancellor was especially vivid, and his opinion moulded in an instant: if succeeding lawyers, then, have acknowledged the ability of his impressions, and courts of review the righteousness of his judgments, we need no more evidence to prove that he was an admirable judge of equity. Nor is this commendation a mere result of our opinion; for, were it so, it would be expressed with much more modesty; it is the unanimous testimony of judges and lawyers, at least of such as lived

' The late Mr. Raithby.

sufficiently distant from his day to be free from prejudice.

Burnet declares, that " he was not learned in his profession;" but Speaker Onslow says, on the contrary, " I have heard Sir Joseph Jekyll[1] say otherwise." The Speaker goes on :—" He had likewise great parts, and made a great chancellor in the business of that court. In more private matters he was thought an able and upright judge wherever he sat; but where the crown or his party were concerned, he was as he is here represented,[2] generally at least."[3] " He was a very ill chancellor," says an author, who must have had a Chancery-suit decided against him by the judge; since he commits every kind of malediction upon the memory of that considerable person. It is next to impossible that an unskilful jurist should have been able to unite so much accuracy with so great a

[1] Master of the Rolls.

[2] That is, by Burnet, as very violent.

[3] In the great case of the attorney-general against Vernon, a patent of lands granted by the crown was set aside, as obtained for a very inadequate consideration, and under colourable proposals. The lord chief justice Jones, and the lord chief baron Montague, men of acknowledged integrity, assisted the chancellor in the inquiry, and gave their judgments in accordance with his.

share of quickness.—*Semper ad eventum festi-nat*, might have been well said of him. There was, moreover, a sense of justice in his proposi-tions so striking, as almost to induce a wish that he had lived in these days to contribute his share of improvement to that fund of alte-ration which has been so ably collected by the Chancery commissioners.[1] Almost as soon as he mounted the bench, he awarded a defendant such costs as he should swear he was out of pocket on the plaintiff dismissing his own bill, instead of the customary but inadequate allow-ance of twenty shillings.—" I will do all I can,"

---

[1] We give an instance of his zeal for just improvement. People acquainted with the affairs of Chancery, are aware that there is some considerable difficulty in drawing up the minutes of the judge's decree; that such minutes are liable to be varied; and that no settled time is fixed for applications for that purpose, whereby delay and vexation are created. Jeffreys, in 1687, observing the evil which was prevalent then also, promulged an order, by which the suitors were bidden to pay strict attention to the reading of his judgments, in order that the officers of the court might not be complained of in future for mistakes; and he ordained, that no petition or motion should be entertained on the subject, unless it were thought right to alter the decree. And not many years afterwards, the time for objecting to the decree was fixed; but this good economy of business hours seems of late to have been much neglected.

said he, on another occasion, "to help an heir
that is disinherited." And he sternly resisted
the vice of gambling. Sir Basil Firebrass, a
citizen, had lost three thousand four hundred
and fifty guineas at play with one Brett, at the
same sitting; but being satisfied that he had
been cheated, he and his servant retook two
thousand guineas from the winner by force.
The successful gamester brought an action of
trespass, and Sir Basil went into Chancery to
stop him, and to have the residue of the losings,
being one thousand four hundred and fifty guineas more. He declared in his bill, that a chain
of fraud had been used to inveigle him; that the
defendant Brett had mixed his own wine with
water, while he plied his antagonist, the unlucky
plaintiff in Chancery, most abundantly; that
Mr. Brett had not above ten guineas in his
pocket to begin the contest; and, in fact, that
he, the plaintiff, was quite unconscious of his
own actions. Jeffreys said, that, as far as he
was able, he would discourage such extravagant
gaming; that the sum of money lost was enormous for persons of their rank; and that the lord
chief justice Hale had checked a horse-race
wager, by threatening to allow the defendant,
the loser, to put off the cause from time to time.'

' By perpetual imparlances.

This alarmed Brett; and he agreed to a compromise, swearing that he took but eight hundred and sixteen guineas away with him. So it was arranged, that each party should keep the money he had got, and give general releases of all actions, suits, and demands.

It is no small testimony to the legal acumen of this judge, that he was considered to be the writer of Vernon's Reports, authorities which have ever borne a very high estimation; but it is said, that his unpopularity was so overwhelming, as to exclude all hopes of their being justly appreciated, if his then obnoxious name had appeared as the author. So sadly true is it, that a man's slippery character or uncourteous demeanour will mar the deepest knowledge and the finest talents.

The year 1688 was now passing away, but great events were in store for the people of England before its close. The acquittal of the bishops had served to show the independence of the country, and their prosecution the obstinacy of James. Finding that his obdurate resolution of forcing a religion upon his subjects was not to be shaken, the public looked earnestly for a deliverer, and the Prince of Orange soon planned his wonderfully successful expedition to ensure their wishes. But the Sovereign was not

without a counsellor of ability : Jeffreys, who
had secretly striven most anxiously to moderate
the royal temper, now urged the calling of a
parliament, and penned a declaration to allay
all jealousies before the meeting. The King
was really struck, but his good feeling did
not last.

On the 22d of September, Lord Clarendon
met the chancellor at the levee, and heard that
the declaration had been altered at the privy-
council board; that the Lord Godolphin had
" broke loose from him, and endeavoured to
trim in the new wording some clauses;" but that
King James had sent for the archbishop of Canterbury, and some of his old friends, to confer
upon the posture of affairs. In less than a week
the chancellor was in despair; some rogues, as
he expressed himself, had changed the King's
mind, who would not yield a point to the
bishops: the Virgin Mary was to do all : so that
the day was lost.

There was a great fluctuation, notwithstanding, in the royal chambers, as two parties were
very earnestly contending for the balance; the
priests on the one side, the bishops on the
other. The monarch would not act decisively :
he issued a general pardon, but he put off the
parliament. And now it fell to the lot of the

poor crest-fallen chancellor to go within the
city gates again, and in most humble mood to
yield up the spoils of his triumph. It was resolved at court, that the charter should be restored : yet it is fair to assert, that he was the
adviser of that honest proceeding ; and why may
we not conclude, that, for the evil he had done,
he was now seeking the most effectual atonement, though he might value himself upon his
influence over the royal mind ? It was with
great satisfaction that he told the Earl of Clarendon on the 2d of October, how several of
the old aldermen were to be carried to court
on that evening, and to be presented by their
old recorder; indeed, he did not doubt but that
he should bring more good things to pass.

The magistrates came ; they received a promise that their charter should be returned, and
the corporation placed in the same situation as
when the depriving judgment was given. When
we hear, then, that the King commanded his
chancellor to yield up the city writings in his
own person, we must give the penitent minister
credit for his good counsel, while we attribute
the humility which accompanied the restoration
to his just apprehensions.

James, indeed, who knew that the bishops
were on the point of importuning him for this

act of justice, professed to make a great merit
of his concession. He told the mayor and aldermen, that he was mightily concerned for the
welfare of their body; and that at a time when
invasion menaced the kingdom, his gracious
boon was a mark of the confidence he entertained of their loyalty. Accordingly, on the
day following this courtly reception, Jeffreys
proceeded to the Guildhall, in great pomp, and
delivered the instrument which put the corporation in possession of their privileges: long
and loud were the acclamations which wel-
comed the deed; though the author was saluted
with a reception which his gorgeous entry had
been calculated to evade. "The sight of the
man," says Dalrymple,[1] "took away the merit
of the concession." He had witnessed, in fact,
an earnest of that strong feeling which the populace held against him, which they were ready
to let loose upon him at the earliest moment
of impunity. He met with treatment as severe
as could then be shown him; conduct, which,
while it evinced a sense of his former tyranny,
no less revealed a ripening contempt for the

[1] Dalrymple declares, that Sunderland prompted these
measures of grace. They were all cowards together, except
the monarch, who, whatever might have been his devoted
bigotry, can never be suspected of personal fear.

z

weak government. Treby was made recorder;
and Sir John Shorter, a churchman, lord mayor
in the room of Eyles, who was an anabaptist.
A simultaneous retribution was ordered in favour of other corporations about the same time.

The fall of the great minister may be dated
from this time: he seems, indeed, to have been
very sensible of his approaching fate, and, in the
recent city transactions, he appeared far less
florid or frolicsome than he was wont to be;
which, for him, was considered a very bad
omen. Soon after this a petition was proposed
by some of the bishops, and other lords: it
was to implore the King, that he would save
the shedding of blood, as the Prince of Orange
had landed. Lord Halifax was asked to sign
it; but he inquired of Lord Clarendon, whether
it was fit that the chancellor's name should be
put to it: that noble earl answered, that,
whether Jeffreys signed or not, it was no concern to him, he should not decline on that account to become a party to it.—" Then," said
Lord Halifax, " I will not join with any who
have sat in the ecclesiastical commission."

The last official act, which fell to the chancellor's lot, was the calling of a parliament.
This was agreed on, in the King's dinner-room,
towards the close of November, and the writs

were issued on the next day. Lord Clarendon spoke with great freedom at the meeting of the council, where this was determined, laying open the principal miscarriages which had embroiled the kingdom; but the King was displeased at his candour. The earl called soon afterwards upon Jeffreys at his chamber in Whitehall, when he was made acquainted with the royal displeasure; but the chancellor added, that he hoped, now the writs were out, His Majesty would be reconciled to his old friends.

The alarm, however, had become general, every one was shifting for himself; and after this all was confusion, till the assembling of the convention parliament, and the accession of William.

CHAP. VIII.

Flight of James II.—The lord chancellor is ill spoken of by the
fugitive monarch—The great seal is consigned to the Thames,
and is found by a fisherman—Jeffreys conceals himself on board
a collier—A scrivener, whom the chancellor had browbeat at a
former time, discovers the fallen judge—He is seized and
carried before Sir John Chapman, lord mayor—He is sent to the
Tower, on a charge of treason—Petition of the widows and
orphans in the west of England against him—Four questions
propounded by the peers to the ex-chancellor—Death of
Jeffreys—Causes of his demise—His place of sepulture—
Anecdotes—Curious writings in vituperation of the fallen
chancellor at the time of his imprisonment—His good and ill
qualities—His splendid talents—Attainder of Jeffreys and his
heirs attempted—His landed possessions—His portrait by Sir
Godfrey Kneller—Some account of his son, John, Lord Jeffreys—*Fable* supposed to have been written by him—He
espouses a daughter of the earl of Pembroke—Conclusion.

IT was now no secret, that *sauve qui peut* was
the ruling principle that prevailed at court. Indeed, it was in operation every where, save in
the camp of the invader.

James, who held the Roman faith dearer than
his dominions, hastened to escape from the land
of protestantism, and to exchange his forlorn

state for the splendid asylum which his brother
of France had proffered. Yet, deserted by his
children and friends, abandoned by the nobles,
and disliked by the multitude, he had not experienced these reverses, till he had himself forgotten the remembrance of past services. When
Duke of York, he had a solicitor who advanced
his interests, and counselled him in the hour of
necessity : when he mounted the throne, he had
the same man for a chief justice, who put down
rebellion by his order, though at the expense
of deep popular odium; and when the seals
were to be disposed of, there was still the same
judge for his minister, whose advice, if followed,
would have ensured the sceptre to his posterity.
Jeffreys was not remembered in the day of danger; for when the monarch left his throne, he
also left a faithful, and to the crowd an obnoxious chancellor. But that the King's undoubted courage is of universal acknowledgment, it might be that personal anxiety would
be offered in excuse for such conduct; yet,
even then, time enough had elapsed in which
the minister might have been warned of his fate,
and assured of a safe shelter. No such intention was held at court ; for there it seemed to have
been well understood that a victim was to be

sacrificed, and that the unfortunate Jeffreys was marked for the atoning scape-goat. When James was seized at Feversham, he acted most consistently with this policy. He called for his landlord, and asked his name. On inquiry, this man turned out to be one who had been fined at the chancellor's instance. Finding this, the crafty prince bade the host draw a discharge as effectually as he chose; and he then signed it with this jesuitical address: " I am sensible that my lord chancellor hath been a very ill man, and hath done very ill things." That nobleman was in the Tower when this happened; so that he was not only betrayed, but even reproached by his master for services, in the execution of which he had been too complying.

The royal fugitive departed from Whitehall on the 11th of December; and it is remarkable, that he gave Father Petre and Lord Mellfort notice of his flight, leaving his keeper of the seals to share those miseries of which he had in part been the instrument. Yet there was, in truth, no keeper of his conscience at this time; for the great seal had been taken from Jeffreys some days before; and far from appointing another, the monarch ordered that the insignia should be thrown into the river:[1] they were discovered by a fisherman, and brought to London: which gives Sir John Dalrymple occasion to observe, that "Heaven seemed by this accident to declare, that the laws, the constitution, and the sovereignty of Britain, were not to depend upon the frailty of man." Had Sir John witnessed our unprejudiced days, he might have heard of a great seal being defaced, and a new one made, without the least apprehension for our great charters. During the short interval which passed between the escape of James and his capture, the populace took their opportunity, and rose, as all mobs do, for the sake of plunder and pillage.[2] Their fury was mainly bent against the papists: they committed every feasible outrage on the priests, whom they held in abomination; and "they rifled the houses of several popish ambassadors."

Indeed, the King owed his arrest to the hatred which prevailed against these Romish confessors; for some fishermen had been out "priest-codding," as they called it, that is, endeavouring to intercept the flying clergy, and so got sight

[1] Reresby says, that Jeffreys took the broad seal along with him.

[2] Order was given by the lords at Whitehall to fire on them with bullet, in case of necessity.

of His Majesty, while the ballast was getting ready for his bark.

And there was one other person whose face the mob most earnestly desired to see : they had a most awful longing for the great terrorist, and used every exertion to get the late chancellor into their power. Need the reader be told, that of all men he was at this time the most execrated? that of stories the most absurd concerning him, there was not one which would not have met the greediest credit? that he was, in a word, the very same devil whom they burnt in effigy in the reign of Charles II. ?[1]

Equally clear it is, that the persecuted noble-man was fully conscious of the mercy he should experience from such a multitude; that he knew well the justice of hanging him first, and examining his conduct afterwards, or, perhaps, not considering it at all; and that Whitehall was of all places the least safe for one so notorious.

[1] The following is an admirable specimen of mob cow-ardice :—

> Now may you hear the people as they scoure
> Along, not fear to damn the chancellor :
> Then women too, and all the tender crew,
> That us'd to pity all, now laugh at you.
> The very boys, how they do grin and prate,
> And giggle at the bills upon your gate !

And, indeed, the public feeling was high in favour of James for leaving such a signal victim to the general fury : for the duke of Buckingham relates, that this act was held to be generous, and that the King was for ever compassionating his subjects who had died in the west. However, the duke freely says, that this "mysterious absconding" cost the minister his life.

The crowd had but a slender hope of laying their hands upon this principal malefactor, as he was reputed; for perceiving how the tide had turned, he left his lodging, and hid himself at a little house at Wapping, whence he might escape beyond sea; upon which it was very naturally rumoured, that he had gone with the King.

And now "George Jeffreys, who boasted his face was of brass," was compelled to clothe himself in the best disguise that he could. He was not merely running from the mob, though that had been wise enough; but from the Prince of Orange, and the lords of the council : he had an equal dread of all the factions. When a courtier asked him, soon after his expedition to the city, what the heads of the Prince's declaration were, he answered, "He was sure his was one, whatever the rest were."

The person now marked out for destruction was rather above the middling stature; his

complexion inclining to fair, and of a comely
appearance. His face showed briskness, but
mixed with an air which might breed a suspicion of some little lurking malice and unplea-
santness. He had a piercing eye, and a brow
most commanding; in the management of which
he showed a great accomplishment, whether
it pleased him to terrify or to conciliate. Some
say, that he was bloated by intemperance;
and if so, he required a most wary concealment, and a faithful guide upon an emergency
like the present. However, he had the sense to
cut off his fierce eyebrows, and to wrap himself
in the garb of a sailor, or a collier : as the poet
sings concerning him ;—

> He took a collier's coat to sea to go :
> Was ever chancellour arrayed so ?

and again :—

> Jeffreys was prepar'd for sailing,
> In his long tarpaulin gown.[1]

His plan was to go to Hamburgh by a coal-
barge, which pretended to be bound for Newcastle, spies being ordered at all the ports by
Admiral Herbert. However, the mate of this

---

[1] James, in his Memoirs, merely says, that my lord chancellor was seized in the confusion, and being committed to
the Tower, died soon afterwards.

vessel was a man of treachery, and gave private information of his retreat: upon which some people applied to a magistrate for a warrant, which the justice refused. Baffled in this, they went to the council-board, and told their story to the lords, who forthwith gave them the authority they desired. Off they went to search the collier; but Jeffreys had some doubt of his security there, and on that night he thought proper to lie in another ship which was near at hand, by which means he escaped the execution of the warrant for a few hours: yet he had the extreme indiscretion to make his appearance the next morning at a little ale-house, with the sign of the Red Cow, in Anchor and Hope Alley, near King Edward's Stairs, and there he had a pot of ale. He was in his sailing accoutrements, with a seaman's cap on; and he put his head through the window to look out. Most unhappily, there passed by at that instant the same miserable scrivener who had been so struck with his face when he came to be relieved from the " Bummery" bond.—" I shall never forget the terrors of that man's face while I live," said he, at that time, to his friend, and now he started at the ominous recollection. This scrivener, and the clerk in Chancery mentioned by Kennet, may be fairly considered

the same person. Nichols tells us, that the
attorney came in to look for a client; and Kennet, that the clerk caught the peeping chancellor at the window. Most probably, having
noticed the remarkable visage, Mr. Trimmer[1]
came in, under pretence of business, that he
might satisfy himself. Jeffreys seems to have
known the scared lawyer as well ; for he feigned a cough, and turned to the wall with his
beer in his hand. But, alas for the poor ex-
chancellor! his hour was come; the inexorable
trimmer proclaimed him aloud, and the rabble
burst in upon him. The occasion of this sad
disaster is said to be, that he waited too long for
the tide.[2] That the discovery was not instantly
crowned with murder ; in effect, that the fugitive was not torn in pieces, limb by limb,—must

[1] This was the name which made Jeffreys call for him in
open court, and express the desire he had to see a trimmer,
which frightened him so seriously.

[2] There is still another account in the London Courant :
that Mr. Gaunt, whose wife was executed for high-treason,
two or three years before, caused the judge to be apprehended, as having passed sentence upon her : but, unluckily
for this statement, Chief Justice Jones was the judge who
gave the sentence upon that occasion. Mr. Burnham was
the name of the solicitor ; and the master of the house was
Mr. Porter, the master of a Newcastle sloop.—See Nichols's
Leicestershire.

be attributed to a kind Providence which interfered to give him a few months' respite; for
(and we cannot be astonished,) the mobile, as he
would call them when chief justice, was disposed very summarily to whip and hang him.
A few doggrel verses written at the time very
sufficiently explain the meaning of the crowd:—

> The mobile and rout, with clubs and staves,
> Swore that his carcass ne'er should lie in graves;
> They'd eat him up alive within an hour;
> Their teeth should tear his flesh, and him devour;
> Limb him they would, as boys at Shrovetide do:
> Some cried, I am for a wing, an arm; for what are you?
> I am for his head, says one; for his brains, says 't other;
> And I am for his nose; his ears another:
> Oh, cries a third, I am for his buttocks brave,
> Nine pounds of steaks from them I mean to have:
> I know the rogue is fleshy, says a fourth,
> The sweetbreads, lungs, and heart, then nothing worth;
> Yes, quoth another, but not good to eat;
> A heart of steel will ne're prove tender meat.

Considering the desperate treatment which
Cinna met with from the Roman vulgar when
mistaken for the conspirator of that name, and
the instant punishment which fell upon the unfortunate Dr. Lamb[1] in the days of Charles I., it

[1] A creature of the Duke of Buckingham, who was murdered by the mob in 1628. The rabble declared, that if his
master, the duke, had been there, they would have given him
as much.

is rather beyond mere hypochondriacal wonder, that this man was not mutilated on the spot. Nevertheless, it was determined to carry him before the lord mayor, which, as we shall see, occasioned another tragedy. He was conveyed in his blue jacket, with his hat flapped down upon his face, in a coach guarded by several blunderbusses. When he came to the mayor's house, the crowd became immense, and their vociferating cries of " Vengeance! Justice! Justice!" were so numerous, as to create some apprehension. The chief magistrate came out into his balcony with his hat in his hand, and begged that the people would retire; he said, justice should be done them, and that their prisoner should be secured till the lords of the council should determine upon his destiny. But the mayor lost his life through this event. He was Sir John Chapman, whom we have already mentioned; and who had a tolerably amicable understanding with Jeffreys. When the hat was lifted up which concealed that minister's face, and he beheld a countenance which was wont to inspire terror into all beholders,—the shock was so great as to occasion a fainting or convulsion fit; and the next day so many fits came on, as to end his life by palsy very soon afterwards.'

' He died March 17, 1689: some say he died of apoplexy. It is supposed that the panic with which this worthy

Ralph writes thus, alluding to the time of Jeffreys's capture : " Every face that he saw was the face of a fury: every grasp he felt, he had reason to think was that of the demon that waited for him : every voice that he could distinguish in so wild an uproar, overwhelmed him with reproaches; and his conscience echo'd within him, that he deserved them all. In this miserable plight, in these merciless hands, with these distracted thoughts, and with the horror and despair in his own ghastly face, that was the natural result of all, he was goaded on to the lord mayor." Notwithstanding this impressive charge of cowardice, it is by no means so certain that this high individual was bereft of a due presence of mind. Fancy will frequently depict the most melancholy appearances, which

citizen was afflicted had so great an effect, as to deprive him of all reason and resolution; so that Jeffreys was actually obliged to assist in drawing the warrant for his own commitment. This was the first warrant. Truly, the lord mayors do not seem to have figured much in those days! Sir Thomas Bludworth, for example, who was so dreadfully scared at the great fire of London! At the tumultuous assemblies for the election of sheriffs in the latter part of Charles the Second's reign, the chief magistrate had screwed his nerves up most painfully before he could do any thing, and was even then backed up of necessity by Jeffreys in all his terrors: and in 1780, living memory can testify that the riots in the city astonished the very worthy man who presided there.

are but shadows, merely because the occasion
seems to call for them. When the seizure was
made, he was asked if he were not the chancellor. He said, " I am the man." He begged
that he might be kept from the enraged populace, and thus came protected by a strong
guard. This account varies in no way from the
former, except that it omits the coloured inter-
pretations of a rabble.

It was dinner-time when the extraordinary
guest was announced at the Mansion-house;
but the hospitalities of the city were not wanting, for the lord mayor begged his old acquaintance to sit at the upper end of the table, where
he received a very honourable entertainment.
Still the people pressed from without; and it was
suggested, that the peer might be dismissed by a
back-way; but a gentleman made his way into
the room, declaring that the chancellor was the
mayor's prisoner, and that the magistrate must
answer his forthcoming with his own blood.'
Upon this two regiments of the train-bands
were sent for to move him to the Tower; a body
most necessary to ward off the increasing violence of the mob. The Lord Lucas received him
on his request : for such an imprisonment was a

' Which he certainly did, if he died of apoplexy.

deliverance from instant death; and soon afterwards, a legitimate order was received from the lords to commit him on a charge of high-treason.[1] There was, however, considerable difficulty in rescuing the state prisoner, even with so powerful a guard, so sternly did the people press against him, at the peril of their very lives. Jeffreys was so sensible of the danger which menaced him on all sides, that he held up his hands, sometimes on one side of the coach, sometimes on the other; and observing the open-mouthed wolves, who were pushing on all sides with whips and halters, exclaimed, " For the Lord's sake keep them off!—For the Lord's sake keep them off!"[2] Oldmixon, who tells us of his

[1] Before the warrant, the following words were ordered to be inserted :—" Whereas the Lord Jeffreys was seized and brought to the house of the lord mayor, and was there in great danger by the insults of the people: to secure him, therefore, from the said violence, and at his desire to the Lord Lucas to remove him to the Tower, the following order was made, &c." Then the warrant. After the warrant, these words followed :—" The lords appointed to examine the Lord Jeffreys, were desired by the Lord Jeffreys *to return to the lords his humble thanks* for their care in preserving him from violence." The lords appointed to examine Lord Jeffreys were, Lord North and Grey, Lord Chandos, and Lord Ossulston.

[2] This fury was not confined to the rabble; for we find Mr. Harbord, a member of the House of Commons,

own habits of compassion for malefactors in general, declares, that he saw these agonizing
alarms without pity. Surely many a brave man
would prefer to be blown from the mouth of a
cannon, to the fate of being swallowed up, or
dissected alive by his own countrymen. As
soon as it became well known that their old
enemy was safely caged in the Tower, the good
people of the west, the women in particular, began to murmur loudly for redress. The same
multitude who were too terrified to join the
Prince for some days, lest the judge with his
hangings of scarlet cloth¹ should come suddenly
down upon them, were now transported with
rage, and demanded that he should be brought
down helpless and unarmed to have vengeance
wreaked upon him.

We give "The humble Petition of the widows
and fatherless children in the west of England.

"We, to the number of a thousand and more,
widdows and fatherless children, of the counties
of Dorset, Somerset, and Devon; our dear husbands and tender fathers having been so tyran-

moving, that two of the judges who approved the King's dispensing power should be hanged, by way of example, at
Westminster-hall gate.

¹ Jeffreys decorated the walls of the courts with scarlet,
during part of the western assize.

nously butcher'd, and some transported; our
estates sold from us, and our inheritance cut off
by the severe and harsh sentence of George,
Lord Jeffreys, now, we understand, in the Tower
of London, a prisoner; who has lately, we hear,
endeavoured to excuse himself from those tyrannical and illegal sentences, by laying it on
information by some gentlemen, who are known
to us to be good Christians, true Protestants,
and Englishmen. We, your poor petitioners,
many hundreds of us, on our knees have begg'd
mercy for our dear husbands and tender parents from his cruel hands, but his thirst for
blood was so great, and his barbarism so cruel,
that instead of granting mercy for some, which
were made appear to be innocent, and petitioned for by the flower of the gentry of the said
counties, he immediately executed; and so bar-
barously, that a very good gentlewoman at Dorchester, begging on her knees the life of a worthy
gentleman to marry him, and make him her
husband; this vile wretch, having not common
civility with him, and laying aside that honour
and respect due to a person of her worth, told
her, 'Come, I know your meaning; some part
of your petition I will grant, which shall be,
that after he is hanged and quartered,   *   *   *

*   *   *   *   *   *   *

and so I will give orders to the sheriff.' These,
with many hundred more tyrannical acts, are
ready to be made appear in the said counties,
by honest and credible persons; and therefore
your petitioners desire, that the said George
Jeffreys, late lord chancellor, the vilest of men,
may be brought down to the counties aforesaid,
where we, the good women in the west, shall
be glad to see him, and give him another manner of welcome than he had there three years
since. And your petitioners shall ever pray,"&c.

These furious women irresistibly remind us
of the *poissardes*, who were by far the most active
of the Parisian rabble at the Revolution; and like
them, they would have delighted in immolating
a victim. And in London the people were in
full expectation of a public execution; nay, according to a poetical letter to the lord chancellor, they continued as intent as ever upon his
speedy fate. Having recommended the nobleman to cut his throat, the writer ends his epistle
thus :—

"I am your lordship's, in any thing of this
nature. From the little house over against
Tyburn, where the people are almost dead with
expectation of you." From such assemblages

the composer of the " New Protestant Litany "
should have said, *Libera nos, Domine!* as well as
from godfather pope, and gunpowder bonfires.

Jeffreys was taken on the 12th of December,
and His Majesty was conveyed back to London
soon afterwards; but it does not appear, that
between the times of this unlucky attempt and
the final embarkation of the monarch for France,
there was any favourable notice of his ancient favourite. Glad to emancipate himself from a kingdom where the heretic flag was triumphant, James
looked forward to no greater pleasure than the
solaces of priestcraft, and lifting up of the cruci-
fix. He had bidden a farewell[1] to old England,

---

[1] THE FAREWEL.

Farewel Petre, farewel Cross;
Farewel Chester, farewel Ass;[*]
Farewel Peterborough, farewel Tool;
Farewel Sun——land, farewel Fool.

Farewel Milford, farewel Scot;
Farewel Butler, farewel Sot;
Farewel Roger, farewel Trimmer;
Farewel Dryden, farewel Rhymer.

Farewel Brent, farewel Villain;
Farewel Wright, worse than Tresilian;
Farewel Chanceller, farewel Mace;
Farewel Prince, farewel Race.

[*] Jeffreys.
George Jeffreys who boasted his face was of brass,
Is now metamorphos'd into a Welsh ass, &c.

and to most of his friends who were not of the Roman communion, leaving behind him a character which would to God the people of this land would hold deeply in their memories!—a prince of bravery, of virtue, and of kindness, where no priest or jesuit interfered; but one whom no tie, moral or political, could restrain, when a zeal for his religion came in question.

It was thought fit to examine Jeffreys on the day after his commitment; and for this purpose a deputation of lords was appointed. Four questions were agreed on to be asked of him. First, What he had done with the great seal of England? To this he answered, that he had delivered it to the King on the Saturday before at Mr. Cheffnel's, no person being present, and never saw it since. He was next asked, Whether he had sealed all the writs for the parliament, and what he had done with them? To the best of his remembrance, he said, the writs were all sealed and delivered to the King. Thirdly, Had he sealed the several patents for the then ensuing year? He declared that he had sealed several patents for the new

Farewel Queen, and farewel Passion;
Farewel King, farewel Nation;
Farewel Priests, and farewel Pope;
Farewel all deserve a rope.

sheriffs, but that he could not charge his memory with the particulars. It was, lastly, inquired, Whether he had a license to go out of the kingdom? And to this he replied, that he had several to go beyond sea, which were all delivered to Sir John Friend, &c. He subscribed these answers thus:—" I affirm all this to be true upon my honour.—Jeffryes."

An order came on the 22d for keeping him in a closer restraint; but he had, nevertheless, the courage to demand his *habeas corpus*, in order to his being bailed, but was not successful.

After he had been in confinement for a few days, he was most cruelly tantalized by the arrival of a barrel as a present, which appeared to contain oysters:[1] seeing this, he said to the bearer, " Well then, I see I have some friends left still," and opened the barrel. The gift was a good able halter.

And now we have arrived at the consummation of this great man's destiny, his lingering struggles in the Tower being little regarded amidst the din of warfare which was sounding without. For James was about to land at Kinsale with the French supplies, when Jeffreys died. It is curious to note the various causes

---

[1] Some refine upon this, and say, " the best Colchester oysters."

assigned by historians for his decease. Some
kill him in his own way, by excessive and intemperate drinking; but his commonly bibacious
habits might have given an easy foundation for
this opinion, as it is most difficult and most un-
wise too for any lover of the bottle to descend
suddenly into the vale of abstemiousness. Others
will have it, that the chiefs of the mobility did
him great injury, and that terror, lest he should
fall into their hands, completed the shock he
had received. Then again, we hear of his dying
furiously and wildly like a raving beast; a report
which must have greatly gratified the superstitious vulgar, who were probably the creators
of it, and doubtless conjured up his unquiet
spirit as a bugbear for a quarter of a century
afterwards. A much more sensible conjecture
would be, that from an unusual imprisonment
he had aggravated an ill habit of body, and
heightened his chronic disorders. Accordingly,
there appears to be great fidelity in the account
which states that fits of the stone came on with
such violence, as to baffle the skill of his physician. Dr. Lower,' an ingenious man, attended
him ; but although his patient was but forty-one

' Richard Lower. Probably the ingenious medical writer
who wrote the " Universal Medicine," which was published
in France and Sweden. He was also the author of many
other treatises.

years of age, he found nature exhausted beyond the reach of medical skill.—" It is generally reported," says Echard, " that he shortened his days, and in a manner dispatched himself, by drinking of the most spirituous liquors; but I have been assur'd to the contrary by a very credible person,[1] who was often with him in his confinement, who said, that the stone was the only bodily distemper that killed him."

Anguish of mind and disappointment are also among the probable bitternesses which harassed him; so that he is said, in some milder relations, to have perished by a broken heart. And far from leaving the stage in a state of frenzied impiety, there are premises from which we may conclude that he died repentant, and under a due sense of religion. For it is said, on the authority of Sir Joseph Jekyll, that Dr. John Scott[2] visited the fallen judge in his prison, who promised to profit by the exhortations of his minister, and review his past life as a seasonable improvement of the situation he had come into. Jeffreys expressed great concern for his past errors; but for one, and that too the greatest of his alleged misdeeds, he could never be induced to

[1] Probably Dr. Scott, of whom we shall speak presently.
[2] Author of " The Christian Life." Sir Joseph heard this from the mouth of the doctor.

yield an unqualified regret. However cruel his
western proceedings might have been thought,
whatever the censures which had been heaped
upon that part of his administration, he solemnly
adhered, in these almost his dying hours, to this
text, that the severities had fallen short of the
King's demand, and that he had extremely displeased the monarch by his forbearance. It is not
to be combated, that the men who fell by the sentence of Jeffreys died by law; and that circumstance makes the distinction between his executions and those of Kirk. Kindness to the human
race was scarcely better understood in those times,
even by persons of reputation, than mercy to
dumb animals* in these, till the rise of Martin.
Forbearance was then esteemed a crime, as
rigorous justice would be at this day. And
truly, it is to be hoped that posterity will kindly
invent some excuse for us, when those who succeed us shall blot out our capital punishments
from the statute-book, and wonder, as we now
do, at the harshness of those who have gone
past.

* Indeed, it is but of late that we have learned to treat our
own children with kindness, and to be persuaded, that however agreeable hardships might have been to the sons of
giants, who wore coats of mail, we of this generation shall be
much wiser in fostering the little strength which is im-
parted to this winter of the world.

The noble penitent, moreover, complained
that he had been urged on by one of the reverend bench,[*] to enforce the rigours of the ecclesiastical commission far beyond his inclination;
and his approved steadfastness in favour of the
established church must strongly call upon us
to believe that this palliation also has some
weight. Indeed, to say that the chancellor had
no religion in the days of his prosperity, would
be an outrage upon history; since we know that
he stood firmly by the Protestant standard, and
that the threatened loss of his place had no
power to wean him from his native creed. To
assert then that he died a reprobate, is a gratuitous slander of his whig enemies, containing
as much truth, perhaps, as the pages of those
speculative voyagers, whose adventurous travels
have been concocted and accomplished by their
own firesides. " God knows how often all of us
have taken the great name of God in vain,"
said Jeffreys one day, in all the plenitude of his
chief justiceship; " or have said more than becomes us, and talked of things we should not
do." Yet some of the good-natured booksellers,
in a few reigns afterwards, seem to have decided

[*] Most likely Crew, bishop of Durham.

his ultimate destiny very unfavourably, placing him in a situation far worse than purgatory. There was published, about the year 1714, "A Letter from Hell, from Lord Ch—r Jeffreys to L— C— B— W——d, relating to James Taylor's standing in the pillory. 4to."

Although this unfortunate nobleman was thus employed in meditating on his past mistakes, he certainly was not quite so far lost to the world as to abandon all hopes of a better fortune. He, therefore, made offers of political disclosures to government; which, it seems, were entertained, and even courted by the parties who were applied to: so that had the Lord Jeffreys lived, he might not have been so near " a place of execution" as his enemies desired; and, in fact, it would not be hazarding a strange opinion to say at once, that he would have escaped with impunity, owing to the turbulent and uncertain spirit of the parliament. Having so long had the *arcana imperii* at his command, it is not to be wondered at that his information would be deemed worthy of notice in such critical times. Illness, however, and death supervened.—The great man died on the 19th of April, 1689, at 35 minutes past four in the morning.

Doubts have prevailed as to the place of his

burial; for there is a tradition that he was laid at Enfield,[1] which seems to be utterly incorrect. Mr. Bayley gives the most satisfactory account of the last rites which were rendered upon this occasion. He was first interred in the Tower privately, and his remains rested there in peace for three years, when his friends, finding that the hot day of persecution was over, begged that they might be allowed to remove the coffin. They had no mind, it seems, to risk much mention of the subject before, as the disgrace of Ireton and other Cromwellians was by no means erased from living memory; and whose bones so likely to be dug up and gibbeted as those of Jeffreys, if the people fancied that they would have it so? Indeed, to gratify the multitude, the government might not have scrupled more in this instance than the successful conquerors of 1746, who elevated the noble heads of the rebellion upon the height of Temple-bar. Johnson, walking near that impregnable city gate some years afterwards with Goldsmith, slily observed, in allusion to their politics at that time of day,—

Forsitan et nostrum nomen miscebitur *istis*.

---

[1] At the east end of the south aisle, in a vault belonging to the manor of Durance. His eldest daughter married the son and heir of Judge Stringer, who was lord of the manor.

A warrant was given, dated the 30th of September, 1692, signed by the Queen, and directed to the governor of the Tower, " for his delivering the body of George, late Lord Jefferies, to his friends and relations, to bury him as they think fit."

He was accordingly disinterred, and buried a second time in a vault under the communion-table of St. Mary Aldermanbury, on the 2d of November, 1693. There was a story very current there, that the apprentices of the parish tumultuously assisted in this removal; but Malcolm, in his account of London, treats this as merely fabulous; adding however, that the apprentices might have run riot upon the occasion, as such conduct was by no means uncommon in those reigns.

One would have thought that the judge's bones might now be considered as undisturbed; and whether his final lot were hallowed or accursed, his remains would at least be suffered to dwindle away in peace: yet curiosity has been more than once gratified with a sight of them, and the leaden coffin has been very recently found in a state of perfect preservation. Malcolm was told by the sextoness, in 1803, that she had seen it entire in its rich clothing of crimson velvet with gilt furniture.

Some years afterwards, in 1810, certain workmen employed to repair the church discovered the place of interment, by removing a large flat stone near the communion-table. The coffin, which appeared to have suffered little from decay, was closed, and there was a plate with the name of Chancellor Jeffreys inscribed. When the public had been satisfied with a view of these remarkable remains, a gaze which some would brand as unhallowed, the coffin was replaced in the vault, and the stone fastened over it. But the body was not seen; for although a sight of it would have highly pleased the ambition of the curious, no one adventured to lay violent hands upon the case which contained it.

When the great Johnson died, many small wits and hungry pens were at work on the instant, to depreciate or to ridicule him. The possessors of these little weapons cared not whether they took aim at his personal deficiencies, or supposed literary errors, provided they had the intense satisfaction of sending forth their poor puffs as speedily as might be. But one circumstance struck all his friends and admirers, and amongst others the late Dr. Parr, whose indignation was kindled at it;—and this was, that many of these critics dared not to have attacked

the doctor in his life-time. Some one made a
slighting remark on him in Parr's presence,—
"Ay," quoth the blunt clergyman, "now the
old lion is dead, every ass thinks he may kick
at him." And it really falls to the lot of most
great men to be served very much in the same
way. No sooner was that man in his grave,
whom all feared alike as counsel, chief justice,
chancellor,—than there sprang up satires and reflections upon his memory, which are vastly at
variance with history, and which he could have
sufficiently answered, but for the stroke of disease or death. And it is observable, that the
scribbling rabble commenced their operations
against him as soon as he went to the Tower,
doubtless conceiving themselves secure from his
vengeance.

The two remarkable papers which we insert,
will be found to contain charges of hypocrisy;
of which, at least of many, Jeffreys can hardly
be deemed guilty:—

The first of these is entitled, "The Chancellor's Examination and Preparation for a Trial."
It was printed for W. Cademan, in 1689, and
runs as follows:—

"As the long imprisonment of George, Lord
Jefferies, the high chancellor of England, has
given him ample leisure for a full and serious

consideration of his state, his examination of his
fatal circumstances, and preparation for his trial,
with all other necessary and due reflections,
previous as well to the appearance, not only before so great a tribunal here, but also a greater
and more terrible one to come, have induced
him to this timely provision of his last will and
testament.

"In the name of Ambition, the only god of
our setting-up and worshipping, together with
Cruelty, Treachery, Perjury, Pride, Insolence,
&c. his ever adored angels and archangels, cloven-
footed, or otherwise, Amen. I, George, sometimes lord, but always Jefferies, being in entire
bodily health, (my once great heart, at present
dwindled to the diminutive dimensions of a
French bean, only excepted,) and in sound and
perfect memory of high-commissions, *quo-warrantos*, regulations, dispensations, pillorizations,
floggations, gibbetations, barbarity, butchery,
tyranny, together with the bonds and ties of
right, justice, equity, law, and gospel; as also
those of liberty, property, *Magna Charta*, &c.;
not only at divers and sundry, but at all times,
by me religiously broken : and being reminded
by a halter before me, and my sins behind me,
do make my last will and testament in manner
and form following :—

2 B

"*Imprimis.*—Because it has always been the modish departure of great men, and greater sinners, to leave some legacy to pious uses, I give and bequeath one thousand pounds towards the building of a shrine and a chapel to St. Coleman, for the particular devotion of a late very great English zealot; for whose glory I farther order my executors to bear half charges in inserting and registering the sacred papers and memoirs of the said saint, in those divine legends, 'The Lives of the Saints,' by the hand of his reverend, and no less industrious successor, Father Peters: that so the never-dying renown of the long-sworn meritorious, though unfortunate vengeance against the northern heresy, (in which once hopeful vineyard I have been no small labourer,) may be transmitted to posterity by so pious a recorder.

" *Item.*—As a legacy to her late consort-majesty of Great Britain (my sometime royal patroness), I do bequeath two thousand crowns to holy mother church, &c.

" *Item.*—In tenderness and hearty good-will to my sometime friends and allies on the other side the herring-pond, I think fit, as a small mite to the great cause, to order my executors, out of my late son-in-law's estate (saved by my own Chancery decree from the Salisbury creditors),

as much money to be remitted over to the true
and trusty Tyrconnel, as will purchase new
liveries of the best Irish frize, completely to rig
a whole regiment of his newly-raised Teagues;
as also the like quantity for the rigging of another
regiment of French dragoons, now sending over
to his excellency's succour; his Gallic majesty
having long since ordered the edict of Nantz,
and all other the parliamentary heretic-records
of France, to be given them *gratis,* to make them
tailors' measures of, in imitation of the English
Magna Charta, sometime since designed for the
same use.

"But, above all, to take care for my own decent funeral, lest my executors, to save the
charges of Christian burial, should drop me
under ground as slovenly as my old great master at Westminster,—I think fit to order the rites
and ceremonies of my obsequies as follows :

"*Imprimis.*—I desire that my funeral anthems
be all set to the tune of ' Old Lilliburlero,'
that never-to-be-forgotten Irish Shibboleth;
in commemoration not only of two hundred
thousand hereticks that formerly danced off to
the said musical notes, but also of the second
part to the same tune, lately designing, setting,
and composing by a great master of mine, and
myself. The said anthem to be sung by a train

of seven or eight hundred of my own making in
the west; who, in their native rags, (a livery
likewise of my own donation, as a dress fittest
for the sad cavalcade,) will, I am assured, be no
way wanting in their readiest and ablest melody,
suitable to the occasion.

" *Item.*—I order two hundred Jacobuses to be
laid out in myrrh, frankincense, and other necessary perfumes to be burnt at my funeral; to
sweeten if possible * * * * * * * * *

" *Item.*—I order an ell and a half of fine cam-
brick to be cut out into handkerchiefs, for drying
up all the wet eyes at my funeral; together with
half a pint of burnt claret for all the mourners in
the kingdom.

" *Item.*—For the more decent interment of my
remains, I will and require, for the re-cementing
of my own unhappy politic head to my shoulders
again, (provided always I have the honour of
the axe, as it is much questioned,) that a present
of a diamond ring be made to Madame Labadie,
for the use of the same needle, and a skain of
the same thread, once used on a very important
occasion, for the quilting of a certain notable
cushion of famous memory.

" To conclude : for avoiding all Chancery-
suits about the disposal of my aforesaid legacies,
that the contents of this my last will may be made

public, I order my executors to take care that this may be printed."

The second paper is, " The Lord Chancellor's Discovery and Confession, made in the time of his Sickness in the Tower;" from which, by the way, we shall only give extracts.

" As for that damned town of London; not Cataline against old Rome, was half so sworn a foe, as I, against that insolent proud city. Really and sincerely, I would willingly and heartily, out of my own pocket, (though I sold my last rag in the world,) have been myself at the charge of a new monument, so I had had but the pleasure of a second same occasion of building it. Nay, verily, I envied the fate of the old Erostratus, and that more modern worthy, Hubart; and could have wished my own name, though at the price of his destiny, engraven in the room of that wisely rased-out inscription, on so glorious an occasion.

" It was then, alas! edged and enraged with a mortal hate, and an avowed vengeance against that accursed and detested city, and more detested parliament: with two such meritorious qualifications, I applied myself to the once great Coleman's greater master, at that time an early, and indeed almost governing pilot at the helm; both infallible recommendations to entitle

me to the highest hopes of the most exalted honours. In short, I entered, listed, and swore
myself engineer-general under that leading
hero's banners; and how hugged, and how em-
braced, my succeeding almost deluge of good
fortune, glories, and preferments, will sufficiently testify.

" And, though the world has sometimes wondered at so sudden a rise, as in little more than
seven years, to mount from a Finsbury petty-
fogger to a lord high chancellor of England;
from bawling at a hedge-court bar for a five shillings' fee, to sit equity-driver with ten thousand pounds per annum, besides presents and
bribes unaccountable, honestly gotten. But,
alas! to rectify the mistakes of mankind, and
suppress their astonishment at so unprecedented
an advance, I must assure them, that as no history affords a parallel of such a crown favourite
as myself, so no age ever yielded such a true
crown drudge neither, to deserve those favours.
Alas! my darling fortunes moved not half so
rapid as my dearer counsels drove; and all the
caresses of my glory were thought but the poor-
est meed and reward of those services that
gained them. But to recite my fatal particu-
ars: upon my first entrance (as I was saying)
of engineer-general, our first great attack was

against the charter of London; and, to the honour of my premier effort, what by our terrible dead-doing *quo-warrantos,* my own invented battering-ram, planted against them at Westminster, and the Tower-hill guns removed and mounted against them on the Tower-battlements, we soon reduced that imperious town to almost as entire a subjection and vassalage, as our own hearts, and our Roman friends could wish.

"Next, for those prorogation-crampers, those check-mates of crowns, called parliaments, there our triumph was absolute : we prorogued or dissolved, and danced them from pillar to post, from Westminster to Oxford, &c. at pleasure, and (Heaven knows) with timely, prudent, and wise care, to hush their too impudently inquisitive curiosity into our Coleman's packets, our Le Chaise and Lewis intrigues, and the rest of our popish plots and cabals, and all, (God knows) little enough to keep our cloven-foot undiscovered.

"Who, alas! but I, with so much unrelenting and pitiless barbarity, triumphed in the blood of those poor miserable western wretches, and sanguined my very ermines in their gore?"—
" Yes, and I acted by the commissioning vengeance that sent me thither, to inform the he-

retick enemies of Rome, how much their blood
tickles when it streams; and to let them know
by the sample of my hand, how keen is a popish
edge-tool.

" Was it not I too, that with so much cunning
and artifice, and by so many rhetorical high-
treason flourishes, wheedled poor Cornish to a
gibbet, and Russel to a scaffold? Yes; and it
was a master-piece! To give the trembling
world a timely warning what Protestant zeal
must trust to, when popish malice is pleased to
be angry; and to convince how easily can a
jesuitical engine wire-draw guilt, when popish
rancour is resolved to destroy.

" Who dissolved all the charters, and new-
garbelled all the corporations, but Jefferies?
And why; but to prepare them to understand
that, (what with our *quo-warrantos* and the rest
of our modelling tools,) we were resolved, at
last, to have parliaments *à la mode de Paris*,
and their dragoon reformers too soon after? Who
invented that ensnaring command to the bishops,
of reading the declaration, and put their refusal
to the stretch of high-misdemeanour, if not
high-treason,—but the chancellor? And why,
think you, but to satisfy them what Roman
eye-sores are the Protestant lawn-sleeves; and
that they shall want neither justles nor stum-

bling-blocks to trip their heels up, and their heads off too, when they stand in our way? Who but the great Jefferies, (in defiance of the very fundamentals of human society, the original laws of human nature, and of the face of *Magna Charta* itself,) got the bishop of London silenced and suspended, without so much as that universal and common right, sacred even amongst heathens and infidels,—viz. the privilege of making either plea or defence; condemned, untried, and unheard? Yes, I did it; to instruct the world what feeble cobweb-lawn are the bonds of justice, law, liberty, common right, &c. in the hands of an imperial popish Samson Agonistes?

" Was it not I too, by my ecclesiastic, high-commission supremacy, (not only against the statutes and customs of the university, but the positive laws of the land,) turned Maudlin College into a seminary of jesuits; and in spite of that bulwark of the church of England, the Act of Uniformity, converted a collegiate chapel into a mass-house? And by the same justice, might not every collegiate, cathedral, and parochial church have had the same conversion, and both the fountains of religion and learning, the mother universities, been deprived · of all her Protestant sons, and re-peopled with the whole race of St. Omer and Salamanca?

"Who did all this? The chancellor! Yes; and
he saved the church of England, and the whole
English liberty by it. The nation was lulled
into so profound a sleep, that they wanted such
thunder-claps, and such a Boanerges, to awaken
them from their lethargy. With these serious
reflections, that these rapid and violent motions
of the Roman cause, are and have been the
destruction of it; who has been the Protestant's
champion—but I? Who has pulled off the vizor
from the scarlet whore, and exposed the painted
Babylon prostitute—but I? And if I drive like
Jehu, it was only to the confusion of a Jezebel.
Who called in the deliverer of our church and
laws, that second Hannibal, that mighty Nas-
sau—but Jefferies? Who has remounted the
sinking glory of our temples, till their pinnacles
shall kiss Heaven,—but Jefferies? Who has united
two such formidable Protestant neighbours with
that eternal link of interest, as shall render us
once more the arbiters of Europe, and terror of
the world—who, but Jefferies? And Jefferies's
conduct has joined those naval forces, those float-
ing walls, that shall one day mew up the French
anti-christian monster, till in despite and despair, he bursts his soul out * * * *!

"In fine, who has cut off the very entail of
popery and slavery from three happy kingdoms—but Jefferies? Three kingdoms did I

say? Yes, possibly has laid that foundation to
the Protestant cause, as perhaps shall one day
make her overtop the seven proud hills, and
strike her dagger into the very gates of Rome."

All the tirade which would seem to connect
the object of these maledictions with papal intrigues are gratuitous, and the offspring of a
malevolence which is so frequently mixed up
with the prejudices of passing times.

Little indeed need be said touching the character of a man whose actions have been so re-
peatedly canvassed, and whom to applaud would
be deemed a political, if not a moral crime. But
his bright sterling talents must be acknowledged; that intuitive perception which led him
to penetrate in a moment the thin veil of hypocrisy, and show things as they were, must have
its meed. Like Thurlow, he had the especial
gift of fastening on the true genius of the cause,
eliciting its nice point, and forming a prompt decision on the right bases of equity and justice.
And he read too at odd unsuspected times; after
a debauch of wine, perhaps, when the share
which would have stupefied a man of ordinary
intellect, only served to give a zest to his ambition, and stimulate the powers of his understanding. That he must have read, appears
from the learning displayed in his judgments:

that he must have read thus, from the even
tenor of his bacchanalian hours; and that due
credit was attached to his abilities, is evident from
the works which were attributed to him by his
contemporaries.[1] He was sufficiently kind to
his friends and dependents, consistent with that
acute insight into the ways of men which he
possessed, which made him restless in the society of dunces, and impatient of intruding ignorance. Had he lived a century and a half later,
though his promotion were retarded or forbid-
den by his debaucheries, he would have held a
name for good-humour and conviviality amongst
his acquaintance, which, however unfit to be
aspired after to the excess of which he was guilty,
is yet no bad recommendation to its possessor;
whilst his sanguinary temper would have lain
dormant in an age when scarce any error escapes
its just scrutiny. It is well known that he was
extravagant, and therefore always needy and
borrowing; but in accordance with the spirit of
the age, every worthy and liberal action which
he did was carefully concealed, according to
Mark Antony's seditious text;—

[1] Vernon's Reports, which are allowed to be most ably
drawn : " The Magistracy and Government of England vindicated," by Sir B. Shower, which drew forth the acrimony
of Sir John Hawles's pen.

The evil, that men do, lives after them;
The good is oft interred with their bones;
So let it be with Cæsar.

Some contributor to the Gentleman's Magazine ventured to ask, some years since, what baronet bore certain arms, describing them, and suggested that he was probably connected with Hertfordshire, or some adjacent county. Being informed that Sir George Jeffreys claimed those heraldic honours, the inquiring correspondent declares, that " the historian of Hertfordshire will now have to record the name of that well-known judge as one of the contributors to the repair of the abbey church of St. Alban, in 1683." He adds, that the arms, with those of his friend Lord-keeper North, and fifty other persons, are fixed against the walls of the choir, *in perpetuam rei memoriam:* but, as we have abundantly shown, the friendship of those two great persons must have been very suspicious; it might, indeed, be more correct to substitute the words, "political opponent," as no two ministers ever differed more, whether in the cabinet, the council, or in their domestic life.

We will now forbear any further mention of

---

[1] On the pillar north opposite to the third pillar, Jeffreys, of Bulstrode, Bart., and two others.—Clutterbuck.

this nobleman as far as his good or ill qualities
are concerned : let such as doubt his talents
examine the grounds and the issue of his judicial decisions; and let those who have agreed to
the general opprobrium which rests upon his
memory, look, for the mere sake of charity, to
discover some redeeming actions, and they will
not be disappointed.

But although death had freed Lord Jeffreys
from public ignominy or degrading concilia-
tions, it was determined in parliament, that
some open mark of reproach should be fixed on
his memory; and it was therefore moved, on
the 16th of the following May, "That the
late chancellor and his heirs may be excepted
out of the indemnity, in order to attainder."
Mr. Boscawen had suggested before, that he
should be " attainted, and reduced to the same
condition as when he began to offend ; and,
moreover, that his posterity should be incapable
of sitting in the Lords' House." So that evil
was plainly gone forth against his descendants,
and their fortunes : yet, disliked as he necessarily must have been, the simple proposition
to except him, as the great offender, was not
pressed at once. Hawles,' afterwards the soli-

' Hawles was born in the Close, at New Sarum, and educated at Winchester-school. He then became a commoner

citor-general, rested on the difficulty of punishing the dead; and, said he, "when you inquire, you will find the chancellor very little
more guilty than those who lately passed the
proclamation, little less than the dispensing
power." The debate was adjourned; and before
the matter was finally set at rest, the western
executions, Oates's dreadful punishments, and
mention of various bribes which had come to
the late chancellor's coffers, were brought upon
the carpet, so that the House became better

at Queen's, in the beginning of the year 1662; but left the
college without a degree, and entered himself a student of
Lincoln's Inn. He soon rose to eminence in his profession, and
found it convenient to adopt King William's whig party for his
political friends. However, he was defeated in a contest for
the recordership of London, in 1691; but the honours of King's
counsel and His Majesty's solicitor-general atoned for the
disappointment. He continued in his high employment till
the end of King William's reign, when Simon Harcourt, afterwards chancellor, superseded him: yet, quite contrary to
the usual practice, he was not advanced to be attorney-
general, when Trevor was promoted to the chief justiceship of
the Common Pleas, Mr. Northey being promoted to that
office; and the same thing had happened to Trevor, who
found Ward placed over his head, after he had been solicitor-
general. Sir John Hawles wrote " Remarks on the Trials
of Fitzharris and others," and " A Reply to the Magistracy
and Government of England vindicated." Anthony Wood
said, that he was turbulent, and inclining to a republic; but
Bishop Tanner erased this character of him from the Athenæ.

prepared to carry their threat into execution. And as several of the judges had been excepted in the interim,¹ it was not likely that any fur-

¹ Wright, Herbert, Jenner, Holloway.

Sir Richard Holloway was the son of a public notary at Oxford, who was very active in the business of the city. Wood calls him " a covetous civilian." In 1667, when the flying coach was set up from Oxford to London, young Richard was one of the six passengers. They started at six in the morning, and were set down at their inn at seven in the evening. Ward was another passenger. It was a great thing for a coach to perform such an immense journey in one day, and public notice of the feat was given throughout the university. In 1677, this gentleman was made serjeant-at-law, there being two other serjeants of the same name, Charles his uncle, and Robert. A few years afterwards he became judge of the King's Bench, whence he was ejected by King James after the trial of the seven bishops, and he was not restored at the Revolution.

There were five Holloways living at Oxford in 1667, and the following curious verses transpired concerning them :

" Sarjeant,¹ Barrister,² Necessitie,³ Notarie,⁴ Mercer,⁵
Gravely dull,⁶ ill spoken,⁷ lawless,⁸ *cum purgere,*⁹ broken."¹⁰

¹ Old Charles Holloway, the uncle.
² Richard, living against Blue-bore, in St. Aldave's parish.
³ Young Charles, son of the old serjeant.
⁴ Old Richard Holloway, the judge's father.
⁵ Francis, brother to old Charles and old Richard.
⁶ In his dotage.
  Censorious.
⁸ So called, because being a barrister and no lawyer, *Necessitas non habet legem.*
⁹ This is not known.
¹⁰ A broken mercer.

ther delay could arise. Sir William Williams,
therefore, the old Welsh antagonist, declared,
on the next consideration of Jeffreys's penalty,
" that no man deserved to be excepted more
than he; but will you begin' with a dead person?"² he continued. The exception was instantly agreed to. Nor did the affair end
here, for Colonel Tipping soon afterwards spoke
warmly upon the fates of Armstrong and Mrs.
Lisle, and finished thus strongly: "He has
raised his estate on the ruin of the law: his estate and honour are the price of your blood. I
move, that you will attaint him." And it was
resolved, that a bill should be brought in for the
forfeiture of his honour and estate.³ How this

¹ The exceptions of the particular day's debate.

² Williams said on a subsequent occasion, when Sir Robert Sawyer endeavoured to excuse himself from being ac-
cessary to Armstrong's fate, that, " all is put upon the dead
(Jeffreys); and the dead must answer for the dead, and ' the
dead bury the dead.'"

³ In Salop, he had the manors of Wem and Loppington,
with many other lands and tenements; in Leicestershire, the
manors of Dalby and Broughton. He bought Dalby of the
Duke of Buckingham; and after his death it passed to Sir
Charles Duncombe, and descended on Anthony Duncombe,
afterwards Lord Feversham. In Bucks, he had the manor
of Bulstrode, which he had purchased of Sir Roger Hill, in
1686; and the manor of Fulmer, with other tenements. He

2 c

attempt failed, we have already acquainted the
reader; but such was the want of due economy,
not only in the chancellor's family, but in his son's
also who succeeded to the title, that all is said
to have been spent and squandered; and some
of the servants who saw the acquisition of a
property no less than 12,000*l.* a year, lived long
enough to hear of its total waste and dispersion.

There are several portraits of this chancellor,
which were taken for the most part whilst he
held the seals; and Nichols, referring to some

built a mansion at Bulstrode, which came afterwards to his
son-in-law Charles Dive, who sold it, in the reign of Queen
Anne, to William, Earl of Portland, in whose family, now
aggrandized by a dukedom, it still continues. And he had
an inclination at one time to have become the purchaser of
another estate,* but was outwitted by one of his legal brethren. Sir Jeffrey Jeffreys, the alderman, lent his namesake
considerable sums of money, and by way of security, had a
mortgage on his Leicestershire estate. When the second and
last Lord Jeffreys died in 1702, Sir Jeffrey took possession of
these lands, and filed a bill of foreclosure against Lord Viscount Windsor, who had married the widow, and others:
the issue of which was, that the noble defendant was ordered
to pay the encumbrances, which amounted to upwards of
13,000*l.* And we have seen, that other estates belonging to
the chancellor were ordered to be sold after his son's death.
The sale took place for the satisfaction of this mortgage
and settlements made by the first lord in 1688.

* Gunedon Park.

of these, says, that " he does not appear that
monster of ugliness and wickedness we have
been taught to think him." In 1687, a whole
length, by Sir Godfrey Kneller, was hung up
in the Inner Temple-hall. It cost fifty pounds,
and was executed at the expense of the society.
This painting, however, was not destined to
remain long in its station; for no sooner had
those reverses taken place which caused such a
general commotion in all societies, than it was
removed to Mr. Holloway's chambers; and in
1695, an order was promulgated from the
benchers to the effect—

" That Mr. Treasurer do declare to the Lord
Jeffreys, that, at his lordship's desire, the house
do make a present to his lordship of his father's
picture, now in Mr. Holloway's chambers, who
is desired to deliver the same to his lordship,
or his order." John, Lord Jeffreys, having obtained the portrait, sent it to Acton; where,
Nichols tells us, the Honourable Daines Bar-
rington often saw it. The Denbighshire estate
being sold to Sir Foster Cunliffe, this painting
was again removed to Erthig, the house of Mr.
Yorke, who possessed another likeness of the
judge by J. Allen.¹ That considerable anti-

¹ The following is a description of some of the portraits
and engravings :—
The Right Honourable George, Lord Jeffreys, Baron of

quary, Mr. Nichols, goes on thus in his note :—
"The picture (that of the Inner Temple) continues in tolerable preservation." Mr. Gough
was informed there was in the hall at Acton a
whole length of the chancellor's brother; and
that an original portrait of the former, removed
from Guildhall in his disgrace, and sold, is, or
was a few years ago, at Mr. Harnage's, at
Belsardine, near Cressing, in Shropshire; one
of whose ancestors married his youngest
daughter. Another picture of him is said to

Wem, lord high chancellor of England, and one of the
lords of His Majesty's most honourable privy-council,
1686. Wig, laced band, habit of office, arms,* mace, and
purse. " POBDAUN ODDVW."—Ames's Catalogue of
English Heads.

Sir George Jefferies. R. White, sc. 8vo.—Granger.

George, Lord Jefferies, &c. lord high chancellor, 1686.
Cooper, large 4to. mezz.

George, Lord Jefferies, &c. inscribed, " The Lord Chancellor." J. Smith, exc. large 4to. mezz.

The lord chancellor taken in disguise at Wapping. He
is surrounded by the mob. H. sh.—Granger.

George (Jefferies), Earl of Flint, Viscount Weikham,
Baron of Weim, &c. G. Kneller, p. Cooper, exc. 1686.
4to. mezz. very scarce.

* He bore ermine, a lion rampant, and canton, sable, with a mullet for
difference on a canton, and the arms of Ulster in an inescutcheon on the
body of the lion.

have perished in the fire which destroyed the manor-house of Durance, about fifty years ago, at the Christmas audit, by putting too much wood on the hall-fire. There were at Stoke Pogis, in Buckinghamshire, in the possession of Lady Juliana Penn, his descendant, two portraits of Lord Chancellor Jeffreys : one a whole length in his robes, holding the great seal; in the other, he is in black with a band, and sitting at a table, on which is a letter directed to him. The present earl of Winchelsea has also a portrait of him; and another is in the possession of Dr. Jeffreys, canon residentiary of St. Paul's.

Whether the reader be curious to know the fate of other persons who have been mentioned in this little history, or be content with the extinction of its principal character, we will offer no opinion. The great novelist of our day has ever been willing to gratify those who have luxuriated in his pages with such information; but as we are dealing with the plain simple narrative of a great man's life, it were far better to say, in imitation of Boswell's farewell,—Such was Jeffreys. Samuel Johnson, however, died childless; whereas the chancellor left a son, who inherited, not only the honour of his title, but some of his bright parts also. A very short mention of this young nobleman shall close the chapter. [1]

Under the management of so jovial a parent, it would have been surprising if John had not fallen into all the gaieties of the times; and he accordingly inherited a love for the bottle, and a propensity to extravagant habits. That very strange story related of him at Dryden's funeral, although proved of late to have been the fabrication of a Mrs. Elizabeth Thomas, his Corinna, [2] is yet quite congenial with his conduct and with the custom of the age, when every young lord was bowed down to like a phœnix.

[1] Jeffreys was twice married. His first wife, Sarah Neesham, brought him four sons and two daughters: John, of whom we are now speaking; Thomas, who died March 7, 1676; George and Robert, who died in their infancy; Margaret, his eldest daughter, who espoused William Stringer, of Durance, in the parish of Enfield (son and heir to Judge Stringer); and Sarah, the second, who married George Harnage, a captain of marines. His second wife, the widow of Sir John Jones, of Funman, in Glamorganshire, and daughter of the Lord Mayor Bludworth, gave him two sons and four daughters, all of whom died infants, except Mary, who became the wife of Charles Dive, Esq.—See Nichols's Leicestershire.

[2] She was in prison, and in great poverty, which might probably induce her to become " the mother of many inventions."

When the great poet died (at least so the story
goes), Sprat, then bishop of Rochester and
dean of Westminster, sent to Lady Elizabeth
Howard, the widow, with a proposal to make a
present of the ground and all the Abbey-fees:
Lord Halifax also offered to bury him with a
gentleman's private funeral, and to bestow 500*l.*
upon a monument to his honour. This liberality being acceded to by the lady and Charles
Dryden the son, the corpse was ready to
move forward, attended by eighteen mourning
coaches; the Abbey was lighted, the choir
attending, the anthem set, and the dean waiting
to bury. At this moment came up the young
lord with some wild rakes, and having learned
for whom the funeral obsequies were performing,
" What shall Dryden, the greatest honour and
ornament of the nation, be buried after this private manner ?" quoth Jeffreys: "No, gentlemen;
let all that loved Mr. Dryden, and honour his
memory, alight, and join with me in gaining
my lady's consent to let me have the honour of
his interment, which shall be after another manner than this; and I will bestow a thousand
pounds on a monument in the Abbey for him."
This said, the people in the coaches, who were
ignorant of the dean's kindness as well as of

Halifax's generosity, alighted, and attended the young man to the bed-chamber of the Lady Howard, who was sick. All kneeled down by his desire, and he vowed never to rise till his request should be granted. The unfortunate woman fainted away, being frightened, but exclaimed, " No, no!" as soon as she recovered. "Enough, gentlemen," said Lord Jeffreys; "my lady is very good; she says, " Go, go." Her feeble voice was, however, drowned in joyous acclamations, and away went all the parties, the hearsemen being bidden to carry the corpse to one Russel, an undertaker in Cheapside, there to be embalmed after the royal fashion. Next day, Mr. Charles Dryden endeavoured to excuse his mother to the bishop and my Lord Halifax; but they would hear nothing in extenuation: and when the undertaker applied to Jeffreys for a fulfilment of his promise, he turned it off ill-naturedly, saying, that those who observed the orders of a drunken frolic deserved no better; that he remembered nothing of it, and that he might do what he liked with the corpse. Charles Dryden then wrote to him, but received for answer, that he would not be troubled about the matter. The result of this extraordinary matter was, that Dr. Garth,

of the College of Physicians, proposed a subscription; and Dryden was at length interred in
the Abbey, followed by a numerous train of
coaches. But as soon as the funeral was over,
Charles sought every opportunity of fighting the
man who had so dishonoured his parents; and
having challenged him in vain, declared that he
would watch and fight him off-hand, though like
a gentleman, and with all the rules of honour;
and then, we are told, that Jeffreys sneaked off
out of the town, and that the meeting, though
sedulously sought for, never took place.

Mr. Malone, who took singular pains to dis-
prove this unhandsome tale, after exhibiting
many instances of falsehood which Mrs. Thomas
had allowed to go forth in print, gives the verity
of the case thus.—True it was, that Jeffreys met
the procession in the street, and that, in con-
junction with others, he was instrumental in
changing the private funeral intended him by
Mr. Montague, afterwards Lord Halifax, into
a public ceremony; but the histories of the
dean, the attendance of the choir, the bed-
chamber scene, and the challenge, were merely
embellishments, or, to speak more to the purpose, gross fictions. The Earl of Dorset and
Jeffreys thought that so great a poet should be
honoured with a signal solemnity; and having

prevailed on the relations of Dryden to suffer
the removal of his corpse, it was taken from the
undertaker's on the same evening to the College
of Physicians, whence it was carried with due
pomp to Westminster, as we have related.[1] The
truth, therefore, is far from being discreditable
to the young nobleman, although he might have
effected his intentions in a manner somewhat
chivalrous.[2]

Like his father, he had the reputation of being
an author, from the force of genius which he
was known to possess; and Walpole has thought
fit to place him in his Noble Catalogue.[3] The
paraphrased fable, however, on King William,
is considered to have been Prior's, having been
found among his unpublished manuscripts after

[1] This account is greatly confirmed by Ward, in his London Spy. He says, he saw the procession when standing at
the end of Chancery-lane, that he heard the concert of haut-
boys and trumpets, and he compliments Lord Jeffreys on his
pious undertaking.

[2] Not unlike Richard—
    " Stay you, that bear the corse, and set it down."
And again :
    " Villains, set down the corse, or, by Saint Paul,
    I'll make a corse of him that disobeys."

[3] But it is in a kind of appendix, where Lord Orford de-
signates his supplemental geniuses as persons he had hardly
thought of noticing.

his death in his own hand-writing, though Lord Jeffreys has long had the credit of it. As it is but short, perhaps there will be no harm in giving it :—

A FABLE.

In Æsop's tales an honest wretch we find,
Whose years and comforts equally declin'd ;
He in two wives had two domestick ills,
For different age they had, and different wills ;
One pluckt his black hairs out, and one his grey ;
The man for quietness did both obey,
Till all his parish saw his head quite bare,
And thought he wanted brains as well as hair.

THE MORAL.

The parties, henpeckt W——m, are thy wives ;
The hair they pluck are thy prerogatives :
Tories thy person hate, the whigs thy power ;
Though much thou yieldest, still they try for more,
Till this poor man and thou alike are shown,
He without hair, and thou without a crown.

The burlesqued epitaph on the Duke of Gloucester has been always understood as the legitimate production of this nobleman. The original by Dr. Bentley is in Latin verse.[1]

---

[1] *On the Death of the Duke of Gloucester, by Dr. Bentley.*

Quid queror ? an proprio sub pondere magna fatiscunt ?
Et Natura labat dotibus ipsa suis ?

What reason have I to complain,
Since in all times it has been plain,
That great and weighty things must soon,
Like jacks, with their own weight, go down?
And Nature, when upon her back
She lays too much, will surely crack.
So little Willy does, and cares
Neither for scepters, nor our pray'rs:
And I shall love him long, for all
The hopes he gave us were but small.
Or rather God, who gave us birth,
Being in wrath with lazy earth,
Takes this occasion, and prefers
Illustrious souls among the stars.
If it be so, I told a lie,
And little Willy does not die;
But mounts alive, and swiftly flies,
On airy horseback thro' the skies.
'Tis the same horse old Enoch rode,
And Asgil keeps to go to God.

Sic moreris, Gulielme, et sceptra, et vota tuorum,
    Destituens, brevis, heu! Spes; diuturnus Amor!
An potius terras Deus indignatus inertes
    Illustres animas ad supera alta vocat?
Nec moreris, Gulielme, volas sed vivus ad astra,
    Ætheriis vectus qualis Enochus equis;
Et positis novus exuviis roseo ore refulges,
    Inter cœlicolas conspiciendus avos.
Interea flendo nos frustra ducimus horas,
    Viventi et cassas solvimus exequias.
Scilicet: at sine te tristi marcescere in ævo,
    Illud erit nobis, bis, Gulielme, mori.

Now see the youth without his clotbes,
How like a new-born flow'r he shows :
See how his rosy cheeks do shine
Among his ancestors divine ;
While we poor mortals here below
Our sighs and tears in vain bestow ;
And empty obsequies are paid,
Just as if he were really dead ;
Which makes it plain, that living on
A hated life, now he is gone,
Will be to us, altho' our breath
Should ne'er be stopt, a double death.

There is really some ground for Mrs. Wise-
man's praise, when, dedicating her tragedy of
Antiochus to him, she spoke of his " admirable
gay humour and eternal vivacity of wit." He
received a similar mark of honour from the author of Bonduca, another tragedy, altered from
Fletcher, which was published in 1696. Yet
while he was an enterprising, he was doubtless
an imprudent lord ; and though his death, which
took place in 1703, averted the distress which
treads hard upon the spendthrift, his estates
turned out to be seriously involved and encumbered. We have seen how he became possessed
of Lord Pembroke's daughter, in spite of all obstacles ; and, whether a state of comfort or unhappiness ensued upon the nuptials, certain it is,

that the chancellor had advanced his son among
the first people of the land, and that his grand-
daughter allied herself to noble blood. John,
Lord Jeffreys, had two children; Herbert, who
died an infant, and Henrietta, who wedded
Thomas, Earl of Pomfret. The death of Herbert
caused the extinction of the title. Henrietta,
the countess, was an amiable and well-informed
gentlewoman; she was the familiar and affectionate correspondent of Lady Hartford,[1] afterwards Duchess of Somerset, whom Thomson
has justly celebrated. Both these ladies retired
from public life in 1737, on the death of Queen
Caroline; Lord Pomfret and his family went to
reside on the continent, while the Lady Hartford remained in England. That nobleman[2]
died in 1753; and two years afterwards, his
noble collection of busts and statues[3] was pre-

---

[1] O Hartford, fitted or to shine in courts
   With unaffected grace, or walk the plain.
                                   THOMSON.

[2] He was a knight of the Bath, and master of the horse to
the Queen, and his wife was a lady of the bed-chamber.

[3] The Pomfret marbles, being part of the Arundel marbles, were bought by Sir William Fermor, Lord Pomfret's
father, and deposited at Easton Neston, Northamptonshire,
the seat of the family, whence they were removed to the
Logic and Moral Philosophy School at Oxford.

sented to the University of Oxford by his widow. She died in 1761, leaving a considerable family, and was honoured with a cenotaph by the college to which she had been so munificent a donor.

THE END.

GENERAL INDEX

TO THE PRINCIPAL MATTERS CONTAINED IN THE

TEXT AND NOTES.

———

2 D

C.

E.

F.

T.

V.

W.

PRINTED BY A. J. VALPY,
RED LION COURT, FLEET STREET.

CPSIA information can be obtained at www.ICGtesting.com
Printed in the USA
BVOW03s0954291013

334930BV00010B/289/P

MEMOIRS

OF

THE LIFE

OF

JUDGE JEFFREYS,

SOMETIME

LORD HIGH CHANCELLOR OF ENGLAND.

BY

HUMPHRY W. WOOLRYCH.

LONDON:

HENRY COLBURN, NEW BURLINGTON STREET.

1827.

Printing Statement:

Due to the very old age and scarcity of this book,
many of the pages may be hard to read due to the
blurring of the original text, possible missing pages,
missing text, dark backgrounds and other issues
beyond our control.

Because this is such an important and rare work, we
believe it is best to reproduce this book regardless of
its original condition.

Thank you for your understanding.

Sir Godfrey Kneller pinxt.   G.W. Smart, sculpt.

GEORGE, LORD JEFFREYS.

LORD HIGH CHANCELLOR in the REIGN of JAMES II.

Published by Henry Colburn, London, June 1821.